To:

Sister M. Elaine

From:

Sister M. Maurina

August 18, 1981

AND

AWAY WE GO

AND
AWAY WE GO

by

Sister Mary Presentina

VANTAGE PRESS
New York   Washington   Atlanta   Hollywood

*
⟶ FIRST EDITION

Copyright © 1975 by Sister Mary Presentina

Published by Vantage Press, Inc.
516 West 34th Street, New York, New York 10001

Manufactured in the United States of America

Standard Book Number 533-01524-3

DEDICATION

To Sister Mary Maurina, O.S.F.,
who has shared forty-four
years of apostolic
labor with me.

CONTENTS

FOREWORD

Historians and others who are interested in the development of religious education in the United States will welcome this admirable account by Sister Presentina, O.S.F., of the origin and growth of the Confraternity of Christian Doctrine in the Diocese of Baker. It is a fascinating story of the heroic efforts made to bring Christ and His message to children and adults in remote areas of the Far West.

It all began when Bishop Joseph McGrath, acting on the request of Pope Pius XI, returned from Rome to Eastern Oregon in 1935, determined to erect the Confraternity in every parish and mission of his diocese.

Shortly afterwards he chose Sister Presentina to pioneer the work. Two years later she was joined by Sister Maurina, O.S.F., and together they labored for nearly twenty years, creating a catechetical structure that achieved national acclaim.

Their missionary activity ranged over 68,000 square miles. Although it was larger in area than New York State, in population the Diocese of Baker was the smallest in the country, only 10,758 Catholics, served by 30 priests and 19 sisters.

By 1950 when the writer of this Foreword came upon the scene, the Confraternity was firmly established and flourishing. Its fruits were evident everywhere. Catholics in isolated places had returned to the Church. Frontier towns had become thriving parishes. Children, even in the most out of the way spots in the diocese, were under instruction. Religious faith and fervor burned brightly.

Today, from the banks of the mighty Columbia River on the north to the California border in the south, and from the snow-capped Eagle mountains in the east to the lovely Deschutes valley in the west, look where you will and you will find the spiritual fruits of the admirable contribution of these sisters to Holy Mother Church.

Father Patrick Gaire, in his *History of the Diocese of Baker*, pays the Sisters the tribute they really deserve: "They have written a glorious chapter in the history of the diocese. Its pages unfold a story of privations and difficulties, yet it is a story mingled with joy as they saw the mustard seed planted many years ago grow into a great tree whose branches extend throughout the entire Diocese."

To that we can only add, may the memory of their sacrifices, dedication and success inspire present and future generations of religious educators in their labors to extend Christ's kingdom in the hearts of men.

Francis P. Leipzig,
Former Bishop of Baker

INTRODUCTION

There is hardly any subject which is more timely or important than that of Catholic Education. It is fundamentally a task of the Church since Christ Our Lord gave it the commission to go and teach all nations and it is fundamentally a task for every Christian who at baptism receives life and at the same time by being made a part of the Mystical Body, like a living cell in the human body, it not only receives life but must of its very nature impart life, or suffer the consequence of internal deterioration and stagnation. Lakes that are fed but do not open become dead sinks, unsuitable for life.

There was a time when a battle raged within the Church between the proponents of the Catholic Parochial School system and the C.C.D. Now, we can be thankful that for the most part we have ceased to fight one another on this point because the hand writing on the wall clearly tells us that we are in a struggle for survival especially as regards the Catholic School. When it was vigorous and growing like a giant and C.C.D. was considered somewhat second rate, it was natural to expect that those who favored, or had no choice except C.C.D., would from time to time take a crack at the Parochial School which looked so fat and opulent. But now we see that each has its place and that either of them, properly conducted, can do a respectable task but only if the parent retains the rightful position of being educator to the children, especially as regards religious education. They must be made a part of the process.

Both the C.C.D. and the school, parochial or public, must reinforce the relationship between parent and child. Whatever helps, aids, gimmicks, efforts, blood, sweat or tears that are expended to bring children to faith, will bring with them their own reward to those who give generously but the success of the task will not depend primarily on such means but on God who gives and the parent who must reinforce the child. The burning question in Catholic Education should be for us, "What can I do to help the parent live his faith in such a way that the child will be drawn to it?" We should be most careful when we teach to see to it that we do not detract from or substitute for the parent, but rather reinforce the parent-child relationship. At the same time we should not forget that God is both the giver of the gift and the gift itself. Whatever system of education we employ should keep these two fundamental principles clearly in mind. We can expend our best energy in teaching children only to find out that what is practiced at home is so clearly contrary to what is being taught that the child is tortured in the whole painful process, being torn between parents, Church and God, each of which the child would like to be a part of, but none of which seem to be in agreement. Likewise if we remember that God is the giver of the gift of Faith we will begin to build a personal relationship between the child and God and will find ourselves in the happy position of introducing them to one another. We become the instruments in the life-giving process of salvation so that we are not shovels or hammers, blunt and uncouth, but living, vital instruments with tact, finesse, courtesy, concern, faith, hope and love as the principal tools of our trade.

In this book you will find all these things clearly exemplified in a practical way in a C.C.D. program which started from scratch and was built step by step into a diocesan program from the grassroots to the executive level. Beginning with the home visitation to get to know the sheep, encouraging their participation, getting them to assume the role of teacher and training them in their task as catechist, supporting and keeping contact through mail where personal contact was impossible, assigning tasks to those who wanted to share the apostolate and were willing to serve others, as members of a team, and contantly working with the chief shepherd and his representative, the pastor of each parish, little by little everyone or at least as many as possible were brought into a program which achieved notable success in its own day and continues, with adaptation, to be successful today. This is the task which three Sisters accepted and which they carried out so well through a period of pioneering in Catholic education among those attending the public school.

This is a book which will always be valuable as an historical record for the Diocese of Baker, but it is much more than that. It will serve even today as an adequate model for any diocese or parish. In fact anyone who tries to implement it will find that they are constantly required to renew themselves according to the model which they have taken, because no one will do it perfectly. The parent will have to return to God for help, reformation and renewal; the teacher will teach best when they model themselves after the Divine Master, Himself, and their lessons will be most effective when they are lived out in themselves; the pastors will best pasture their flocks when they know their sheep and lay down their lives for them daily, and the sheep who are pastured are not, after all, sheep, but people who must give their own response and the message will be accepted or resisted as each one is offered the bread of life. Everyone then involved in the task will have the responsibility to grow and will find themselves more or less effective as they return to the Giver of life to be renewed in themselves so that they can bring Him effectively to others. They will learn, then, "to speak to God about men before they speak to men about God," as has been well said.

To all those who are interested in being effective instruments, I recommend this book. It is not the last word to be said, but it is a practical example of what a little group of devoted Sisters were able to do in a diocese that was rural, far flung and disconnected, but where willing bishops and pastors were looking for a means of finding a green pasture where

their flock might be nourished and refreshed at the springs of
life. I commend it to your study.

Most Reverend Thomas J. Connolly, D.D., J.C.D.

Bishop of Baker

April 20, 1974

AND

AWAY WE GO

Chapter 1

In The Beginning

It was May 10, 1937. Little did I know what the day had in store for me. Sister Rosella, the school directress of Sacred Heart Province in the West, and I were leaving Pendleton, Oregon, the site of the province headquarters of the Sisters of St. Francis, of Philadelphia, to go to Baker, the episcopal city of the diocese of the same name. It was a glorious morning for travel—the air heavily redolent with the fragrance of locust blossoms and lilacs in full bloom. The "Portland Rose" was more than an hour late, assuring our arrival in Baker long after 9:30 a.m., the time at which the Second Annual Regional Conference of the Confraternity of Christian Doctrine was scheduled to open.

The train ride, however, was delightful. I sat next to the window so as to enjoy the scenery to my heart's content. There were mountains, wooded glens, forested hillsides with log cabins, and woodpiles neatly stacked nearby; seemingly, flowers and budding shrubs were everywhere. A turbulent stream made music, tumbling, racing, splashing over the rounded stones that lay in its course. At Kamela, near the crest of the Blue Mountains, the train stopped its puffing pull. We alighted with the idea of experiencing nature at her best.

"Don't go too far," the conductor called after us. "We'll be here only five minutes."

"We'll be back in no time," Sr. Rosella answered with a smile. "We're going only a short distance."

Down a graded incline we went. To my delight, there in the midst of this primeval forest of pine was a hastily constructed cage with two black bear cubs romping about in happy abandon. We enjoyed their antics awhile before making our way back to the train just as the conductor's stentorian voice announced, "All aboard."

The train was ninety minutes late even though the engineer made good time in the valley from La Grande to Baker. As we alighted, a tall, distinguished clergyman came smilingly toward us. When greetings were over, he turned to me saying, "Yes, you are late, but please do not worry. We simply adjusted the program and put you on as the principal speaker for the afternoon session. At least, you are in time for the luncheon." We had hardly expected the Chancellor of the diocese, Father John D. Lee, to come to meet us. I was dismayed; I was flabbergasted; I had nothing specifically prepared to say to the meeting.

Little is more embarrassing than to find that as a main speaker at a conference you are late. Still it is more than a little bewildering to learn that you are the late main speaker when you did not know you were to be a speaker at all. Father Lee hurriedly explained that the Bishop was waiting to hear what I had to say.

Right there and then I wanted to take the train back to Pendleton. But that is not the way it is done. Long ago I grew up with the belief that a Bishop could be right, so with a little soul-searching and trepidation I decided to go along with the idea to address the assembled delegates on "Christ the teacher par excellence." I had been using this concept with the novices and postulants at Pendleton in "Methods of Teaching Religion." In retrospect I can pronounce the audience as most appreciative, listening with rapt attention to the "Wise One from the East" as I had been introduced by the presiding of-

2

ficer. It was an exciting challenge that acquainted me with many people whom I would meet again and again. I was grateful for the experience.

My thoughts kept pace with the grinding whirr of the train on our ride back to Pendleton that evening. One train of thought took me back to my coming West in January 1937. A long illness had many speculating whether I would ever teach again. But then I had not come into contact with Mother Casimir, the Provincial of the Sacred Heart Province in the Far West. She met me one day in December 1936 at our Motherhouse in Glen Riddle, Pennsylvania, and quite casually said, "Pack your trunk; we need you in the West. I am ready to take you along."

I mused. "We will have to see about that. What does the Mother General think?" Then to no one in particular, I added, "I always wanted to go West. If Mother Immaculate, the Superior General, approves, I'll be ready."

There were some who thought me foolhardy. "You'll never make it. You'll drop by the wayside," was my immediate Superior's comment, to which Sr. Rosella encouragingly replied, "You have everything to gain and nothing to lose by coming with us. Besides, it is only for six months. You'll be back in August."

Mother Casimir left the East to be at her administrative post in Pendleton by Christmas. Sr. Rosella stayed on to accompany me after New Year to a new home with new horizons. We left for the West January 2, 1937, arriving by train in Pendleton at the Provincialate January 6 in a blinding snowstorm. I made it. I did not fall by the wayside. The story has a happy ending. I recovered my health and instead of staying only six months as predicted, I stayed thirty-four years in addition to the six months. My sojourn in the West has but happy memories; I enjoyed every minute of it.

Oregon is a beautiful state. Approximately two-thirds of the state forms the diocese of Baker. The Cascade Mountain range is Oregon's most impressive feature, dividing the state into two distinct regions. In fact, it is the Cascades that form

3

the boundary between the Archdiocese of Portland in Oregon and the diocese of Baker. Lakes and streams abound and are famous for their yield of salmon, steelhead, brook, and rainbow trout. Game includes quail, grouse, Chinese pheasants, duck, geese, deer, bear, elk, and, if you really wish to play the game, cougar.

There are numerous state reservation areas, which to us later on as Confraternity travelers were a haven at lunchtime and a lift of spirit as we moved from one end of the diocese to the other. Our enjoyment of the great outdoors added zest to a day of traveling that could have been boring. We were always ready to stop to admire some great scenic attraction. If you are ever passing along Rogue River State Park, don't travel on without stopping long enough to look down into the canyon of that river. It is deep; it is breathtaking; it is magnificent. You will never regret the extra minutes added to your trip.

After my arrival in Pendleton in January, I was stationed at the Provincialate there. From the end of January to mid-June of 1937 I had an hour's class daily with the novices in "Methods of Teaching Religion." One day the bishop of the diocese, the Most Rev. Joseph F. McGrath, D.D., was walking across the campus. Hearing the class in an outdoor session, he stopped, listened for a while and did an about-face. He had been conferring with Mother Casimir about the needs of his far-flung diocese; now he was returning to take up again the discussion with Mother Casimir.

"That's the Sister we want for our Confraternity program," he blurted out.

"But Sister is just loaned to us from the East. Her return after six months was the principal condition on which she came West," explained Mother Casimir.

"Can't you ask for her? You know we need her," the Bishop replied.

Mother Casimir smiled enigmatically and murmured something that sounded like, "We'll see."

An hour later, as I was returning from class, the Bishop met me. He was all smiles. Patting his breast pocket, he greeted me and said, "I have a letter here to your headquarters in the East asking that you remain in the West to promote the Confraternity program. What do you say?"

"I would like that very much," I replied without hesitation. I was enjoying the good mountain air, so exhilarating and bracing. I had found it easier to breathe with the air dry, never humid.

"When you were in Baker for the conference, I asked you to consider what you think would be a good catechetical program for our diocese. Have you given the matter any thought?" the Bishop asked.

"Before I could possibly submit a catechetical program for the diocese, it would be necessary for me to know the diocese," I remonstrated.

"You wouldn't have to know much," the Bishop resumed. "The diocese of Baker City extends north to Washington, east to Idaho, south to Nevada and California, and west to the eastern slopes of the Cascade Mountains. There are only nineteen parishes and twenty-eight priests, including a few Capuchins and Jesuits in an area of 66,826 square miles. In that vast stretch of land there are only four parochial schools. Can we go into your study? I have something to tell you."

No sooner said than done; into the Administration Building we went. When the Bishop was comfortably seated in a big chair opposite me, he began, "In May 1934 when I made my ad limina visit to Rome, I had a private audience with His Holiness, Pope Pius XI. Before him on his desk lay the report I had submitted to the Sacred Congregation of the Council. The Holy Father was gracious and listened most attentively to my oral report. He had been properly cued in by the Cardinal Secretary. He knew the answers to the questionnaire on the teaching of Christian Doctrine for children in the parishes, in Catholic schools and colleges, in public schools and for adults, from the form filled out by individual bishops in making the quinquennial reports of their dioceses throughout the world.

"With great solicitude the Holy Father asked, 'Tell me, what do you do about the religious education of the children

5

not in Catholic schools, of the children in the isolated rural districts of your diocese?' The Holy Father had touched the core of our problem.

"With heavy heart, I admitted that the religious instruction of these children left much to be desired. Pastors and their assistants did what they could to teach the children their faith, but other pastoral duties frequently crowded out the regular, systematic religious instruction, particularly in rural areas. Instantly the Holy Father offered a suggestion, 'Go back and establish in every parish and mission the Confraternity of Christian Doctrine. Enlist the aid of lay people, good Catholic men and women, to assist the priests in functioning as teachers fulfilling the magisterial office of the Church.' To me, the Bishop of Baker City, one of the most missionary dioceses in the United States, these words of Pius XI were the words of the Heart of Christ Himself to my own heart. As I knelt at the feet of our Holy Father that early day in May 1934, I heard clearly and unmistakably the command of Christ, 'Go back and establish the Confraternity of Christian Doctrine in your diocese.'

"That was more than three years ago. There was much opposition to efforts on my part to establish the Confraternity. But on January 12, 1935, the Sacred Congregation of the Council issued the decree 'Provido Sane Consilio,' on the better care and promotion of catechetical instructions. This decree given at Rome furnished me with another foothold to put into action the advice given me by Pope Pius XI. It did not take me long to assure the furtherance of this work. In February 1935, I ordered the erection of the Confraternity in every parish and mission of the diocese. During the month of March, Miss Miriam Marks, secretary of the National Center of the Confraternity in Washington, D. C., toured the entire diocese with me, hoping to generate interest in this apostolic project. We also held Deanery Conferences both in 1936 and this year. But we need something more than decrees, we need someone to show the people in parishes what to do and how to do it. I have prayed and done much penance for God's blessing and success in this work. I have asked Sisters and priests to undertake this project. No favorable answer from anyone. Now I am asking you, 'Will you help?' "

My heart was in full accord with Bishop McGrath's request. The Confraternity of Christian Doctrine was not a new idea for me. In September 1907, before I entered the convent, I had been corralled to teach a Confraternity class at my home parish, St. Joseph's, Lancaster, Pennsylvania. I knew the objectives of this now world-wide organization. I remembered 1907-1908 and the happiness that my class gave me. What could I say? The Bishop was waiting; he had no idea the train of thought his question engendered.

"I will try; I will do my best." That was early in the summer of '37. On August 26 of that same year, I submitted a "Plan for Training Lay Catechists" to Bishop McGrath. Since he was in Baker and I in Pendleton, 104 miles to the west, I sent my plan to him by mail. The Bishop lost no time in answering.

He wrote, "Permit me to say that your program is ideal; just what is needed and a God-sent answer to prayer." Further on he added, "My whole idea is that lay catechists teach these mission children under proper supervision as you have so perfectly outlined . . . I await your next visit to Baker with great interest."

I regarded the Bishop's letter as a generously polite reply acknowledging the plan I had so idealistically outlined. But I little knew Bishop McGrath or the Provincial, Mother Casimir. Between them they arranged that I should make Baker my base of operations and that I should be in residence at St. Elizabeth Hospital there. By the early part of September there I was, bag and baggage, to help launch a new program in a new part of the country.

Baker is the county seat, situated in Baker Valley. Its leading industries include lumbering, stock raising, and farming. The population hovers between nine and ten thousand so that no one place or institution is far from any other. So it happened that Bishop McGrath's residence was only a stone's throw from St. Elizabeth Hospital. He came to see me post-haste on my arrival to plot my course of action.

"Welcome to Baker! Welcome to the Confraternity field of labor! We are glad you came." The Bishop was expansive. "Now, put your ideas into operation at once."

I demurred, "I can help. But it is really a priest's work to introduce the procedures of administering a school of Religion to his brother priests. I do not think I could tell priests how to run this or any other organization." In the thirties, Women's Lib was only a name, not as in the seventies when women desire to be in the fore at all times.

With a twinkle in his eye, the Bishop said, "Listen carefully. If a priest went into another priest's parish and told him how to run his Sunday School, he would be killed. He would never get away with it. It is your idea. You must make that idea of yours a reality. No one else can do that for you." That is how I received my commission to be Confraternity Supervisor in the diocese of Baker City. Things were moving fast; I was in the midst of all the upheaval.

Every Catholic knows that the bishop is the principal guardian of truth in his diocese. Ever cognizant of that principle, Bishop McGrath came to my headquarters almost daily to inquire what progress I was making. In other words, Bishop McGrath made himself available to clear up difficulties, to give me an encouraging smile or word, to steer the work according to the prescriptions of the Holy See. "What does Rome say?" he would ask, just to be certain that we were not following our own tendencies. "Be sure that the teachers know that they are teaching Christ and not themselves," he counselled. Then, thinking of the practical aspects of my program, "Make this program work in the Cathedral parish and at least in one of its many missions, preferably Jordan Valley or John Day; then you may go to any other parish to see what you can do."

One day Bishop McGrath casually remarked that Father John Curran would be in Baker soon to take up his duties as Executive Secretary of the Confraternity of Christian Doctrine, commonly known as the CCD. Father Curran was a priest worth knowing. He was young, quick, fiery, and easily moved to action. His red, unruly hair bristled and stood up on end most of the time. It was smoothed back only for certain occasions, such as Midnight Mass at Christmas, at funerals, and on state occasions. He had a natural ability to ferret out the people in a parish who were capable of meeting any and all requirements. He never stood on ceremony. He called a spade a spade and had no use for euphemisms, excepting in satire.

I still smile at the waitress at the depot lunch-bar in Huntington who asked, "Who is that priest who talks like a railroad man? Without preliminaries, he straddles a stool and calls out, 'I want a cup of coffee right away.'"

Another view of the man came from Mrs. D. P. O'Leary who had been dragooned into becoming chairman of teachers at Klamath Falls in the southern part of the diocese. She recalled, "He refused flatly to take 'No' for an answer. He sat on my doorstep, day by day, and virtually wore out my steps coming to my door. Finally I relented and said, 'Yes.' In my day I had been a teacher; I had the techniques and experience of teaching. I was Father Curran's choice."

I find it interesting to re-read Father Curran's notes. He was adamant in his criteria for selection of board members:

Always have a successful businessman as president;
For vice-president, select an outgoing businesswoman;
For treasurer, again choose a man with some knowledge of banking;
For secretary, look for a young woman, pert and active, with an attractive personality, good-looking, and generally petite with short curly hair.

Women's Lib might find fault with his division of labor, but practically it was effective, and generally productive of good results.

When Father was not analyzing the catechetical problems of the missions connected with the Cathedral parish in Baker and scanning the registers of the various missions for potential CCD leaders and members, he came daily from the Cathedral rectory to my headquarters at the hospital to brief me on what he discovered to be excellent prospects for the organization and to see what I had accomplished since his latest visit in outlining a detailed curriculum. This kept me from dawdling; I had to show something for the hours I had been at my desk.

Shortly after my arrival at Baker, I was assigned as assistant and companion-secretary Sister Emmanuel Mary, very young and capable, who stayed for a year in the CCD program. Sister Mary Rosetta, a native Oregonian, who replaced her, was excellent and worked in the diocesan office from 1938 to 1952, with the exception of one year, 1941-1942. Sister Mary Maurina came West from our Holy Trinity High School in Roxbury, a suburb of Boston, to act as Supervisor of Catechetics in the Baker diocese from 1940 to 1956 when she and I were assigned to the Spokane diocesan office of the CCD. Among our "house-mothers" at Holy Family Confraternity House, where we moved from the hospital after a few years, Sr. Mary Kathleen stands out. On two different occasions for a total of ten years, she made the house home for us.

Others from among our Franciscan Sisters came to help or to experiment with their ability as CCD workers. Those who rendered invaluable service were: Sister Therese Marguerite, Sister St. Anne, Sister Laureen, and Sister Perpetua. Sister Maurina, Sister Rosetta, Sister Clare Inez, and I stayed on through the years, rain and shine, from one year's end to the other. Sister Claire Inez remained at Baker after Sister Maurina and I were transferred to Spokane. Incidentally, she was still there in 1971-72 giving unstinted service to the CCD program in Baker.

This, in capsule form, is the history of the diocesan CCD personnel. As it stood in September 1937 there was a threefold team: Father Curran, Sister Emmanuel Mary, and I.

All three of us read and re-read everything that we could find on the CCD. I devoted myself to studying Father Curran's reports on Baker and its missions. His remarks on the CCD were incisive and exact:

The CCD was organized in Baker in March 1935 by Miriam Marks. Officers were appointed for the missions of Huntington and Jordan Valley. These people never knew they had an office, and knew nothing about CCD. In Huntington a high school girl was teaching all grades from "Jesus and I" as the text. In January 1936 there was a conference in Baker. It was poorly attended, poorly managed. Reports concerned activities of nuns; priests did all the talking.

Father Curran's reports on the Baker unit were neither flattering nor optimistic. Usually they concluded that training of teachers and more organization were necessary.

With a stout heart and clutching at straws, I agreed to begin the training of teachers in October. A preliminary course of six lectures was announced. The Rev. John D. Lee, rector of the Cathedral, contacted all possible prospects to attend the lectures. I approached Father Curran toward the same objective; his answer was dynamic and very encouraging. When I suggested that he announce the coming lectures, he answered laconically, "You bet. They'll be here if I have to corral them."

We scheduled the lectures for Tuesdays and Thursdays at 7:30 in the evening in one of the nurses' classrooms. This arrangement gave a pleasant setting and was of great advantage to me since I was living at the hospital. I had little notion of what I was getting into, but this was definitely a challenge: to create a system whereby good, willing people would promote the proper attitude toward teaching children the truths of their holy faith, children who for various reasons would not be attending Catholic schools.

I talked to many of the Sisters stationed at St. Francis Academy, Baker. "You're going to have a hard time convincing anyone that they should teach these youngsters."

I talked to Father Curran. He scratched his head, then blurted out unceremoniously, while winking at Father Lee,

"That's your problem. I'll get some prospects there. You keep 'em."

I walked the floor. I recalled what one woman had told me: "No one attends anything like that in Baker. They hardly help with the Red Cross; how do you expect to get them?"

I prayed and studied and tried to put myself in the place of the lay people. I tried to imagine how I would want someone to tell me what the CCD was all about; why I should at least learn about it; and how I could best go about teaching a class of religion.

Grasping in memory for every aid, I came up with the dictum of a famous educator—I believe it was Father Schwickerath's—"I think best, pencil in hand." Pencil in hand, I made jottings under the heading, "Methods of Teaching Religion." The heading itself sounded formidable. But one way of clarifying ideas is to define all terms used.

Methods. What were Methods? In the midst of my attempt to refine the idea, Sister Cuniberta, directress of nurses, dropped into my room for a short visit, that became extended as we batted our ideas back and forth. We probed "method" in her field; method is used in taking a patient's temperature, in making a bed, in baking a pie, or in teaching. Method, we concluded, is the procedure in pursuing a certain end.

"That's right," Sister exclaimed. "These people will understand what you are doing, what you are saying, if you use plenty of down-to-earth examples. They are homey people, with families, close to the earth, and not given too much to technical terms."

Out of this ping-ponging of ideas, I had the fundamental thoughts for my first talk. With method brought down to earth, the term "Religion" offered more challenge: what it meant in everyday living, what it really entailed, and further, what study it demanded. More pacing, more pencilled notes, more prayers, and ideas started to concretize.

Long ago as it was, I recall my first class. About 35 attended—all of them very attentive, eager and responsive. Many of them were married; in age, they ranged from 35 to

12

40, although a few were over sixty. The notables attending, Bishop McGrath and Father Lee, did not occupy places of honor; rather, they took places to one side, like coaches along the sidelines. It gives me a bit of satisfaction to recall that one young woman, Miss Rita Neault, later on as a married woman, served first as a Confraternity teacher in St. Charles Parish, Spokane, then taught in the parochial school as an aide.

Usually in conducting the classes, I talked or lectured about half an hour; then I encouraged the class to ask questions. On one occasion when I was talking on Motivation, Bishop McGrath raised his hand and asked, "What is motivation?"

I was so taken up by my subject that I was really unaware of the source of the question. "Motivation is a play upon the will. It is a cogent reason 'why' we should react this way or that. Motivation is anything that induces the pupil to learn. Whatever impels a pupil to learn is a motive."

All the while I was answering the Bishop's question, I made sure that everyone listening would get the explanation. Turning to the Bishop, I asked directly and pointedly, "Do you understand?" That question is instinctive to any teacher following an explanation. It was only when I kept looking at the Bishop nod and smile behind his hand that I realized to whom I was giving the challenge. However, Bishop McGrath was one of the easiest persons to get along with as long as you tried half-way. I will not be detoured here; an appreciation of the Bishop can come later. I will note only that it is to Bishop McGrath that I owe so much for his inspiration, his encouragement, his interest, and so many of the guidelines we observed in CCD work.

On the occasion of that first talk, questions followed one after the other. "How many Catholic children are there in public school here in Baker?" According to Mrs. George Black, Chairman of Visitors, and Mrs. Dreisbach, the total was about 35 or 40. However, this did not include the children from Durkee, Haines, Pleasant Valley, Keating, Muddy Creek, and other nearby stations. Nor did it include the children who lived in the mission areas.

Others in the group could hardly wait to ask questions, which were practical and pointed. "How many teachers will be needed for these children; where will classes be held?" Happily I had anticipated this type of question. "If there are forty children, you will need at least five teachers, one for Grade 1; one for Grade 2; one for Grades 3 and 4 combined; one for Grades 5 and 6; and one for Grades 7 and 8. Each division will study from a text designed for children in that grouping."

A woman in the third row ventured, "When I was going to school, we always started each year in the front of the book, but never finished it. I got as far as 'The Communion of Saints,' but nothing more. Each year the same story. Begin at the beginning; study as much as you can get in from mid-September to the end of May; the next year repeated the process."

I admitted the flaw in the process: the entire course of instructions based on the Baltimore catechism was never completed. No wonder the children could glibly affirm, "We had that last year; we never learn anything new; it is always the same old thing."

I went on to show that to overcome that difficulty, we planned to divide the matter of the then-used catechism into four parts. Part 1, treating of the Creed, would be the subject matter for the first year. Attention then would be focussed on Part 2, the Commandments, during the two full weeks of Religious Vacation School. Classes during the following scholastic year would be studying Sacraments in general and in particular: Baptism, Confirmation, Holy Eucharist, and Penance. Finally Holy Orders, Matrimony, and the sacrament of Anointing of the Sick would form the basis of attention for the Second Vacation School. In two years each child would have studied the whole range of the Catholic faith on his own age level. By dividing the content, no child need say, "We had the same old stuff last year."

14

Of course, children in Grade 4, coming back to school in September, might say, "We had that book last year. We know what is in that book." To persuade the Fourth Graders, I continued, "that this was not the case, we must show them that in the third grade they went just as far as the middle of the book, no further. Now in the fourth grade they would begin in the middle of the book and go to the end. Usually children are satisfied when this is explained to them."

"You would like parents to understand the function of the CCD. How do you go about that?" asked a questioner in the last row. My mind was working fast. I answered at length.

When Bishop McGrath briefed me on the diocese he was graphic. "Here is a difficulty we must understand. There are some children living seventy-five miles from the nearest Catholic church. Their nearest Catholic neighbors may be ten miles east of them with another Catholic family sixteen miles to the north. It is impossible to form these children into classes. What can be done for them?"

Instantly came the reply. "Then we will have to train the parents how to teach the elementary truths of our faith to their children in their homes. Teach parents how to teach!" Then and there I made a mental note: Stress the role of parents as teachers of Religion. In answer to your question I would say that parents should be acquainted with what the CCD is doing. Get some of them to attend these classes. By divine authorization, parents are the primary teachers of Religion. Sisters are merely supplementary to the parents' work. Sisters can seldom substitute for one's parents; they supplement, they never supplant parents.

"But more of that later on. So far, so good. In the next session on Thursday we will look at Christ as the teacher par excellence. May we call on Bishop McGrath for the closing prayer, please."

Bishop McGrath graciously complied and thus ended our first formal class in teaching lay people how to teach. I was delighted with the response; I had made a beginning and no one could foresee just what this beginning would lead to. My

15

heart sang a song with the refrain, "In the beginning, we made a beginning; nothing else."

Subsequent lectures and discussions embraced these topics:

Characteristics of a catechist;
The use and abuse of textbooks;
Lesson plans and class programs;
How to vitalize the teaching of Religion.

How did we manage all we hoped to do? I do not know.
In the beginning we worked as though all success depended on us, and we prayed as though everything depended on God.

16

Chapter 2

And Away We Go

Early in November 1937, Sister Emmanuel Mary and I packed our belongings for a twelve-day visit to one of the outposts of the Baker diocese—Jordan Valley. This small settlement of about 350, two miles from the Oregon-Idaho border, is a colorful little community in which Basque settlers and their descendants form the predominant element. Sheep-raising is the basis of the area's economy, for the desert is kind to sheep herded by the Basques who were brought over from Spain because of their long traditional skill in caring for sheep and their needs.

Before the outset of this journey, Father Curran, the Executive Secretary of the CCD, had been down to Jordan Valley at least twice since September to arouse interest in the work. He pictured Jordan Valley to us in rather dismal and bleak outline. "Remember, I had nothing to do with shunting you off to Jordan Valley. The people down there are not ready for you. If they give you the cold shoulder, don't look for me. I have no shoulder to cry on."

"Well, can't you at least wish us good luck?" I countered. "We are going at the Bishop's request. His Excellency put it this way, 'You can go anywhere in the diocese to promote the Confraternity program if you make some headway in

Jordan Valley, organizing classes, and training teachers.' Jordan Valley is supposed to be a difficult place.''

Despite the challenge in my words, it was with some questioning that Sister and I finished stowing books, charts, and bags of clothing into the trunk of the car and climbed into the back seat of Father's car for the formidable unknown. As rector of the Cathedral parish, Father Lee had the responsibility to see that we had transportation to Jordan, although he shared Father Curran's sentiment that he had no shoulder to spare for us to cry on.

The day was gray, chilly, damp, and hardly promising; in fact, a fine drizzle threatened to become a steady downpour, with the possibility of a flood. Off we were, off into the unyielding, gray yonder, since we did not even know in what direction our path lay until we retrieved a road map of Oregon. Yes, we were this way before—Pleasant Valley, Durkee, Lime and Huntington, all east of Baker.

At Ontario, Father Lee told us that we would make an overnight stop at Caldwell, Idaho, at the home of Mrs. Burns. Since it was already getting dark, this offered a pleasant interlude.

The next day, Friday, saw us up at the crack of dawn to resume our journey. A swing in the road westward brought us back into Oregon. The skies were still leaden, but the rain had stopped. As we skirted the eastern border of Oregon, we had eyes for every chasm, lava butte, and scraggly juniper or pine tree along the way. We were in the desert—forbidding, dry, cold, and sandy. Every now and then a forlorn shack loomed up in the distance near the hills covered with sagebrush and tumbleweed. We judged they were lambing-sheds, used by the sheepherders to provide some shelter for the ewes and their offspring. Now they were empty, not to be used until the spring. As we were jolting along on one of the shelves of a high canyon, at the bottom of which a trickle of water found its way among the rocks and stones, I turned to the right and looked up, up, up. There were stones, rocks, sand outcroppings — a little bit of everything and not much of anything. Drab color of all kinds, here, there, everywhere, a dull lifeless green heightened by some pink splashed with brown and yellow that forced me to exclaim, "I know this must be the place where God threw all the things He had left over after making the rest of the world."

"How much longer will it be until we get to Jordan Valley?" I ventured. By way of diversion, Father Lee regaled us with some of his innumerable stories and experiences. He was entertaining, but we could not be entirely distracted from the surroundings. We were again in the wide, open country where there is one outstanding feature—the quiet. Minds attuned to city clatter revolt in the utter stillness. Our homes are filled with gadgets that whirr, grind, spin, tick, or flash. No wonder either the desert grows on you, or else you want promptly to say farewell to the "sea-like pathless, limitless waste of the desert." I could appreciate Longfellow's estimation of the desert and was looking forward to a town or hamlet.

We became more conscious of the interesting lava formations running along both sides of the road. Father Lee reminded us that Jordan Crater, one of the youngest volcanoes in the continental United States, was nearby and that in this rugged terrain about ten miles to the southwest was located Antelope Reservation, offering fishing and boating, not much else.

Jordan Valley itself is picturesque in an old-country way. One main street runs east and west, and is bisected by about twenty side streets and alleys. The post office anchors one end of the street, and St. Bernard's Catholic church, a stone-structure, the other. At least that was the picture in 1937. A drug store, grocery store, saloon, restaurant, and movie theater, open only on Saturday afternoon and evenings, were in between. The public schools, in separate buildings for grade and for high school classes, were on a side street, but more or less centrally located in the town.

This was Jordan Valley as we came to know it in the following days; on our arrival, our view of the town was as damp as our spirits. A heavy downpour of driving, slashing rain had started near Sheaville about 12 miles north of Jordan Valley. By the time we reached Jordan Valley, a rich brown oozy mud was everywhere.

Suddenly Father Lee announced that he had not been able to make any contacts to arrange for our stay in Jordan, but that he was sure someone would provide for us. He drove to the home of the altar-society president. No; she did not know we were coming; she was sorry, but she could not accommodate us. However, she compromised, "Let the Sisters wait here until you find a place for them."

Since Father Lee had some acquaintance with the townspeople, he was confident that he would succeed in finding a place. In an hour he returned, buoyant and cheerful. "Well, Sisters, no one has room for you. But I did find a tent in the back of the city jail which you may use. There are a few rents in the tent and the water is dripping in, but I have some Band-Aids that will remedy the situation."

Looking at Father Lee and trying to capture some of his cheeriness, I suggested, "It's getting rather late. Let's go and see what there is. Perhaps we will have to call on St. Paul for help; he was a tent maker, I believe." Our hostess of the past hour looked a bit nonplussed in the face of this bogus cheeriness; she had no more idea than Sister Emmanuel Mary and I what was in store for us.

Out in the car, Father Lee chuckled, "You are going to the home of the postmistress. She has a vacant room and you may stay with her. By the way, there is only one telephone in town and that is out of order. That is why no one here knew you were coming. Might tell you that there's only one bathtub in town in the home of a Mrs. Skinner, the mother of one of the American families here. Mrs. Skinner is a young Catholic woman, a nurse, and you may go there any time you want a bath."

Our introduction to life in Jordan Valley was sudden and abrupt; we were speedily introduced to its limitations: limited electricity, no indoor plumbing, lack of so many "accepted amenities." But then there were no jukeboxes! Yet we were to

20

know music, for these Basque people love real music and enjoy it. Every family had its own singing group, music and dancing all in colorful costumes, to the accent of castanets and tambourines. They had brought with them from the Basque country in the western foothills of the Pyrenees in Spain and France their native skills and customs. Originally imported into Idaho, northern California, and Nevada, as well as Oregon, for their skill in sheepherding, they tended to form a solid, ethnic group, keeping to themselves and seldom mixing with the Americans or Irish in their midst.

Down the main street we went to Mrs. Lee's home. Considering the condition of the weather and the resultant underfooting of squishy brown mud, it was fortunate for us that her home was very near to the church, with only a large field or meadow between. It was still raining as we took our overnight bags and extra wraps into the house. The charts, teaching materials, and books would be left at the church where we hoped to conduct training classes for parents and teachers. Instruction classes for children would be held there also. Mrs. Lee was at home and welcomed us warmly; she invited us to a cup of tea and some cake just to take the chill out of our bones. Then followed a climbing of stairs to stow away our things and to look over the accommodations. It was a large room with a double bed and a few chairs. Mrs. Lee told us that she would bring us water for washing when she heard us up and about in the morning.

It did not take us long to look around; it was clean and we had a quiet place to sleep. Downstairs we went to Father Lee who was waiting to accompany us to the church. A fence with a gate protected the church which in good weather presided over a meadow on three sides, frequently taken over by a few stray cows and dogs. Today the church was standing in sodden land with water in puddles and small lakes of muddied water. It was good we wore galoshes and leggings. A big key opened the gate that creaked and groaned on its rusty hinges. The door to the church was finally opened.

A vestibule hardly prepared us for what was awaiting us

in St. Bernard's. I thought the church was beautiful. The walls were frescoed in bright colors that appeal to the Basques. They were geometrically portioned off in rectangles clearly outlined in thick black paint. Half of the first block in the second row was under the second half of the first block or rectangle in the first row. Color was also alternated so that the general effect was variety, yet unity. I forget how the sanctuary was done, and I do not recall whether the windows were stained glass or not. At any rate there were statues vividly decorated.

In back of the sanctuary was a combination sacristy-office-living room for the visiting priest, but frequently taken over by the children of the parish. The sacristy consisted mainly of a row of closets for vestments used by the priest who celebrated Holy Mass and for cassocks and surplices for the servers, although these usually landed on the floor of the closet. A nondescript table, with two long benches, was used for arranging flowers for the altar. The "office" was graced by a bookcase filled with quite an array of books, including catechetical material, pictures to illustrate lessons, and a complete set of *Catholic Encyclopedia*, deluxe edition. A rocker with its innards trailing on the floor, and a few chairs of questionable vintage completed the living room.

To the extreme right of this multi-purpose area we followed a stairway leading to a large bedroom and to a long, narrow kitchen alongside it where a wood-stove, two chairs, and a rickety table gave service. There was an assortment of dishes in the cupboard fastened to the wall. Later, in subsequent visits, these two rooms were our housekeeping quarters, not at all bad for two Sisters camping with the Lord.

Our first night at Jordan Valley was cold, damp, and chilly; but we left the bedroom door wide open to capture some of the heat from the kitchen and the living room since there was no heater in our bedroom. Mr. and Mrs. Lee had their bedroom on the first floor. Like them, we were safe and snug in bed by ten o'clock. At about midnight I awoke with a drip-drip on my chin. Not wishing to disturb my partner, I put my feet on the floor searching for my "Angel Treads"—better known as bedroom slippers. I had hoped quietly to study and solve the drippy situation. Without warning, something bit my foot, hard and sharp. Nothing came to my mind but a rattlesnake. Sister awoke with my alarm.

"Something bit me," I announced. A cautious survey of the floor revealed no rattlesnake, but a large nest of wasps come alive out of their somnolent state from the extra warmth coming their way. A hasty look around, and we decided the best place for us was in bed, pulled out of the way of the drip.

Six-thirty came too early, when Mrs. Lee brought us a pitcher of hot water and other necessities for our morning ablutions. By seven o'clock we had donned all the accoutrements of Arctic survival. A stiff wind was blowing the rain toward us. We sloshed along, hoping the church would be warm. Father had a fire going, but since there was mainly sagebrush in the bin, the air was thick with acrid smoke. The stove was in the back of the church; we moved to the front. Holy Mass began at 7:15, and at eight o'clock we were sloshingly paddling our way back to Mrs. Lee's for breakfast. Hot cakes made appetizingly tremendous with melted butter and syrup, washed down with steaming hot coffee, did the trick. We felt much better and were ready to tackle the tasks of the day. For they would be "our" tasks, since by 9:30 Father Lee was on his return trip to Baker. We regretted his going for that would mean that we would be deprived of Mass that first Sunday as well as during the week; however, the Blessed Sacrament was on the altar so we were not entirely alone.

Father Lee had left us the names of families he wanted us to visit. The Ellorriages, Elordis, Madariagas, Eicurans, Yturraspes, Zaticas, and many others. All of them had children in school. It would be great to meet them in their homes and to give them an idea of the religious education program. We stopped at the post office for directions. The Zatica home was the one we came to first. A rap at the door, a short, silent prayer, and the door flew open. Jimmy, about three, a cute little fellow, motioned us to come in. It was the living room of a large family, with several of the children playing on the linoleum-covered floor. Mr. Zatica, reading the newspaper, looked up and made us welcome. Yes, he wanted the children to go to release time instructions, and so did Mamacita coming in from the kitchen with flour on her hands. She was making a special Basque dish for dinner and invited us to stay. We would have been happy to accept her gracious offer, but had already put our name in someone else's pot; however, we would come back another day.

I'll never forget Mr. Zatica. He was a typical Basque, of sturdy and stocky build, rather heavy. He complained of our lax religious practices in America. He demonstrated this by making a genuflection. Straight as a poker, he genuflected, making sure that his knee touched the floor with a loud crack like a pistol shot. "That is how we do it at home," he said and repeated the action. At the end, the children were in hysterics; they thought "Pop" was so funny; we thought he was splendid.

From Zaticas' we went to Yturraspes'. This was a home with three teenagers—Delphine, Beatrice, and a third whose name evades me—helping to take care of an invalid mother. "Yes; of course Mommy will be glad to sign the paper asking the school to release us for an hour's instruction each week." We had to assure the mother, "No, the girls will not be punished for missing school. We want to be sure that every parent signs the request for attendance at religious instruction classes and that you understand Oregon law allows this. Any questions? . . . Yes, we will be in church tomorrow at 10 o'clock for a service. Did you get your notice? Fine, we'll see you then in church at 10, rain or shine."

Saturday afternoon was spent visiting the various members of the school board, to acquaint them with the Released Time program and to gain their cooperation. This was done with individual members and with several small groups of men. Several men on the board, all of whom were non-Catholic, were encouraging. They saw no reasons why the request would not be honored. However, there was one gentleman who was not so sure. He was tall and dark, with deep-set black eyes that narrowed to mere slits as he scanned me sternly and with severe disapproval. It took some tall talking, with the proviso that the parents of the children concerned would not protest, to bring him around to at least a grudging, "Go ahead."

Protests did come from some of the parents: "They will punish our children for being absent," or "They will keep our children back; they will not be promoted." However, when the parents learned that this program would not take place until the next school year, all—both parents and members of the school board—wisely determined to thrash out any problems they might have at the meetings held in the interim. The outcome of the meetings was that by September 1938 the Released Time program won approval on a tentative basis.

When we came to Jordan, it was arranged that we would have breakfast either at Lee's or that Sister and I would prepare our own breakfast in the kitchenette on the second floor loft in back of the church. Members of the Altar Society took it upon themselves to supply a substantial luncheon at noon in the living room at the rear of the church; and various parishioners invited us to their homes for the evening meal. Girls generally came to us with a basket containing luncheon at noon, while the boys supplied us with pails of water for all our needs. If that combination living room-sacristy-office could talk, it would have many a tale to tell. Here it was that I held the training sessions for teachers; here it was that the children came for "stories" after school; here it was that we met all and sundry who wanted to see either one of us. Meetings of the parishioners had to be held in the church that could accommodate a goodly number.

The evening meal that Saturday was at Madariagas' home. It was typically a Basque feast with fish, lamb, vegetables, biscuits, homemade bread, and butter; and the characteristic wine-skin was passed from one diner to another to take his fill. The sheepherders had come into town so that at least eight burly men were there in from the desert along with four women and six children gathered at the long table groaning with food. The wine-skin was full and expertly used and handed from one to the next. I judge there were at least two to three quarts of wine in the pouch. Attached to the pouch was a long rubber tube with a nozzle to facilitate drinking. The wine-skin was lifted to one's shoulder, steadied by one's head and one hand; the free hand was used to convey the tube to one's mouth. Tipping the head back slightly, the possessor of the wine-skin drew a deep breath to enjoy the nectar of the gods in Basque fashion. No, I did not try my hand, or my mouth, at the art, although the skin was offered to us each time around.

There was much gayety, good-will, and laughter during the meal, followed by sprightly conversation among the men. They were kindly gentlemen who did lots of reading out on the range and they could talk intelligently on any subject. After seeing the wine-skin go the rounds, it was interesting to find that their favorite drink at work was tea. They are out in the wind, cold, and snow; at camp there is a special kind of sheet-metal stove that holds a fire well; on the stove is a big kettle of tea. One grizzly old herder told of his riding back to camp to drink a few cups of the "brew that cheers, but does not inebriate" whenever he was cold, thirsty, tired, or lonesome. I enjoyed his laudatory dissertation on the benefits of tea. Scalding hot, it warmed him, relieved his thirst, and the several trips to get tea helped wonderfully to pass the time. His idea of hospitality was to ask a stranger to his camp to share with him a cup of tea. For him, tea was the touchstone of his social life.

Mrs. Madariaga was a good cook and outdid herself for the occasion. We sat down to table at 6 p.m.; when Sister and I left, it was 8 p.m. It was not far to the Lees' home. We found the wasps and their nest had been cleared out during the day, so we could hope that it would be a quiet night, free from any disturbance such as wasps . . . or rattlesnakes.

Mr. Lee gave us the informative bit of encouragement, "It's too cold for snakes, now hibernating. You can find plenty of them in late spring and summer. There's a den of rattlesnakes on the way into town in one of the lava formations, but at this time of year, you are safe."

The roads were still soggy and slushy the next morning, Sunday. When the rain stopped before dawn, the water evaporated somewhat and gave promise of its being dry underfoot. However, some dark clouds strayed our way and we were deluged with another downpour. That was our regular weather for the next two days.

The people knew there was no Mass that Sunday morning, but we had written an announcement that went out to every Catholic home. In it we scheduled:

1. A rosary devotion;
2. Reading of the Gospel of the Sunday; and,
3. Explanation of our visit to Jordan Valley, giving our aims and plans.

We tackled a few of the older girls coming into church. We asked, "Wouldn't you like to help say the rosary?" There was a nod dubiously given, but a nod nonetheless. One of the boys was invited to read the Gospel. He did it very nicely; we were proud of him. A general instruction and questions from the worshippers were next in order.

One of the youngsters wanted to know why the sanctuary light was burning. A lovely little curly-headed girl of about seven called out, "I know; that shows the Sisters are in town."

"Well, it certainly shows that Somebody is in town," I answered. "It shows that Jesus is in the church in the tabernacle. It shows that our Lord is in town, in this church."

In turn, I did some questioning—a lesson with visual aids followed, aids immediately at hand. "Who of you children can show me the altar? The candlesticks? The cruets?" The Mass servers volunteered to point to the cruets. "That is good. You are very alert." I added, "Who knows what pews are?" A boy of about seven volunteered to identify the pews.

You should have seen the parents' eyes sparkle the minute

the children went into action. "What do you call this?" I asked, pointing to the crucifix. "Cross," thundered from the children's area. Then, holding my crucifix for all to see, I explained, "This is a crucifix; it is a cross with Jesus on it." That led to the sign of the cross and the proper way to make it. A girl from one of the upper grades volunteered somewhat anxiously to demonstrate the fashion in which the Spanish people sign themselves with the cross. "Form a cross by placing your thumb of the right hand under the forefinger of the same hand. Kiss it; it reminds us of the cross of Christ. Make a small sign of the cross on your forehead, lips and heart, saying, 'From the snares of the evil one, deliver us, O Lord.' Then make the large sign of the cross, saying, 'In the name of the Father, and of the Son, and of the Holy Ghost. Amen.'''

I was delighted with the response. I knew that some Basques made the sign of the cross in that way, but had never seen it done. Even in America, after years away from the homeland, some Basque families are proud to pass on this custom to their children as part of their ethnic heritage. My esteem for the people of Jordan Valley, both Irish and Basque, was growing. I certainly liked what I had learned about them thus far. I must say that the mothers especially did a creditable job teaching their children their own way according to the dictates of the heart and common sense. Before dismissing the group at about 11:15, I spoke of our plan to initiate a program of religion teacher training for them. They indicated that 3 p.m. Sunday afternoon in the sacristy would be a good time to begin. Their good-byes indicated the end of the Sunday morning service; however, their trailing "See you again" ushered in a period of quiet and relaxation.

Sr. Emmanuel Mary and I found ourselves happy exchanging accounts of our work in this isolated colony of pioneers. Sister had been busy in the so-called library area, sorting according to their categories the books on Father's shelves. She showed me the list of names, children's and mother's, who had been present that morning. We had lunch of a hamburger, a glass of milk, and some fruit, quite ample

28

and enough to do us until the evening meal at Pilar Elloriaga's. We had a short time to say Vespers and then to welcome our would-be trainees for the course in teaching Religion.

Three o'clock came—and only three prospective catechists showed up—a Mrs. Joyce, Mrs. Skinner, and Pilar. After an introductory talk explaining the purpose of the course and the general principles of religious education, I listened attentively to the all-over complaint that the Basque children, as a rule, are not required to study at home. This was a problem, but there was the larger one. Was I discouraged that not even a handful of interested prospects came to class? Not at all; it simply urged me on to remedy the situation.

When we closed up for the day, it was 4 o'clock. If we wanted to do something about the lack of returnees for our introduction to teaching, we had to make up our minds fast; we had no time for dallying. Without delay, we decided to use the rest of the afternoon to find out first why some of the women were absent when at the morning session they had indicated that they would be present at the afternoon session. The early morning shower had subsided; a bright November sun was peeping out between the remaining clouds. A walk would do us good; away we go.

I'll never forget the reaction to our visit at the first house. Answering our rap, a well-proportioned woman, neatly dressed, opened the door. She said nothing, but started to laugh as though there were some kind of joke. She had had no intention to attend the class; neither did she expect us to come looking for her. At any rate her good-natured laugh told us volumes; she could not be bothered teaching other people's children. However, our visit to her had one good effect; by the time we had visited the third home on our list, she had already been there telling her neighbor that we were on the way to see why they had changed their minds. "Oh, I thought you would be satisfied with my promise; I had no idea you expected me to keep that promise." Sr. Emmanuel Mary and I may not have had the last laugh, but we were satisfied to smile happily when finally these ladies took over the teaching quite effectively.

The next day, Monday, saw us visiting the schools, both grade and high. Our purpose was to meet all the children. The elementary school had three classrooms, two on the first floor, one on the second. The teachers were most gracious and cooperative. The children were gloriously happy to see us. Yes, they would come to church after school; and they kept their promise. It was true that through the years the religious instruction of children was not wholly neglected. At the turn of the 20th century, priests from the Baker diocese ministered more or less regularly to the spiritual and religious needs of the faithful here. Now, however, we hoped to establish a program for the regular, systematic teaching of religion there. The children loved every minute of the time we could give them, and the church became the regular stopping place every day after school. They were beautiful children, free as mountain goats and fresh as daisies in spring. When they saw us on the streets, they would run to catch up with us, shouting some unusual greeting, as, "Sister, are you guys going to stay all year?"

I must say that I loved the people of Jordan Valley. Different in so many ways from the Bostonians and Philadelphians I had known. Now it amuses me no end when thinking of my first few days with them. Thoughtfully, seriously, one evening I was struck with the idea, "I am sure my mother would be worried about me tonight if she knew where I am."

I cannot help recalling here, digression though it may be, how on one occasion a few years later in downtown Portland, Oregon, I remarked to my companion, "It feels good to have cement pavements under my feet; makes me think of Philadelphia." By that time I had traveled many roads, unpaved and hard to navigate, in eastern Oregon.

I also paid a visit to the high school. The boys thought it funny that I found some difficulty in pronouncing their family names. But that fact formed a bond between us. I couldn't pronounce their surnames; they couldn't recite the Confiteor or Act of Contrition.

After ten days, during which we battled a second deluge that lasted three days, Sister and I decided we had done as much as we could do on this first venture into the area. We had visited every Catholic home with children at least twice, visited the schools and the school board members; we instructed the women how to bring home to their children the truths of our holy faith and introduced them to formal classes. Sr. Emmanuel Mary kept the record of all activities and prepared teaching aids. Now it was time for us to move on. In view of the fact that each of us had two suitcases and a box of educational material to lug back to Baker, we decided that a car was needed for the return trip.

How to get a car? That was the question. A telegram was sent to Father Lee: "SOS—torrential rains—Come for us at once." That brought action. The telephone at the grocery store had been restored to use and we got word that Father Lee wanted us to call him back. A squishy walk ensued.

Father Lee, I believe with tongue in cheek, phoned. "Take the bus and come back."

Our answer: "We could never get on a bus with all our things."

His rejoinder: "I told you not to come crying to me if you found your task unbearable."

Our reply: "Our work is finished here. We are delighted with the response we received. We do not intend to cry on your shoulder or on anybody else's."

Father Lee: "In that case, I will be in Jordan Valley tomorrow."

It was twelve days since we had left Baker. We were glad to be going back; we had finished our first missionary exploit. The feeling of accomplishment was most rewarding; we were glad that we had come. We promised the people, parents and children, that we would repeat our visit to them in the spring.

That promise was carried out when we returned to teach Religious Vacation School the last week of May and the first week of June the following year, 1938. From then on, Jordan Valley had its place in our yearly calendar. It was delightful to go back among friends and to have Alice O'Connor and Mrs. Joyce help us with the teaching. Religious Vacation School in Jordan Valley was a novel idea. For several years the children from the Valley had attended the summer sessions in Religion at St. Francis Academy, Baker, where they were boarded for two weeks. The Sisters of St. Francis taught the children during the day and washed their clothes and mended them at night.

While the Vacation School was occupying the children, I used the evenings from 7:30 to 9 p.m. to finish the course of instruction for lay teachers that I had begun in November 1937. I thought that with the help the teachers were now getting, they could initiate the Released Time program in September 1938 and be prepared for any emergency. During the time Alice O'Connor helped us teach during the day, she stayed with us at night and also helped with our meals. A cot had been placed in the kitchen for Alice; two cots in the adjoining room provided sleeping accommodations for us. Someone provided two new basins for daily ablutions, with our names printed on the bottom. I still have a picture of the basins, sitting atop a chest of drawers with all the dignity of some sort of ceremonial urns.

We spent the two weeks literally with the children. Besides attending school, they found their way to church for daily Mass. They were great. Some of the boys served at Holy Mass and Benediction. They sang, prayed, and sang some more to their hearts' content. And then they'd go home romping, playing along the road, to come back in an hour or so with some casserole, or biscuits, or salad to round out a meal. In between, the little ones would come in for a story.

One afternoon about 4:30 three little boys came bounding into the "sacristy" for a story. No place was private to them. This was their church, their sacristy, their bedroom, their kitchen. There were several low chairs in the sacristy for the servers. The boys requisitioned them for their story hour. These little boys and one Sister around a small table were soon engrossed in "The Boy Who Ran Away from Home," Suddenly two of the three legs of my stool parted company and I landed on the floor with a bang. The little boys stood up and studied me in the prone position on the floor. I was laughing; it seemed so funny. Making sure I was not hurt, all three wanted to help me up. But I had to laugh some more. Then the oldest of the three gave me his hand, saying, "Come on," and I was restored to my feet. Finally, assured that no damage had been done to me, they burst into laughter which they struggled to conceal, until they realized they were laughing with me.

Is it any wonder I said the children of Jordan Valley were lovable? A few days later when we left town, they followed us on the highway to the bridge, shouting their "Good-bye, Sisters; come back soon again." That did something to me. How could I ever forget them? They won their way to my heart, dancing, singing, smiling, with the happy characteristic of children everywhere.

God bless you all, I prayed, as we rode along hardly aware of the desert country we were traversing. In a few hours, we would be home in Baker to recoup our forces, for we "had miles to go," we "had promises to keep."

The catechist's prayer was beginning to take on new meaning for me. Each teacher I instructed meant a duplication of myself. It goes something like this:

> "Jesus, before the record of my life
> Is chiseled on a rain-worn stone
>   In two mute dates,
> Let me be a bearer of Thy Name
> And light within ten-thousand hearts
> Thy Love's Eternal Flame."

Chapter 3

Do You Know What You Are Doing?

The years 1937-1940 could be called the round-up period in the Baker diocesan CCD. Sr. Mary Rosetta had come to join the staff in 1938, but by 1940 the work had expanded to such a point that a third Sister was required and happily acquired when Sr. Mary Maurina bade farewell to Boston and joined us at Baker.

These were years of new and exciting experiences for all of us. They were years of calling to account, of taking risks as part of the sacrifices demanded for bringing the love of Christ to the children and their parents in far-flung eastern Oregon. They were years that transformed one's parochial school mind-set to an all-children-comprehensive mentality on a diocesan-wide basis. Under the circumstances, as they are even today in the Baker diocese, parochial schools do exceptionally good work; but they take care of only a small fraction of the total number of Catholic children in the diocese. The rest must be taken care of by the CCD—the organization recommended by Pope Pius XI to Bishop McGrath.

Instead of thinking solely of the children who could come to us in our schools to learn Christ, we had to consider taking Christ to the Catholic children not in Catholic schools. Where could we find them? In their homes after school, in church at

35

Holy Mass, and even in the schools they attended. Naturally, if we could contact the children in a group, we could reach more in a shorter time than by visiting their homes. We did both, whichever lent itself best to our purpose. I shall give an example or two.

One bright October day Sister Maurina accompanied me on our visit to Pendleton, Echo, Hermiston, Heppner, and Ione. Mrs. Jack Kennedy volunteered to take us by car. She was not only apostolic, but truly was anxious to visit friends and relatives along the way. In another twelve months we would have a car of our own; for the nonce we depended on the Union Pacific Railroad, the Greyhound Bus Lines, and volunteers with cars. On this trip, we had done our stint in Pendleton and were now going to Hermiston, about thirty miles west.

As we come near to the Echo public school, I said to Sr. Maurina, "How about going in here? We might find some children we want."

Sister Maurina panicked at the thought. She had just come from staid and conservative Boston, where Sisters did not go traipsing through the country as we were. She was still new to this wide, open country. Baker City diocese was wide enough to embrace all the states of Pennsylvania and New York, with some hundreds of square miles left over for good measure. Towns were a rarity in the open area from Pendleton to Hermiston with its rich wheat lands that were exposed to deeply darkening duststorms which could bring havoc to the newly-plowed farmlands. Placing her hand on my arm, Sister asked concernedly, "Do you know what you are doing?"

"Come and see," was my reply, as we headed toward the high, high steps into the school. It was a typical no-nonsense public school of the early 1940s. We looked around inquiringly for the office. The drone of voices in recitation came to us from both sides of the hall. We rapped at a classroom door; the teacher was surprised to see two nuns, but came to our rescue.

"The principal will come from the gym in a few minutes.

36

Wait in the office, two doors down to the right. He is the coach and also physical ed instructor, but should be in the office by ten o'clock."

To the office we walked, as carefully as two miscreant students might respond to an invitation to that office. Before we had time to get our bearings, in bustled a very businesslike person, a man who might have been middle-aged, but was vigorously young in manner. His movements were definite, brisk, energetic. His cordial greeting put both of us at ease. "Sisters, I am happy to meet you. What can I do for you?"

My heart gave a hop, skip, and jump. I was overjoyed, encouraged. His offer of help seemed warmly forthright. Out came the story, "We are Sisters of St. Francis from Baker in charge of the religious education of Catholic children in public schools." No hedging or apologizing for our assignment. Be open and see what happens.

"We would like to make an appointment to meet the Catholic children in attendance here at a time most convenient for you, for the teachers, and for all concerned. We are teachers and know what it means for anyone to come to a school unexpectedly. We can come back anytime, any day within the week."

He was quick and alert. He took a moment to mull over the idea, checking possibilities. "How about meeting the children today? In fifteen minutes you can meet the children you want to see in the lunchroom; there are tables and chairs there and ample room."

Then by way of explanation, he added, "You see, I am not a Catholic, but this summer I was in a music class at Portland University with Catholic nuns. They were great women; lots of good fun studying together. I shall ever remember them. One of them stands out in particular, a music-teacher from Baker, Sr. Faustina."

"That's right. Sr. Faustina is a synonym for music and fun. We are glad you met her." Then, gathering our briefcases, we followed the principal's directions to the lunchroom. This was a sort of barracks affair, useful, but no chrome, no high polish, no glitter. Long tables with benches on either side to accommodate about ten children per table filled the greater part of the room.

Shortly, the children came; they came in all sizes and formed a lively group, pushing, jostling, and laughing. Big and little, exuberant and subdued, boys and girls: in all there were about twenty. They were from homes in the small towns of Echo and Stanfield and from all the settlements nearby.

They eyed us carefully, speculating what we wanted with them, probably anticipating a holiday or release from school work. "Yes, we know who you are," some of the children said in answer to my questions and opening remarks to establish rapport. "You came to see us at Vacation School."

"Why are we here? Can't you guess? We are here because we like you. We want to help you learn about God, our Father, about Jesus, His Son, and about the Holy Ghost. The study of religion is not only for vacation school, but also for year-round classes. We shall see what you need in the line of books and teachers. Perhaps classes will be held in some of your homes. But first we must know who you are, what grade you are in, where you live, and how old you are.

"We brought slips of paper and pencils with us. Sister Maurina will give a paper and pencil to each one. On the first line where it says 'Name,' write your name; on the second line, write the grade you are in. Yes, numbers will do. On the third line, write your address, giving the street on which you live and your house number, together with the name of your town; at the bottom, write age, putting how old you are."

A glance noted some children apparently willing, but confused, puzzled; this occasioned the additional remark, "Here are a few little boys and girls who cannot write all of that. Maybe the brothers and sisters of these little ones will help them write what we want to know." It was really a task to wring this information from them. Later on, we provided registration slips that they could take home to be filled out and returned to us. The answers to the basic questions were a veritable gold mine of information to the pastor at Hermiston, the parish of which Echo is a mission.

We arranged to meet the children at their little mission church three days later after school hours. Then they would receive their religion texts and be shown how to study. It was with singing hearts that we said good-bye to the children and their principal as we fairly skipped down the steps of the Echo Public School. It was close to noon when we got back to the car; the waiting periods and the conferences had taken up almost two well-used hours. During that time, Mrs. Kennedy had been visiting with the Cunhas, family friends of long standing.

At any rate, we could say "Mission Accomplished" when we reported in at Our Lady of Angels rectory, Hermiston. The Capuchin Fathers are in charge here and the pastor was delighted that we had visited the children. Before we partook of a luncheon, he arranged with Mrs. Kennedy to take us to another mission to see what we could do for the children in and around Irrigon.

Irrigon, some ten miles or so to the northwest from Hermiston, is situated on Highway 30 along the Columbia River, a road that is a scenic delight, unless you are in a hurry to make a schedule and have eyes only for the clock and the odometer. Here there was another station, later on to become a mission for a small community of scattered Catholics.

The public school at Irrigon was of that period—a square, two-storied structure, set well back from the road. It was a thrill to go into the school to discover what the reception might be here. We did not have to wait. The principal was coming down the hall; he looked as though he knew what he was there for. Straight to the point he went. In a low-keyed, well-modulated voice, he asked, "May I help you, please?" His tone of voice and inflection indicated readiness to serve.

As quietly and as quickly as possible, we told him our names and mission. Then with a smile we ventured the query, "Would it be possible for you to arrange a meeting for us with the children at a time you can spare? We know schools are busy places, time is at a premium, and many teachers do not welcome interruptions."

Without waiting for further explanations, the principal broke in, "Of course, I'll see what I can do. Come with me into the office, please. According to this schedule, we have supervised study in half an hour. I'll send a message to the teachers asking them to see that all Catholic children come to Room 26 for study period. How does that sound to you? Is that arrangement satisfactory?"

Then, as if an afterthought, on leaving the office he mumbled something. At first I didn't know what; then it dawned on me that he was asking a favor. "May I come in too? I would like to hear what you have to say." We acquiesced with a smile. We might feel that we were under scrutiny, but what else could we do except be equally gracious?

A hasty conference made us decide to take a general subject for discussion with the group. Seventeen boys and girls, an assortment in age and size, made their appearance with the principal at 2:30. The Commandments of God, or at least some examples suitable for children, were on the agenda.

Sister Maurina, smiling broadly, began, "Do you know who we are?" After several children hazarded answers, Sister continued, "Yes, we are Sisters. We are your Sisters, just for you. Perhaps you know some children who go to St. Joseph's Academy in Pendleton. These children tell you about their school. They speak of 'our Sister', or say 'My Sister says this.' Well, just the same as your friends talk about 'our Sister' so you may think of us as 'your Sisters.' We are Sisters working, thinking, planning, and praying just for Catholic children in public school. We are 'your Sisters' and we are visiting with you; we are happy to be here."

It was a pleasure to see their eyes gleam and sparkle as they listened to Sister. "Try to remember always that you are special; you are children of God and God loves you, every one of you, very much. Do you know how we show God that we love Him? . . . Yes, that is right—by keeping His Commandments, by doing what God wants us to do."

A hand waved frantically and a child called out, "S'ter, S'ter, we show God we love Him when we behave."

"Very good; now tell me what we do when we behave?"

"We try to be good," one little fellow called out.

A little prodding brought out further responses, "We tell the truth," "We obey."

"Can you tell me what 'obey' means?"

"Yes, obey means to do what you are told to do by your parents, by your teachers, by those who have the right to tell you what to do."

"We should tell the truth," one of the little ones contributed.

"Very good; when do we tell the truth?" The questioning kept on. "A little boy in the last seat spilled some ink on the floor, and he tells Mr. Quinn he did it. He does not blame it on someone else. Is he telling the truth?"

A unanimous, explosive "Yes" came from the children.

"All right. Martin had a peanut butter sandwich in his lunch box. When he went for the sandwich, it was gone. Martin felt bad that somebody had taken his lunch. No one would say what had happened to the sandwich. How about that?"

A bright little girl with bright red hair in a pony tail spoke up, "That was not a lie. That's taking what does not belong to you."

"Very good for you. Do you know what we call that?"

"Snitching," piped up one voice.

"I'd call that stealing," volunteered another.

"What about fighting with your brothers and sisters? Being mean to them? Calling them names? Do you think this is one of God's commandments? Remember, being good, behaving, being loving and kind begin at home. Boys and girls who do what their parents ask them to do, who are kind and loving to their brothers and sisters, should have little trouble in school."

There was much discussion of and suggestions about ways

41

and means of being good. "Put wet towels on the rack and not on the bathroom floor," announced one little girl with a housekeeping flair.

"Feed the cat; put her food in the dish on the back porch," came another hint.

"Rock the baby while your mother is getting dinner."

While we were encouraging pertinent responses, a fidgety boy tremulously offered, "Put out the garbage without spilling it on the way."

Then, to our surprise, the gong sounded for dismissal. Since many of the children went home on school buses, our summary had to be brief. I thanked Sr. Maurina and the class for the good review of the commandments, and told the children what arrangements had been made for their year-round classes.

There seemed to be some unresolved questions in the minds of some children. "Are you going to be in church next Sunday?"

"Do you want us to come?"

"Yes," they chorused. "Do come."

Sister satisfied their curiosity, "We do not know exactly when we will have time to visit you on a Sunday, but this much I can say: We intend coming back some Sunday to visit you at class; yes, it will be some Sunday before Thanksgiving. Tell mother and daddy that we visited you in school today, and tell them we are pleased that you know that a good Christian not only knows his faith, but also lives it. Good-bye and God bless you. You were very attentive. We are happy."

With that, the children began to depart and the principal came forward. "Sisters, I cannot understand why all our children cannot come in to hear you. I know the children's behavior will be better after your visit. All our children could profit by the talks you give. Thank you for coming."

We were made more than happy by the principal's reaction. He liked particularly the positive approach. We found further encouragement when the principal added as we bade him a grateful farewell, "Come back whenever you can. You are always welcome."

Outside, our faithful charioteer, Mrs. Kennedy, closed the book she had been reading during the long wait and asked for directions. It was nearly 3:30. We decided to return to Hermiston where a few days' work was cut out for us, giving intensive training sessions to the CCD teachers and strengthening the executive board. We stayed at the McKenzies and Mrs. Kennedy visited with relatives.

But first to the rectory to report our activities and to plan our schedule for the next few days. The pastor, the Rev. Alban Cullen, O.F.M.Cap., was pleased with our report on the school visits and offered us every help. We ate meals at the rectory with the Capuchins. Our stay with the McKenzies was a happy arrangement since Mrs. McKenzie was chairman of the teachers present at the CCD sessions. Father Cullen, or his assistant, graciously offered to take us to visit the families with children in the parish. We stayed three full days in Hermiston before going further, encouraging teachers to continue better efforts, solidifying the functions of the executive board, and promoting parent education. We were ready to move on in accord with our practice of not delaying at a parish or mission once our work was completed for the time. We sent word to Mrs. Kennedy. Incidentally, such demands on our driver made us realize the need of our own transportation.

Our itinerary had us scheduled to go to Condon. We could go there either cross-country and save some mileage, or we could follow the Columbia River highway to Arlington, then turn directly south about forty miles to Condon. No time was to be gained by going through open fields and unpaved roads of the wheat country, so we followed the scenic highway to the secondary Route 19 leading south. At one time, Condon was known as Summers Springs, when it was a stage-post and trading point for the surrounding territory. Many early families are still in and around the town. Among them are the Cooneys, who are Mrs. Kennedy's brother and family, the

Greiners, the Quinns, and the Fix family.

Upon our arrival in Condon we went at once to St. John's rectory where the pastor, the Rev. John B. Wand, lived with his assistant, the Rev. Thomas McTeigue. Father Wand was an elderly man and a veteran from pioneer days in Oregon who had done untold missionary work in the diocese. He was crippled from the austerities that he endured in making the rounds of the mining center at Cornucopia and other outposts at the turn of the century.

On one occasion he was in his bunk, trying to get a few hours' sleep before starting off in the early morning for Richland when a dark figure drew aside the curtain and raised a knife or stiletto above him. Of course, it was a mistake; the angry man had gone to the wrong bunk.

Another time he had gone to Cornucopia, a little settlement high amidst the Blue Mountains, to visit the miners working there. It was bitterly cold; hands and feet became numb during the night and in the morning Father Wand had two frozen feet to contend with. No doctor in sight, he applied the miners' remedy—snow. Even though his feet were frozen, his heart and will were not. There was work to be done; as soon as he could amble about, he was off and away, making light of his experience. However, as a result, he was crippled for the rest of his life, dragging himself laboriously from one place to another.

His middle initial "B" stands for Baptist. When you laid eyes on him for the first time, you thought of the patriarchs of bygone days. At any rate, he looked like a patriarch. He had a long beard that covered his chest. One time in talking with him, I asked, "Father, what do you do with your beard at night? Do you put it under the covers, or do you leave it outside your covers?"

He answered, "I really don't know." The next day he informed us that he could not get to sleep for the longest time, wondering what he should do with his beard.

The thought of Father Wand has caused this detour; it is

difficult not to flounder in memories of the grand people of the area, lay and clerical, with whom we came in contact.

Here in Condon, we had a room at the home of Judge James Burns and his wife, Mary, and their children. At least breakfast was to be at the rectory. Next morning at 7:30 we were trudging along the dirt roads to church; Mass was scheduled at 8 a.m. At exactly 8:45, we were in the very modest rectory for breakfast, spiced with pastoral suggestions on how to spend the day. I have noted that Father Wand was handicapped; however, no handicap ever kept him from doing his work.

Suddenly there was a rap at the door. At Father's booming response the door opened and three beaming girls of high school age were there. Be it noted, the dining room was a multiple-purpose room: it was living room, office, and dining room all in one. Without hesitation, Mary Eaton began, "We would like Sister to come to the high school this morning to address the students. Many of them have never seen a Sister. If she does not come, the students may never have another opportunity." This was a new angle to our visiting schools. We had gone into them with the idea of meeting children living in areas where they were remotely scattered to acquaint them with our plans. This invitation, what did it mean? Mary continued, when she noticed the slight hesitation, "The principal told us to come over and to ask you; the boys and girls are assembled."

"Whose idea was this?" I asked.

"Ours," she replied with a coaxing smile.

"Well, all right; we will come in five minutes. We must finish our coffee first."

I'll never forget Father Wand as he encouraged us to go. "You will know what to say when you get there. I will pray while you are in the school."

We had only to cross the street and go through a large unused lot to reach the school, then up the stairs to the second floor to the assembly hall. Bright sunshine came into the room;

all the windows were open. The principal, a professional-looking man, came toward us. "Sisters, I am happy you came. The students asked for you."

As he was ushering us to the platform, I questioned him, "Have you anything in particular you would like us to stress?"

"Nothing in particular, Sister. We are confident you know what students can use."

Teachers and pupils alike had an attentive air about them. I knew I would enjoy talking to this group. Introductions finished, I began, not without asking myself, "Do you really know what you are doing?"

"Both Sister Maurina and I are glad to be with you. Both of us come from large eastern cities where we were teachers in high school, St. Maurina in Boston, I in Philadelphia. But I am wondering what you want us to say to you. Perhaps you would like to know what I think makes for success in a high school student. All of us desire success in one way or another. From experience and observation I would say success in high school depends on three things:

1. The ability to learn;
2. The opportunity to learn; and,
3. Most important—the will to learn."

These three factors that spell success were amplified, illustrated, and explained fully. Finally, I gave the assembly this formula for success: Inspiration plus aspiration plus desperation plus perspiration equal sucess in any endeavor—with 90 percent perspiration.

The applause was tumultuous. Sr. Maurina won the students over with her beaming smiles during the talk. Now the principal took over. He thanked us most graciously; then, turning to the students, he addressed them, "When Sister came up to the platform, she had not determined the theme of her talk. She asked me what I would like her to stress. I gave Sister no definite topic. Sister gave us a perfect example of an im-

46

promptu talk. There was an introduction, an excellent discussion, and a forceful ending."

Afterwards, Mary Eaton and her companions introduced us to their classroom teachers and the physical ed instructor. He was elated. "I must give a talk tonight at a banquet for the athletic teams of Gilliam County. After listening to you, I know now what to say to them. Thank you so much. You both were great."

I was pleased with the outcome as I was at a similar occasion when I spoke as a Catholic educator to the entire student body, and not as a Religion teacher to a group of Catholic students. At La Grande the invitation was extended through the pastor after the parents of the Catholic students had suggested my name to the principal; here it was at the instigation of the students themselves. Here I spoke on the factors that make for success in a high school student; at La Grande, I selected the topic: "The Ideals of Washington," since it was the day before his birthday when Father McMahon accompanied me to the high school for the talk.

The Catholic students at La Grande had invited their mothers to attend the assembly at 1 p.m. There was a large student body of several hundred and the hall was crowded. The students on the whole were more or less sophisticated and curious but polite. The atmosphere was electric, the students springing to attention as soon as Father McMahon introduced me.

"Dear boys and girls, parents and teachers," I began. "I am very happy to be here, to have the opportunity of talking with you and of visiting your school. I feel at home in a school anywhere, for in a school I meet young people, eager, intelligent, and inquiring, on whom the hope of America is built." I could see them settle comfortably in their seats, they were ready to listen.

"Tomorrow is Washington's birthday. As the Father of our Country, he demands both our respect and admiration. If I were to ask you to tell me one thing you admire in Washington, what would you say? I am sure you would mention his

47

courage, his bravery, his patriotism."

After discussing each of these points, I continued, "Besides these characteristics there is one more I would like to mention, his reverence for God and his spirit of prayer."

From a somewhat restless group in the very beginning, they were unusually attentive, interested and equally alert as I finished with a genuine "Thank you. I enjoyed being with you. Have a happy holiday tomorrow."

Were I asked, I would have to say there was no cast-iron rule· that we followed in going into a public school. I recall one small one-room schoolhouse that we passed on our journeys through the diocese. We were in the Burns parish and the pastor there, the Rev. Vincent C. Egan, asked Sr. Rosetta and me to visit two little girls attending the school. He cautioned, "Do not talk to the children in school. Ask the teacher to send them out to you." Father Egan was conservative to the nth degree in regard to the general interpretation of the principle of "Separation of Church and State." He was most solicitous in following the more rigid interpretation, hence his injunction to see the children outside the school building. But Father Egan did not reckon with all the parties concerned. There was another person to be dealt with.

Quite unexpectedly the teacher came out of the little whitewashed school building. She was energetic and purposeful. Directly and unmistakably she came to the point, "Here are the two girls. However, why don't you come in to see all of the children? They have no visitors at all. It would be valuable experience for them."

Put that way, there was nothing to do but acquiesce. Sister Rosetta got busy with instruction for the two girls while the teacher was suggesting a compromise, "Tell the children who you are, what you do, and anything else you wish to add." A pleasant fifteen minutes awaited me in the classroom.

There was nothing bleak about this school; the room was cheery. Window-boxes with bright red geraniums helped to make this classroom the cheerful place it was. There was a sandbox in one corner depicting city life with its well-laid out streets, municipal park, and public buildings constructed of corrugated paper. A balanced aquarium enlivened another corner with various forms of marine life. The children, about twenty of them in Grades 1 to 6, seemed eager, happy, and receptive. Sister and I both spoke to them briefly, complimenting them on their wide-awake appearance, and telling them how fortunate they were in their teacher.

Father Egan was pleased that we had this contact, and so were we. Little had we thought that we would have the opportunity to enter a public school in Harney County. Little did we reckon with the ingenuity and resourcefulness of the teacher in charge. This incident happened as long as 34 years ago, but the memory of the visit stayed with me.

No matter where we went in the diocese, our reception by the public school authorities was usually the same—courteous, cooperative, and very considerate. No wonder I could say to Sr. Maurina, "Come and see," when she asked me on the steps leading to the Echo public school, "Do you know what you are doing?"

There are many other encounters with public school pupils in their school situations, that will ever be cherished in memory. The principal at Prineville in the central part of Oregon would take one look at us and say, "Oh, yes; I know what you want; you want to meet the Catholic children." Frequently he would send them to us, grade by grade, right in his office. As a rule, he was present at our meetings. One day he said to me, "Now, Sister, have you some way of knowing whether the Children are Catholic?"

"I think we can tell pretty well," I assured him.

Before the children present, I held up my rosary. "Look at these beads. Have any of you seen anything like them before?" Heads nodded.

One youngster spoke up. "Grandma has one of them hanging on her bedpost."

Another curly-haired mite of six whispered quietly, "Mommy has a rosary; it's real pretty. She takes it to church."

Very informative, I noted. Where the rosary is hanging on a bedpost, there must be some Catholicity, although I happen to know a non-Catholic boy of ten, who always carries a rosary in his pocket. The mother who has the "real pretty" rosary and takes it to church has in all probability a Catholic child.

A few of the children did not recognize the rosary. I was not discouraged. "Look at me; watch what I am doing." I made the sign of the Cross. "Has anyone of you seen anyone do this before?"

They became clamorous. One lad with a crew-cut shouted, "I can do that. We do that when we go to church."

"Very good." I was pleased until I noted one shy little girl with the face of one of Botticelli's angels who was misty-eyed and close to tears. I drew her to myself and asked her name. The family name was unfamiliar. I told her she was a very nice little girl, but that she should go back to her classroom. I had no reason to believe that she was from a Catholic family. Sometimes children came to us simply because their friends were coming, or because of curiosity; they did not want to miss anything.

Amusing little incidents occurred when we met children in their schools. Sometimes we went to tell them we were in town and we would be glad to see them at the church at some convenient time, at 4 o'clock for example. At certain places the children actually ran from school to church. Then we would explain the scope of their studies for the year and the general structure of the CCD program. The children generally were quite responsive. They knew us and we knew them.

It once happened that we visited Lakeview, with its militantly Catholic enclave, and as usual made arrangements to visit the public schools. The principals were most generous. "Come whenever it is most convenient for you." That is all we needed. Sister Maurina and I decided to go to the two schools directly after luncheon. In the schoolyard even the non-Catholic children greeted us as we passed through.

That day, one girl of about ten was not in school. The

50

next day one of her non-Catholic friends met her with the announcement, "Oh, Mary Ann, you missed the Catholics!"

Mary Ann shook her head, "Uh-huhn, they are staying at our house."

Her companion was delighted; Mary Ann was just what she hoped for—a board of information. "Tell me," she importuned, "why do they always wear the same clothes?"

In reporting this incident to us at the supper table, Mary Ann confessed, "I really did not know, but I said that shows you belong to God."

Many other incidents could be told, but I hope the reader has some idea of what we did when we entered a public school. We found the teachers, principals, and superintendents superb and magnanimous in all our dealings with them. They were idealistic and practical, too. We recognized them as educators, dedicated to the service of our children and youth. In the eleven-year period from 1937 to 1948, we made 389 visits to public schools.

No wonder the principal at Ione, a mission in the sheep country of Heppner, would say, "Come in; you are always welcome. All of our children need the lessons on truth, obedience, and honesty that you stress. When they hear you, they somehow listen. They have us all the time; you are special."

Chapter 4

It's the Mass That Matters

In the Middle Atlantic States where I had grown up and in New England where I worked as a teacher, I had come to associate the offering of Mass with churches, larger or smaller, or with convent chapels, some quite small. I had to go West to come to some idea of the circumstances of Mass in the colonial days in those same states when missionary priests riding the circuit offered Holy Mass in the front room of some home, the lounge of some inn, or vacant room in a village post exchange. There are churches and convent and institutional chapels in the cities and relatively larger towns of eastern Oregon; but in rural districts such as Richland, Drewsey, Mitchell, and Grass Valley, Mass was offered wherever a group of people could gather. Such occasions were inspiring, with a stress on the meaning of "ecclesia" (the calling together, the assembly); certainly they brought home the meaning of community and were experiences to be shared, as reminders of the past and presages of the future.

It was late fall in the early forties. Our day-by-day account of CCD activities sets the time as October 10-15, 1941. Sister Maurina and I had set out with the Rev. George A. Murphy for CCD activities in his parish of St. Elizabeth at John Day, a one-time mining community when the gold rush was on. The ride from St. Elizabeth Hospital, Baker, to the parish house at John Day was breathtaking over Dooley Mountain with its narrow, winding road, south for 26 miles. Mountain pines and other evergreens clung to the slopes on both sides of the road, which was built ledge-wise into the mountain on the left, with deep canyons opening out on the right. After that stretch, the road was more or less level for about ten miles until we came to Dixie Mountain with Whitman National Forest traversing it. Occasional campsites were to be found by anyone wishing a drink of fresh mountain water, or a rest in the open air with no breath of air pollution. We passed through several little towns, exuding charm and a certain quaintness, before coming to John Day in Grant County.

We knew that as soon as we arrived at the parish house the work there would be different. The reason for that was none other than the pastor, Father George Murphy, an energetic, bustling, apostolic priest. No monotony, when you were working with or for Father Murphy. His ideas—and he was usually bristling with them—were innovative, original and frequently startling.

He lost no time in acquainting us with the procedures for catechetical instruction. "I believe in the dictum that parents are the best teachers of religion for their own children. The parish is so far-flung that it is impossible to have formal classes. Every child of school age has the books according to the diocesan course of studies, and follows the Directed Home Study Course. They bring the completed papers with them to church for me, and take home the corrected papers with them. You'll see how it works on Sunday."

"Do the parents actually comply with your wishes that they teach their own children?" I asked with great interest.

"Many of them do. Those who don't lose out in the end. Are these your bags? I'll take them upstairs for you," he announced.

"Upstairs" had several rooms, sparsely furnished, but adequately enough to take care of one's needs. It sometimes

54

happened that a woman with children, for example, would come to see Father. Food and shelter were given, when needed, for a few days and nights. Father believed in being practical.

After supper, which his mother cooked, Father said, "Get a good night's rest. Tomorrow we will visit families along the way to Johnson's at Long Creek. We stay with Jim and Catherine overnight."

That did not mean much to us. We knew as much as we did before. We knew neither Jim nor Catherine. The next morning after Mass and breakfast, we started off. A surprise awaited us. Coming out of the house, we stopped short at the sight of our equipage. Sister Maurina put her fingers to her mouth to smother an "Oh, my." Consternation did not last long.

"Sisters, we are picking up a horse to take him back to the ranch. The Johnsons gave me 'Major' to lead the Labor Day parade in John Day; we're killing two birds with one stone—taking you for catechetical instructions, and 'Major' back to the ranch."

Imagine the picture: two Sisters in the front with Father driving, and our new companion's chariot attached to the rear. The few people we met smiled; happily the children were in school so there were no comments from them. In my wild overactive imagination I could hear them shout, "Hey, kids, here comes the circus."

Toward four-thirty that afternoon, the car nosed its way up a rocky, winding road to reach a rambling farmhouse that was to be our haven for the night. Here a warm welcome awaited us and a supper such as only a farm-wife can dish up was bubbling on the coal-stove. We ate with the family —Catherine, her husband Jim, and their little boy. During the meal, Father briskly announced his plan of action for the morning.

"Holy Mass at 8 a.m. in the kitchen; confessions beforehand in one of the bedrooms. The Sisters will explain the working of the Home Directed Study Course before we leave"; this last was directed toward Catherine. "If you have any questions to ask, now is the time to ask them."

After dishes had been washed and the usual evening chores done, Father and Jim had a discussion about the state of the Union while Catherine spoke to us about her two children, the boy and a girl, attending St. Joseph's Academy, Pendleton. She spoke to us of life at the ranch, raising chickens, milking cows, baking bread. After we had rested comfortably and chatted pleasantly for a while in the kitchen, Catherine remarked that both she and her husband had an errand to take care of. She directed us to our room.

A huge bed with blankets and comforters invited us to make ourselves comfortable. However, on the wall above the bed was a·rack holding a varied and formidable assortment of guns! We eyed it apprehensively, our one hope being that none of them would go off accidentally during the night.

Next morning the house was astir with activity. Father was busy, first hearing confessions in a spare bedroom, then in discussing various problems with our young hosts. In the kitchen where we had dined the night before, the table was cleared for a different kind of meal. Father moved about in a very business-like fashion. As he prepared the table for Holy Mass, he explained everything he did—a good demonstration lesson in using visual aids. In the same way, while he was vesting, he made informative remarks about each vestment, giving its name, use, and symbolism.

Mass began. Little Jimmy was seated on a stool in front of his parents; Sister Maurina and I, a little in back of the parents. We five formed the congregation. After the Gospel, Father indicated that he would give a short talk. He spoke on Peace, developing the thought that ideally all of us should be at peace with God, with our neighbor, and with ourselves. Jimmy listened intently, his little head cocked to one side. Suddenly in a shrill, piping voice he spoke out, "Father Murphy, give me a piece." The sermon ended then and there. Holy Mass with Holy Communion was continued to the accustomed "Ite, Missa est."

Usually Holy Mass at a home is attended by all who are Catholic living in the surrounding area. A flash flood during the night had produced hazardous driving; bridges were down, roads were washed out, and communications were at a standstill since many of the telephone lines were down. We had hoped that Mrs. Johnson's mother, who was staying at another ranch, would be able to attend the Mass. Here was Mass celebrated for the lucky five. How fortunate can one be! Sister Maurina and I years later were fortunate to be able to assist at Mass on the feast of Sts. Peter and Paul, celebrated by His Holiness, Pope Paul VI, at St. Peter's in Rome. We were faced with the realization that the majesty of the Mass did not depend upon the setting. Mass is Mass anywhere.

A fortnight later, a different tour found us doing CCD work in Burns, at Holy Family parish. Burns is in the heart of the Oregon Desert, about 131 miles north of Lakeview and 131 miles northeast of Bend, the seats of neighboring parishes. Holy Family parish extends over 12,000 square miles and encompasses the mission of Juntura along with Drewsey and many stations. At various times Drewsey was a station or a mission depending on the availability of priests to say Holy Mass there.

There was a nice little church in Drewsey, but on the occasion of this visit, Mass was not celebrated there. When, along with Father John T. Curran, the recently appointed pastor, we reached Drewsey, we found we were to stay with Molly Kent. It is with warm appreciation that I recall the many homes that served us on our journeys as Holiday Inns with gracious welcomes. Here, our hostess put us into a room reserved for visiting priests and Sisters. It was spotlessly clean and homey. What caught my eye were the starched pillow shams over the bolsters: one sham embroidered "Good Morning," the other, "Good Night." I forget which of us picked which.

When we were settled for the night, something seemed to have come close to our window and screamed its presence. It wasn't really a scream—more like a howl of distress. We sat up in bed, terrified.

"What was that?" Sister Maurina whispered in awed tones.

"Nothing; nothing much," I lied unhesitatingly. "I believe it's some prowling coyote telling the world the desert is his domain."

We were glad to be safe indoors, leaving the desert to the coyote. I was more or less familiar with the cry of the coyote. Often in the early mornings they would call back and forth frequently to each other. It is a zippity-zip sound sent in an exchange of conversation. Sometimes it was some social chit-chat bandied back and forth; sometimes it must have been an amusing story, producing sounds of gleeful laughter; again, there seemed a situation deserving a scolding reproof. "You and your big feet," a large fellow complained to his coyote pal. "By stepping on that rock that rolled down the cliff, you scared that little brown rabbit just as I was ready to pounce on it. I'll say it again; you and your big feet." And then came the yipped reply, "And yours, too."

After reassuring ourselves that there was no immediate danger of the coyote gaining entrance to our room, we listened to the sounds made by the little woodspeople scurrying in the desert night, and fell asleep.

Neighbors living thirty or forty miles from Drewsey had been notified of our coming. When we left our room in the morning, we found about 25 men, women, and children assembled at this thoroughly Catholic home. The early assembly let them have advantage of confession before Mass. The people were standing in little knots, talking, visiting. Father Curran had corralled the sheepherders who had come down from the high country. He took his place in the living room; as one penitent ambled out, another shuffled in.

We Sisters herded the children together to aid them in their preparation for confession. The children had their own notion of sin. We tried to instill confidence in God's love and mercy, showing them that confession was a matter for joy, and

58

not for fear, that it was Jesus Who listened to them and forgave them.

"That's right; our sins are forgiven in confession, if we are sorry. How about saying a prayer to the Holy Spirit Who helps us to know our sins? Then, when we know our sins, we must be truly sorry for them and sincerely confess them. That, of course, means to tell them without hoping to hide something, or even to make it out worse than it really is.

"Now, let us think how long it is since our last confession. Is it a week, or a month, or was it at Religious Vacation School? In that case, you would say, 'My last confession was made four months ago.'"

A little hand fluttered. "I don't know how long it is since my last confession, but this is my fourteenth confession." We noted that the number was not important, but that the time elapsed gave the confessor some idea how frequently they had failed.

After the grown-ups were finished, the children went to confession. While Father was not a frequent visitor, the children liked him and seemed to have no nervousness at approaching him in confession.

Then, Mass was celebrated on a table in the living room; the congregation gathered round the temporary altar, filling up the corners of the room. Molly had seen to it that all was in readiness for the offering of the Holy Sacrifice. She had asked us Sisters to give a running commentary during the Mass to insure attention from everyone. The commentary of necessity had to be impromptu.

As soon as Father had recited the Confiteor, Sister Maurina led in saying our community act of contrition. This was in pre-Vatican days and there were no handy missalettes. I gave the running commentary during the Mass; Sister Maurina led the prayers at the Offertory and in the preparation for Holy Communion. These were taken from *Jesus and I*, Father Heeg's book, one familiar to the children. At Holy Communion the entire group come forward to receive, the children first, then the adults of all ages, with creaking knees and rheumatic

59

joints adding their bit to the general atmosphere of sacrifice and prayer. It was crowded quarters, but each communicant graciously made way for the next. There followed the blessing and a thanksgiving when the oneness of this gathering through Christ was almost palpable.

That community spirit, that is made so much of today and sometimes artificially produced, carried over to breakfast, cooked and set out for everybody, young and old. Everybody stayed for the social hour that followed. It was only at such times that neighbor was united in fact with the group of neighbors. True, they met at grange meetings, but the spirit was not the same. At least 35 people were present for breakfast—better called brunch, for sausage, pancakes, bacon and eggs, toast with homemade butter and jelly, along with hot biscuits and coffee unlimited, were spread out in abundance. Pitchers of whole milk were there not only for the children, but also for the sheepherders. Such an occasion gave me insight into the Agape as related in the epistles of St. Paul.

Holy Mass was offered in many places like this one. The priest arranged to offer Mass on different days of the week at various homes in areas where people lived twenty to fifty miles, or sometimes seventy miles, from the parish church or mission. The hostess found such a gathering not a burden, but a welcome privilege. The families were brought together and went away to their farms and ranches, scattered over wide distances, with a deeper sense of community.

Another, out of many such instances, comes to mind. I am thinking of Richland, about forty miles east of Baker on the North Powder River, not too far from the Idaho border —about fifteen miles. Now there is a mission church, named after St. William, at Richland, built in 1954. But as early as 1912, Mass was celebrated in Richland, even though there was but a handful of Catholics in the area.

Forty years back, Mass had been offered about once a month at the home of Mrs. Richards. What has been written about the gathering at Drewsey could be said about Richland. Confession, Mass, instructions, followed by breakfast, was the order of the day. Everyone came from nearby—and nearby included up to a radius of thirty or more miles. If someone had not appeared, a sharp ring on the telephone would confirm that the latecomers were on the way, or would remind them literally to "get on their horses." When I say that "families" came, I mean "family" in the original sense, for the hired men came, too—often even non-Catholics.

Richland provided an improvisation that stayed in my mind. At the solemn parts of the Mass, since there was no bell or gong, a teaspoon was used to strike a teacup to regain attention. No dearth of initiative at Richland; if you did not have a gong, invent one; and actually it was the Mass that mattered, not the clanging of a bell.

By way of an aside, I can mention that with Richland, I always associate the novel way that the principal of the high school had for acquainting me with the religious affiliations of the pupils. Opening the rollbook, he went down the list; I do not recall the correct names of the students, but the designation of their affiliation never left me. In a quick, clipped manner of speech, he started:

"Abbot. . . . pagan
Bennet . . pagan
Coyne. . . . Catholic
Chander . . Methodist, I think
Davis. . . . . pagan
Reed. . . . . . Catholic
Etc."

In all, he mentioned only four Catholics out of a total of seventy. This little incident does not detract from the devotion exhibited in Richland for the Mass, but rather emphasizes the strength, the power, the holding effect of the Mass in a community predominantly non-Catholic.

Another little town, Arlington, on the Columbia River, about twenty-six miles west of Boardman, conjures up many satisfying memories of our work. Like Longfellow in "The

61

Midnight Ride of Paul Revere," I do not hesitate to say of the people of Arlington, "Hardly a man is now there who remembers that day and year" (a slightly accommodated version). Properly, Arlington was within the parish limits of St. John's at Condon, some forty miles to the south. It was a station where Mass was celebrated about once a month. At that time, there was no chapel.

A small dining room at the Vendome Hotel was the site for Mass, or, when more space was needed, the Legion Hall. Alas to say, the Vendome has been sacrificed to the needs of progress; several new dams have been built between Bonneville and McNary Dams, with the result that when water was released, lower Arlington was no more.

I shall never forget Mass at the Legion Hall. I noticed that Mr. Hazen stood at the door and handed the people as they entered a rectangle of cardboard. When he presented one to us, I thought, "What's this for? What am I supposed to do with this? What now?"

It did not take us long to find out. The floor of the Legion Hall was rough and cold cement. The cardboard was to kneel on. I discovered that you had to stay put when once you had decided on the spot where you wanted to kneel. The cardboard was not so large that you could afford to shift weight from one knee to the other. If you did move over, you found that the cardboard hadn't and you had no protection for a rheumatic or an arthritic knee.

The furnishings of the Hall were not strictly ecclesiastical, even in the most futuristic sense. There were a long table or two, some chairs, a pinball machine, a vending machine for dispensing sour-balls, bubble gum, salted peanuts, and in the corners of the room, some athletic equipment. Yet at once attention focused on the table being prepared for Mass. Father William Roden, the pastor, vested in full view of the congregation, quite like a bishop in his cathedral. Then Mass proceeded, with priest and people oblivious of the setting in which it was offered. In due time a collection was taken up; I forget just how it was handled. No one interested in the building of a small chapel would fail of a ready response.

That was the general procedure if Mass was offered on a Sunday. If, on the other hand, it was a weekday on which Mass was to be celebrated, some good woman would welcome us as guests to her home. I recall one such occasion. We had come to Arlington to inaugurate CCD classes. The pastor coincidentally was in town. His schedule of mission visits did not allow him to offer Mass that day. However, he proposed to present a "dry Mass" for instruction of the children.

A woman who was not a Catholic kindly threw open the ground floor of her house for our use. The children of the town came to us at one o'clock instead of going to school for the usual classes. They crowded into the downstairs living or rumpus room, where close together they sat cross-legged on the floor. Father had asked us to prepare them for confession before his arrival at two o'clock. Instruction was easy; there were no disciplinary problems. We opened with a prayer to the Holy Spirit, and followed through with an examination of conscience, act of contrition, and silent prayer.

Classes ended when Father Roden bustled in, more than promptly, at a quarter to two. He was ready to hear confessions, but where? A look around revealed a bedroom, off to the right—dark, windowless, gloomy. Father went in, found a box to sit on, and the children lined up for sacramental confession. When the line was giving out, I entered the room. When I closed the door, the darkness confused me; I wondered where Father was. If only I could see! Then his kindly voice gave me assurance and I knelt alongside to receive absolution. Sister Maurina followed after me to join in the search for God's love and mercy. I might observe that one child after another came out—smiling and, surely, happy. After they had all completed their penances, we sent them outdoors for a break.

At 2:30 we stepped outdoors to call the children in. The next item on the agenda of instruction was a "dry Mass." Father went through all the motions of the Mass, but did not consecrate. He was teaching, explaining, elaborating. The children understood that Father was giving meaning to what he did on Sundays in the Legion Hall. The so-called dry Mass was a success. To this day the woman in whose home all of this took place is not a Catholic; I can wonder whether she ever had an idea of all that took place in her home.

One day early in the forties, I received a letter, post-marked Mitchell, Oregon. Now, Mitchell to me at that time was only a name, but the writer knew how to bring her hometown to our attention. "Mitchell," she confided, "is in the land of rimrocks, sagebrush, and rattlesnakes. It is in the land of no man's hopes, but of many a one's despair. It is in the Oregon Desert, the high desert, sprawling over one-fourth of the State. Come and see for yourself."

That was enough to make us curious. "When would we visit Mitchell? And why? What would we do? Where would we stay?"

We didn't have to wait long for more specific arguments to accept the invitation. Two weeks later, another letter came from Mitchell: "I have a nine-year old child who should make her first Holy Communion. Please tell me what to do."

Then Father John O'Donovan, pastor of St. Thomas church, Redmond, Oregon, contacted us: "Come down our way soon. I need some help at Mitchell." There it was again: Mitchell. Conclusion: We go to Mitchell. Father O'Donovan arranged to drive us down. Along the way, he outlined the plan of action. Mass in the morning would be at the O'Connells' ranch, where we were to stay overnight.

Many of the ranchers and some of their hands from nearby spreads, as well as sheepherders pasturing in the area, had received notification of the Mass. I have always been impressed by the desire of the men to attend Holy Mass on occasions such as these. Father had also notified a Catholic family living in Twinkenham to bring with them their two girls; he was letting the twins make their first Holy Communion. So this was going to be something special.

Where the O'Connells put up all the people I don't know; that was their problem, not ours. Sister Maurina and I decided to explore the environs before nightfall set in, and found our way to the barn where the milking was under way. Suddenly one of the milkers turned and said to his companion milker, "My cow is scared, no milk. It must be the Sisters." That was enough for us; we turned back toward the house to look over the flower and vegetable gardens. Before long we learned that the cows were once again happy and contented, giving full measure of milk.

Dinner was announced at 7 p.m. It really would take Charles Dickens to do credit to the creaking table with its savory wholesome dishes of roast beef, gravy, browned potatoes, corn on the cob, creamed asparagus, and all the side dishes of relishes and jellies one could think of.

Gravy appears to be a universal favorite among outdoor men. No pert gravy bowls here; a large mixing bowl was used for this hot steaming sauce. As a matter of fact, large mixing bowls were used as vegetable dishes, and there was no dearth of mixing bowls that night. But then, there were a few at the table who had not broken bread since morning. What a feast!

After dinner, several of the men helped with the dishes while the women of the household put the food away. No mean task in any household, but here it had tripled.

Bedtime came early. By 10:20 Sister Maurina and I were nestled quite snug in our beds. But sleep was another thing. It was quiet and still—deadly so. Squeaks, scratchings, whirrs, and small cries of terror came to us, creating the impression that minute chaos was erupting, all in an area apparently devoid of life. When sleep finally came to us, I do not know; however, when dawn's early light filtered through our windows, other sounds and scrapings, more familiar, greeted us. Breakfast preparations were under way.

The living room large, airy and spacious, was being readied for Mass. Chairs were lined against one wall. A table was covered suitably for the Holy Sacrifice. Father borrowed a missal from one of us so that he could read the Epistle and Gospel for his congregation. He installed himself in one of the bedrooms to hear confessions. Everybody went; the men first, then a few of the women, and lastly the school children from near and far. These last were unperturbed and seemed to know what they were doing. Our little spastic friend came next, followed by the twins with whom Sister Maurina had spent every minute she could spare, introducing them to what was going to take place.

Holy Mass followed. Father came into the living room, asking, "Who wants to receive?" Hands showed. Father counted about thirty-six hosts—no, add two more, Mrs. O'Connell and her assistant were still in the kitchen. Then, in a Celtic whisper, meant for Sister Maurina, said, "Say the prayers for the First Communicants, please. I want to be sure the twins know what is going on." While he vested, he said the prayers loud enough for everyone to hear.

In a loud voice, Father began, "Introibo ad altare Dei." The great drama had begun. At the first sound of the celebrant's voice, everyone present knelt, no matter how stiff the knees, or ungainly the posture. These people knew what they were here for: to acknowledge dependence on their Creator, to ask His blessing, to thank Him for the good things that came their way, to ask His forgiveness. Yes; these people knew why they came together on this weekday with faith that was living and true

During the course of the Mass, Sister Maurina expressed simple, easy prayers aloud, with the congregation—old and young—silently phrasing the words on their lips that signified the dictates of their hearts.

At the Gospel, Sister reminded them that the Gospel is God's word and that we all stand at that time to show our respect and love for it. We listen to God's word; we listen to the priest while he explains the word of God.

At the offertory, Sister, as commentator, stressed the offering of themselves along with the offering of the priest of bread and wine. She recalled to them that the bread and wine would be changed into the Body and Blood of Christ. At the approach of consecration, the group was reminded that the bell would caution them that soon Jesus would be upon the altar and suggested that they express simply whatever came to their

66

minds in appreciation of His coming. All heads bowed at the consecration, not only the scrim-bedecked curly-heads of the twins, but also of the bronzed, weather-beaten faces of the adults bent forward in attitudes bespeaking their faith.

As Communion time came, we kept on praying aloud, especially having in mind the little girls for whom this was a first Communion: "Jesus come to me; I love you so much." Supplementing the short instructions they had had, we whispered, "Yes, that's right; open your mouth wide and make a table with your tongue. Jesus is here in the little, white round host. He is coming into our hearts." The little spastic girl was wheeled forward by her mother. It was fitting that her mother receive Our Lord with her, for she had prepared little Eileen for this occasion.

While the most of us spent some time in thanksgiving, a few women were preparing a regular rancher's breakfast. Everyone stayed. Two long tables were arranged from boards on sawhorses in the kitchen and on the porch. Conversation flowed easily in this little community meeting, infrequent and welcome and with a sense of a deeper, more significant union than at a casual get-together. Still, there was nothing forced or solemn about their talk.

One of the men thought he heard a coyote on the rimrock, talking to one of his cronies, silhouetted against the sky, perhaps a mile away. "I bet he's saying, 'Come on over this way, Big Fourpaws; everyone is gone for some doings and we should be able to get the pick of the flock while Cherubino is away.' "

One buckaroo wondered, "A bunch of cows and calves will be lying down grazing. All at once, as though an alarm had sounded, all the cows will get up and leave for water, all except one. She stays to look after the little calves. I'd like to know how they decide which one is to stay. Maybe she doesn't have a calf. Perhaps they pay her for baby-sitting."

No sheepherder could let a cowhand out-talk him. I am aware of the tradition, greatly amplified by western books and movies, that no love is lost between sheepherders and cowhands. Yet actually in some parts of Oregon in the desert, they frequently work in the same grazing lands; and this was a very special occasion when rancher and sheepman had been shoulder to shoulder at another Table.

Food and conversation flowed round the table; the talk went from coyotes, sheep, and cows to chipmunks. One of the boys present, a little nine-year old, told of his pet chipmunk storing great quantities of nuts away for the winter in his cache. A rancher observed, "Food-storers are not friendly with others of their kind. They do not believe in sharing. Their formula for this behavior is, 'What is mine, is mine.' "

Finally, Father O'Donovan brought the hubbub to an abrupt halt with a loud tone, giving thanks to God, and to the O'Connells. Chairs were pushed back, and everyone present took his plate, cup, and saucer to the kitchen sink, where they were stacked in orderly piles for the dishwashing crew. Amidst a flurry of good-byes, we Sisters left the ranch where we had had a short course in livestock.

Before we got under way, Father O'Donovan charted our work for the day. "We shall visit some families along the way. Get ready for a long ride." By ten o'clock, you could not see us for dust. Father O'Donovan did not believe in going "easy."

Among the various "small Masses" that we shared, one stands out in mind. Close to Baker, about 23 miles east, lies Durkee, a small hamlet with a mission chapel, dedicated to the Sacred Heart. Its dedication Mass had been celebrated by Father Wand, rector, December 3, 1911.

The chancellor of the diocese, Father John Delahunty, had charge of the spiritual welfare of the few Catholics living there about 1943. One Sunday, Father invited the Sisters to attend Mass at Durkee.

Sr. Rosetta and Sr. Kathleen had gone to Huntington for the weekend leaving Sr. Maurina and me to hold the Baker fort. Thus we got to make the trip with Father in his car. Father Delahunty bared his concern for Durkee. "A few old men and women come to Mass and about six or eight children.

They seem so apathetic during Mass that I was thinking it would help if one of you gave a running commentary during the celebration." Sister Maurina expressed herself as quite ready to fulfill the task.

In the congregation, there were four old men in the fourth row, several old women in front of the men, and about seven children in the second pew. They were very attentive and enjoyed Sister's commentary. At the end, Sister said to the children, "Wait for a few minutes after Mass; I want to see how much you remember of what I told you."

To Sister's surprise, everybody stayed. The old men as well as the women wanted to see how the children would answer. To Sister's first question, "When was the Holy Mass instituted?" an old man waggled his fingers at Sister and in a stage whisper volunteered, "At the Last Supper."

Sister was pleased and responded "Very good," and smiled as she gave him a holy card, one of those she had promised to the children for good answers. After everyone had an opportunity to answer, Sister asked them whether they liked what had been done and why they liked it. This time an old woman in a cracked and croakily sibilant voice quavered, "I liked it because it did not seem so long and I learned a lot."

Everybody went home happy, even the elders, happy with a medal or picture commemorating their understanding of the Mass. Father was happy that we had gone to Durkee with him. Sister Maurina and I were happy that the little congregation realized at least to a limited extent that it is to our advantage to know what the Mass really means and represents. This is what matters.

Chapter 5

The Spice of Life

Previously for years on end, Sister Maurina, Sister Rosetta, and I had led lives that were marked by regularity in performing our teaching assignments, by a certain uniformity in teaching procedures and techniques, and by a steadiness in daily work that made for security, a permanence and a sense of satisfaction in achievement. With the appointment of each Sister to the diocesan CCD office in Baker, drastic adaptations had to be made by each of us. Variety, risk, change, and modification became the order of the day.

Instead of "staying-put" at one location or school, the new assignment required that we move about from one place to another, for we had twenty parishes and about fifty missions and stations to visit. At these various parishes and missions we met and trained lay teachers of religion, usually selected by the pastor, and supervised the classes taught by these teachers. That was quite different from teaching only one or two classes in four or five subjects day in and day out, and being responsible for them alone. Not only was the work different, but also the accidentals of a great part of our daily living were subject to variation.

When we were at Baker, we ate, slept, prayed and had fun together with the community in our own convent home.

On the road, we ate at rectories with the pastors, at homes with families in the parish—often every meal at a different home, or at some inn or restaurant, according to the arrangements made by the pastor whose parish we were visiting. In the convent, we had the luxury of our own sleeping accommodations; on the road, we sought whatever shelter for the night was offered, accepting new quarters sometimes as often as three times a week. These changes frequently spelt frustration and anxiety, but not unhappiness, for we soon learned to live out of a suitcase, to enjoy the challenge every new situation presented, and to "roll with the punches." Every change brought inspiration, engendered hope, and inflamed our enthusiasm to a white heat for further and better efforts to promote the Confraternity program, thus sharing in the magisterial office of the Church. As each in turn made adaptation, she could take the changes in stride without a murmur or sigh. Change was accepted as spice that added zest and verve to life. We revelled in the change as a means to get our work done.

Days did differ. April 3, 1944, was an entrancingly fresh spring day. Still Nickie, the Holy Family Confraternity House cat, was crouched guardedly, ears perked at the unusual stir, eyeing the kitchen door so as to be ready for a hasty retreat to his lair down the cellar steps. Something was afoot with everyone in hurried motion. No fire, no earthquake. Simply, Sister Rosetta and I were preparing to leave on a three-week tour to Lakeview, Merrill, Klamath Falls, Chiloquin, and their missions.

"Going away?" boomed Mr. Frank Grant as he passed by our home and noted Sister Maurina and Sister Kathleen, our Martha, trudging out to the car with boxes of books, handbags, and other paraphernalia that we would need riding the circuit. Mr. Grant had two daughters in our community and had the idea of sending along a greeting.

"Looks as though we are going to stay awhile," rejoined Sister Rosetta. Actually, by the time we got back home, we would have logged one thousand five hundred miles.

"What in the world have you in this box?" protested Sister Maurina with a groan.

"Just a few teaching aids and some books. You know how difficult it is to get even a piece of chalk in some places," I explained, as I checked off the boxes, suitcases, packages, all to be safely stowed away in the capacious trunk of the car.

Sister Maurina supplemented my check-off, "Have you everything you need? Have you forgotten anything?"

Down-to-earth Sister Kathleen was heard from: "What about your lunch?" and went pell-mell into the house. Out she came with a box of ham sandwiches and some pineapple upside-down-cake, a specialty from Sister Maurina's art. That, together with a thermos of hot coffee, would take care of us until we got to Lakeview.

"Thanks a million for everything," we called, with Sister Rosetta adding as we pulled away, "I know there are not too many desirable eating places along the way; that hamper will supply our needs."

We were glad to be going on this Oregon safari, not hunting for rhinos or elephants in Africa, but in an area just packed with problems and possibilities and hard work. A great deal of work goes into making the rounds of the parishes successful; work not only on the part of the Sisters from Holy Family Confraternity House, but particularly on the part of the pastors or directors, and of the lay people we visited. They were great—very great.

The last homey voice we caught as we turned at Fourth Avenue was Sister Maurina's: "If you don't come back, write." Then we headed off to the southeast toward the agricultural area that surrounds Ontario. There we made a rolling stop to visit the pastor of Blessed Sacrament parish. He had figured in Sister Rosetta's spiritual odyssey, since he had administered Baptism to her as a young girl in Merrill. Her life, the fragments of which I gathered especially on our long rides together, runs like a book. Often Sister remarked, "If we had had the Confraternity when I was a schoolgirl, I would not

73

have had to go round looking for a church that would accept me as a member." Understandably, we stopped to pay our respects to Father August Loeser at Holy Rosary Hospital when we could, before he died the following year after a long illness.

From Ontario we swung in a westerly direction to Vale, then followed more or less along the Malheur River to Juntura. Malheur National Forest is nearby with its scenic appeal and untold opportunities for outdoor recreation. Fossil beds of prehistoric plants are there. Although we share a love for exploring natural secrets, we could not tarry.

"Wait till we get to Merrill," promised Sister Rosetta as we rolled along to Juntura. There are extensive lava beds there worth exploring.

Juntura is quaint; Juntura is unique. Here is a colony of Irish who in 1914 purchased ground to which a parish-owned schoolhouse was transferred and remodeled into St. Patrick's church. In the rear of the church were two small rooms to be used by the priest when he came for Holy Mass once a month. I said Juntura was unique; Juntura is fantastic. It is a very small, placid country spot, one main street running along the highway for about four city blocks with a few intersecting roads. Unique? It's the only place I have been where by simply ringing the churchbell we could announce our arrival, or call for aid in calamities. When it sounded, women and girls would come from nearby houses to learn why the bell was clanging.

Once it happened that while in Juntura, Sr. Rosetta and I decided to make a fire in the stove to take off the chill. Before many minutes the church, sacristy, and adjoining rooms were filled with thick, acrid fumes.

"What's happened, Sister? What shall we do? How can we correct this?" I asked with anxious voice.

"I guess this is a time when ringing the bell will bring the answer," was Sr. Rosetta's reply.

At least three women came hurrying to the church. They saw our predicament and remedied this by shutting off the valve, opening the bottom door to the stove, and making other minor adjustments. Friendly banter came with the good fresh air through the opened windows. Once more we were comfortable, all sneezing and coughing gone with the smoke.

This day, however, we did not go into the church; we simply drove into the church grounds to enjoy our lunch. It was around noon, but since we had still some two hundred miles to go, we could not tarry long. It was a delightful picnic grounds. Buttercups of gold glittered in the sun; birds twittered their joyous notes of cheer; baby lambs frisked about a front lawn and long-legged calves stood big-eyed, wondering what this world was all about. Soft billowy clouds gathered in an azure sky presented a typical bucolic scene that Horace could have described so ably. Coffee, hot and steaming, from a thermos touched the right spot as we did justice to the box luncheon.

To get from Juntura to Lakeview involved a sixty-mile run eastward towards Burns and then one hundred thirty miles south to Lakeview, with about ninety per cent of the drive through the Oregon Desert. I was settling myself for a long, fairly tedious afternoon when Sister Rosetta broke the silence; evidently the spell of the Gaelic settlement at Juntura was still upon her.

"I'll never forget my first stay in the back of the church in Juntura," began Sr. Rosetta. "Sr. Maurina and I were tired after a long, hard drive. Father Denis Sheedy from Burns asked us to stop there to teach the high school girls how to take care of the sacristy, how to lay out the vestments for Mass, how to launder the church linen. We found the three girls, the lovely Joyce sisters and a companion, refreshingly delightful.

"We explored the possibilities of St. Patrick's and thought them very promising. The girls brought dairy products, milk, butter, eggs, and a large loaf of homemade bread," she continued.

"How long did you stay?" I wanted to know.

"Oh, just a day," she answered. "After the session with

the high school girls, we resumed our journey homewards.''

"Where did you stay for the night? Surely not in the back of the church?'' I asked.

"Of course,'' Sr. Rosetta replied promptly. "That's the story. There were two narrow iron cots there—one in the narrow two-by-four sacristy, the other in the kitchen. At least, Sr. Maurina rationalized, we will not put any family to extra work by staying here. Furthermore, we will not have to go to bed in the sagebrush.

"With that we got ready for the night, Sr. Maurina in the kitchen, I in the sacristy. Everything was still and very quiet and dark. No street lights in that area. At first we were trapped in a blanket of heavenly silence, desolately so. But our ears became attuned to the stillness until every night sound was magnified a hundred-fold.''

I lived the story as Sister Rosetta recounted it. "Get on with your tale. I can imagine all sorts of things.''

"Boards creaked,'' Sister continued, "dozens of little outdoor folk were creeping, crawling, flying in the inky blackness of the woods nearby. A few low-hanging branches of a tree were brushing the roof of our abode. Then a night owl screeched to add fantastic images to overwrought minds.

" 'What's that?' nervously asked Sr. Maurina from her boudoir in the kitchen.

"In not too steady a voice, I assured her, 'A pack rat, I guess. It sounds like one to me. The next minute, he'll jump across your bed.'

" 'A pack rat! Do you mean a real pack rat? Well, he'll not jump across my bed. I'm coming in with you,' shouted Sr. Maurina. 'Move over, I am not going back to that haunted kitchen.'

"Flashlight in hand, Sister was now investigating where all these noises came from. Playing her light on the surrounding area outside our headquarters, Sister announced in exasperation, 'Listen, Rosetta, I think there's a cow massaging her side against the door.'

"With that said, Sr. Maurina nudged me to move over; I moved halfway out of the cot into outer space. Sister slid in alongside of me, holding on to the iron frame supporting the not-too-heavy mattress and went for further space to the outer regions about us. In the morning, we were two bedraggled-looking Sisters, bleary-eyed and too weary to care what happened next.

"As Sister Maurina was going into the kitchen to dress, I called after her, 'Don't be surprised if a shoe or your eyeglasses are missing. Pack rats are notorious for carrying off anything that strikes their fancy.'

"However, all her belongings were intact and there were no unpleasant surprises—rather, a very pleasant one, for Mrs. Joyce had sent a penciled note telling us to stop at her house for breakfast. And that put a happy ending to our night out in the town of Juntura."

We had covered a good stretch of our way by the time Sr. Rosetta's tale was told, and we were now approaching Burns, which might be considered the capital of, since it is in the heart of, the Oregon desert. For those who have eyes to see, there are untold things to study and behold. It's true the predominant color is gray. All the typical plants like sagebrush are gray; deer, lizards, and rattlesnakes are a marked gray, dappled with light brown, protective coloring, no doubt. However, at dawn and dusk, the desert skies are resplendent in a riot of color. Wild streaks and splashes of vivid hues enhance the beauty of desert skies. Life on the desert is rough and tough; life itself is never gray.

Suddenly, I saw something big and white, glistening in the sunlight—a cow skeleton, vivid reminder that the weak and the injured do not survive in this land, reminder that this is a waterless waste.

"Take it slowly," Sr. Rosetta cautioned. I had taken over the wheel a few miles back. "Take it easy. We don't want to miss anything."

"What's that off in the distance, to the right? I'd like to

know," I said, nodding my head in the direction.

"I am not sure, but it might be the remains of a ghost town," Sister conjectured.

"Ghost town?" I repeated. "Who would ever dream of building a town in the desert?"

Sister Rosetta was a native of southeast Oregon and well versed in Oregon lore. "Ghost towns," she informed me, "are at their best sad commentaries on the misfortune that befell homesteaders. In some places, a broken dish, a torndown shack with its broken foundation, a false storefront, often suggest the site where a town might have been. A ghost town speaks of blasted hopes and of failure. Homesteaders, as a rule, were wonderful people. They came to farm, but there was little, very little, water; so, no farming. The Oregon desert has its share of ghost towns, like Butte near Wagontire, and Fremont about six miles west of Fort Rock," Sister continued.

"The post office in Butte was established in 1911 and discontinued in 1922; not enough business. In Fremont the post office was established in 1909 and again discontinued in 1915. A stock-watering windmill is all that is left in Fremont.

"Not deliberately changing the subject, but over there is Abert rim, the highest fault scarp in the United States. That site alone would give any interested person many hours of study. Not far away is Alkali Lake that maintains no life of any kind. Deep deposits of alkali ring the lake."

Sr. Rosetta explained, "The formation of a scarp is a geological fact that encompassed thousands of years. At first the land was covered by two thousand feet of lava that spread out from cracks in the earth's crust. The lava cooled but in the process broke into huge blocks, and the pressures below, operating unevenly, tossed those blocks about, as ice blocks are tossed when the ice breaks up on a frozen river. When one side was pushed up, adjacent to an edge that remained stationary, we have the enormous faults or scarps.

"The most famous is the scarp line that starts southeast of Lakeview and runs northwest past Goose, Abert, and Alkali lakes. We are opposite this scarp now. The face of this scarp, in places, is three thousand feet high and there are many sheer cliffs where a careless step might be six hundred feet long."

Sr. Rosetta was reciting the marvels of Abert Rim as though she were reading from a science magazine but this area was well-known to Sister. "Is it any wonder," she remarked, "that this territory would give any interested person, especially a geologist, many hours of study?" I was fascinated to say the least, but that is as far as it went.

I pulled over to the side of the road to let Sr. Rosetta take over. It was now 5 o'clock and we were nearing Lakeview; not a large metropolis, but I preferred to let Sister hunt her way through the streets to St. Patrick's church.

The Reverend Felix L. Geis was standing on the porch, watch in hand. "You're late," he told us, "It is now 5:35 p.m. Your letter stated you would be here at 5 p.m."

Discounting his reference to our schedule, we called out as we came up the steps, "Good evening, Father, we are sorry; hope we didn't ruin your schedule."

One would have to know Father Geis to appreciate him. Tall, on the portly side, with a gruff exterior, he could scare the daylights out of itinerant tramps or unwanted solicitors ringing his doorbell. He had a subtle sense of humor and really was friendly though his mannerisms seemed to suggest the opposite.

"Well, come in. I've made arrangements at Hunter's to have dinner at six. You can stay here, for we have plenty of room."

"Thank you, Father. We'll be ready in five minutes to go with you."

"All right," he responded.

As we reappeared in the front room, Father said genially, "I scheduled no meetings for tonight, so we can relax and take things easy."

This announcement came as a pleasant surprise for us. After having travelled nearly four hundred miles that day, we welcomed a free night. We had a delightful dinner at Hunter's, an attractive hostel with restaurant facilities. A striking feature of Hunter's was the use of a natural hot geyser on the grounds to furnish heat for the building. It was a bit chilly in early April, so that the moderate warmth was welcome.

Refreshed and relaxed, we were back in the rectory by 8 o'clock. The housekeeper had come in and had seen to it that our luggage had been transported to our rooms. At Father Geis' invitation, we went to the living room to plan our activities. Long-range planning could be done at Baker, more detailed plans worked out along the road, but always when we got to a particular location, we had to learn the "ground rules" and the hazards and helps of the given place.

"What would you like us to do while we are here?" I began.

"You'll want the teachers. I sent them word to come to the church at 7 tomorrow evening," he grudgingly admitted. "But the children, what about them?"

"If there are no objections, Sister Rosetta and I will visit the public grade schools and meet them there. While I take the lower grades, Sister Rosetta will take the upper grades. Yes, of course, we will arrange to have the children come here to the church with their religion texts for another session."

"Well, I don't know how you will do that; that is your business. But I would like you to give some time to Paisley, Silver Lake and West Side if you can work it in."

I replied, "We have a week to give to the parish; we'll see what we can do."

Paisley was a mission of Lakeview about forty miles north of the city; Silver Lake was about eighty miles in a northwesterly direction from the mother parish; West Side was only ten miles from the home base in a southwesterly direction. If things would go as well as we hoped, we would stay two days in Paisley, one day in Silver Lake, and the rest of the week in Lakeview.

Father was anxious that we should be happy working in his parish. Everything was planned. Gruffly he announced, "Mass is at 7:30 in the morning; breakfast here; dinner in the evenings, as well as lunch, at various homes." Addressing Sis-

80

ter Rosetta, he continued, "Your Uncle Mike is home from the ranch for a few days. Have dinner with them sometimes."

Drowsy by now, Father continued, "I have a report card from my grandfather when he was a boy in Germany. Some of his marks are good; it says so—*Gut*; but there is one thing I cannot decipher." Turning to me, he asked, "Can you?"

"I don't know; let's see it."

Father held on to the card. "What is *fleiss*? and what does *mittelmässig* mean?"

"*Fleiss* means industry, application; and *mittelmässig is the German way of saying a student* is average."

Father Geis was delighted to find out that his grandfather was only average in his application. He laughed all over and enjoyed the idea immensely. I have never seen him so exuberant before. A good note to end the evening on. After saying goodnight to Father, we went to our rooms, tired from the long day of driving.

Morning came, it seemed, much too early. By nine o'clock we were ready to start our visits to the two grade schools and the one high school. We also held an executive board meeting with Mr. Carl Fretsch as chairman, and a teachers' meeting with Mrs. Crystal Carmody as chairman. Besides these meetings, we held personal conferences with individual teachers who needed help. Two days were taken up completely with our visit to Paisley and Silver Lake. While working in Paisley, we stayed with the O'Learys, a family with growing boys and girls from pre-school to the eighth-grade ages. The father, Jeremiah O'Leary, taught one of the CCD classes at Our Lady of Lourdes in Paisley.

I'll never forget our visit to Silver Lake. While there, we stopped in the public school to meet the Catholic children. The teacher was very obliging. "Wait here in the lunch room until I get them."

The lunch room was a small affair, one long table, two benches on either side. In a few minutes three children came in; a girl, Kathleen, and two boys, Bart and Connie; the latter was on crutches as a result of a broken leg. These were the

81

O'Keefes of whom the Rev. Edward O'D. Hynes, the former pastor of Lakeview, had often spoken in glowing terms. It was that day, Kathleen, a girl of fourteen, confided to me that she would like to be a Sister. Today Kathleen is a Sister in our community and is doing good work in the diocesan office of Religious education in Baker.

From this brief outline of our days at Lakeview, it can readily be seen that no two days were alike. In fact, this could be said of our days all through the years or working with the CCD in the Baker diocese. There was so much variety that that in itself guaranteed zest for the work. Monotony was unknown to us as CCD supervisors and coordinators.

As Father had planned, we had dinner with the various families: the Flynns, the Lynches, the Barrys with their twins, Philip and Andrew, and the Carmodys, who graciously extended their home circle to include us; nor should I forget Aunt Bridgie and Uncle Mike who claimed Sr. Rosetta as a member of the clan. Some evenings, not tied up with meetings, we enjoyed stories, games, music, and reading in the family group. Not only did we hope to encourage families in their work of teaching Christian living by word and example, but we also could learn much. At the same time, we could aspire to show that teaching involved giving witness, that fathers and mothers and children too could best teach by living their teaching.

The time allotted to our stay rushed by; it was with regret that we tore ourselves away from Lakeview. But this was a tour of duty, and Merrill to the west, near the California border, was our next stopping place. From Lakeview, the distance is a little better than a hundred miles, or about three hours driving over Quartz Mountain and through parts of Fremont National Forest. The latter is famous for the Gearhart Mountain Wild Life Area, dedicated to preserving the forest in its natural state. We were on schedule, and that meant we had no time to tarry, not even at Bly where there were a number of Catholic families. We had added reason to get on to Merrill, since we were to stop with Sister Rosetta's mother and family and our stay would be limited to three days.

As we drove along, Sister Rosetta warned, "You won't like it in Merrill. You are from the East, and this is the West."

"I haven't seen a thing yet that I didn't like in the West," I replied. "I will most likely fall in love with Merrill. Don't forget I've already met your sister Nora and Dan Cashman. We stayed with them the last time we stopped here. Your mother and dad were. away at the time, so I didn't meet them."

I smiled to myself as we rode along. It has always seemed to me one of the blessings of Religious life that we have a predilection for members of the families of our fellow Religious. Possibly, through knowing the parents, brothers and sisters of these Religious, we know a great deal more of the Religious themselves. So I had no worry, since we were going home for a few days.

Sister Rosetta was not so sure of what accommodations we would find. She wanted to prepare me. "It is a rambling, big house; all the rooms are large, particularly the kitchen and dining area. Some bedrooms are right on the first floor."

"Suits me to perfection," I assured her. "Your parents are no longer young; we couldn't expect them to fix up, just because I happen to be with you. I know I'll be happy with your father and mother."

The church, St. Augustine's, was down the highway about a mile. We stopped at Sr. Rosetta's home first. From there we went to see Father James M. O'Connor, the pastor. He was happy and very proud of the parish. He told us that Merrill had the distinction of having the best general line of teaching equipment in the diocese. St. Augustine's, a solid, brick church, which had replaced a wooden structure under the title of the Holy Cross, had a stable set-up.

Getting down to work at Merrill proved to be a pleasure. Looking at Father John T. Curran's notes, which I have before me, I find that he and Father George A. Murphy had begun early to set up a good catechetical program there. As Father

O'Connor said, there were "tools of the trade"—a ditto machine, stamping set. teacher manuals, and pictures for classroom use. I suspect much of that went back to the days when Father Curran was assistant pastor at Sacred Heart, Klamath, and had charge of the mission church at Merrill. No wonder we would find a well-developed Confraternity at St. Augustine's.

It was quite easy to follow out the regular outline of activity for visiting a parish CCD here. On Sunday after Mass, I spoke to the entire parish. I was pleased that all the men, even the farmhands and sheepherders in from the range, stayed for the talk. Shortly after, we visited the Sunday school classes and took the opportunity to encourage parents, children, and teachers alike.

Immediately after the end of the classes, one of the teachers accosted me, saying, "I want you to know that I don't seem to be getting anywhere, but I am doing my best."

"Angels can't do more," I observed. "No one expects anything else; keep on; you are doing more than you think." I truly meant what I said.

She brightened up, gathered her books, and went out into the sunshine with a smile. I smiled since I was but repeating Bishop McGrath's reminder, "No effort in this direction is ever lost."

Our work in Merrill consisted mainly in encouraging parents, children, and teachers to continue in the work they had begun. Teachers were given various practical aids to help children enjoy their studies. We emphasized the idea that children tend to repeat anything that brings them happiness.

The evenings, or part of them, we tried to keep more or less free to enjoy visiting with Sr. Rosetta's parents. Mrs. Barry could not have been better to us. We took our evening meals with her and her father, Little Mike, who entertained us with his observations on life in general, and on Shakespeare in particular. I was told that he had a complete set of the English bard in his possession when herding sheep, far from human habitation and from the usual means of communication. It was while at the camping site that he read both Shakespeare and the Scriptures.

One evening he was in a reminiscent mood, and I was a good listener. He began slowly, reverently, "I imagine you know the twenty-third Psalm. That psalm is the touchstone of the shepherd's calling. David knew sheep; that is why 'The Lord is my shepherd' is so meaningful to us who make sheep our living.

"Sheep graze from early morning until about 10 o'clock. Then they must lie down and rest for several hours. That's why you have the words in the psalm, 'He maketh me to lie down in green pastures.'

"Sheep will not drink from running or gurgling water. The sheep appreciate a herder who finds still water for them.

"The sheep approach the herder for attention. The herder rubs the sheep's nose and ears, scratches its chin, whispers endearments into its ear. The sheep will nibble at the shepherd's ear and rub its cheek against his face. No wonder the sheep's soliloquy continues, 'He restores my soul; he leads me into righteous paths for his name's sake.'

"In some places there are narrow defiles and deep gullies the sheep must traverse. However, the sheep fear no evil for the herder is with them. Sometimes sheep fall and land in the gully. The shepherd has to be there to aid and protect them with his staff and rod.

"Frequently you find poisonous milkweed and other harmful plants on grazing lands. When such conditions prevail, the herder goes ahead and with his mattock digs up the deadly weeds. 'He prepares a table for me,' muses the flock as it is led into newly prepared pastures.

"Every sheepfold has a big eastern bowl of olive oil and a large jar of water. At night, the sheepherder examines each sheep for snags, cuts, or scratches, or for weeping eyes from dusty winds. Each sheep's lacerations are carefully cleaned. Then, dipping his hand into the bowl of olive oil, he generously anoints the injury with the oil, all the while talking, whispering encouraging words into the sheep's ear. A cup is dipped to overflowing; the sheep drinks until fully refreshed. No wonder the psalm puts it this way: 'He anoints my head with oil; my cup runs over.'

"When all the sheep are at rest, the herder lays his staff on the ground within easy reach, wraps himself in his woolen robe, and lies down across the gateway, facing the sheep, for his night's rest. 'Surely mercy and goodness shall follow me all the days of my life; I will dwell in the house of the Lord forever.' "

I was stirred to the depths by Mr. Barry's interpretation of this wonderful psalm. "Thank you; thank you for letting me share this beautiful piece of the Old Testament literature. I need no meditation book tonight; you have provided some beautiful thoughts for me to ponder."

To both Mr. and Mrs. Barry for being so graciously hospitable to us, I continue to be appreciative. I am sure that Sr. Rosetta was aware that I enjoyed sharing her home.

Merrill, practically on the southern border of the diocese, was the turning point of our tour; from there we headed northward the short distance to Klamath Falls. There we stayed at Sacred Heart Academy, operated by the Sisters of St. Francis, the community to which we belonged. That would mean "home" away from home, with a heyday of laundering, brushing, and cleaning our belongings. We were carrying with us a lot of dust from Alkali Lake. I must admit that some of the dust and dirt was acquired when we went hunting and found an artifact of the days when Indians maintained these areas. In fact, the vacuum cleaner had to be used on our black habits, to free them of the fine dust and silt.

Klamath Falls is in the south-central part of Oregon. There are actually no falls in the city, but there are rapids on the Link River which connects Upper Klamath Lake and Lake Ewauna. Definitely this is a bird paradise. The white pelican, which often has a wingspread of ten feet, is frequently seen on nearby lakes and rivers. Ducks and geese congregate here by the millions each fall during their migration south. Not only fowl abound; this is open country for deer, bear, and elk.

The largest city in the Baker diocese, Klamath Falls is rich in history. Indians, who once held sway in the area, made friends with the early pioneers, showing them the easiest way to procure food from the lakes and rivers. As in other places, where settlers began to increase in numbers, there was the Church. As early as the mid-eighties, Father Blanchard, the parish priest for Jackson, Klamath, and Lake counties, visited Klamath Falls once in three or four years, and said Mass for the Catholics of Klamath county. In 1881, Archbishop Seghers visited Klamath Falls and ministered to the few Catholics there. In 1938, on our first visit, there was a flourishing parish, with a beautiful church and rectory, and Sacred Heart Academy had been quite some years in operation.

Warm, cordial greetings were ours from the Academy Sisters. As soon as we were settled in our accommodations, we went down to the rectory to report our arrival to the pastor, the Rev. Timothy P. Casey. At the same time, we outlined our agenda for the visit for his approval. I must say that we looked forward to our meeting with Father Casey. He was a true pastor and always was very congenial and happy to cooperate with anything that would promote the faith. He himself superintended the assembling of the Catholic children from the public school for the Saturday classes. Any Saturday morning found him in front of the church, counting the happy crowd of children that came pouring out of the cars. One Saturday morning, Father brought twenty-two children in his big shiny limousine.

"How are you, Sisters?" was Father's friendly greeting, as he walked into the rectory parlor. As we were leaving after discussing plans, he made several parting inquiries about Little Mike and the rest of Sister's family. All the priests of the area knew the family well; their homes were places to stop on a cold day for a cup of good coffee and a good word. With confidence that things at Klamath were really lined up, we headed back to the Academy which was separated from the church and rectory only by the school yard.

By the time we got back, Mrs. Percy Murray, chairman

87

of teachers, who had succeeded Mrs. O'Leary, was waiting for us. It is a warming pleasure to recall the women who gave many years of service, teaching Confraternity classes. They were Mrs. Paul Landry, Mrs. Winnie Hooker, Mrs. Kann, Mrs. Howard, and certainly Mrs. O'Leary, who at Father Curran's persistence, had been chairman prior to Mrs. Murray's effective carrying out of that office. Mrs. Murray had brought us stacks of work done by the children; she wanted us to see how creative and original the children were. She brought also roll books, lesson plans, and a list of regular absentees from Saturday classes, hoping that we would offer comments and suggestions to the teachers how best to cope with the various problems they faced.

Before plunging into the task of checking all this material, Sr. Rosetta and I took time out to visit with the members of the community. There were letters, memos and variables to be delivered from the Sisters in the Academy at Baker. They took us on a tour of the plant to note the improvements made since our last visit. All very pleasant, but there was still our homework to be done in order to get an overall picture of the CCD in Klamath. So we pitched in.

There was a regular hodgepodge: roll books, lesson plans, examinations, and even some extra projects. Quite enough to keep us busy not only that afternoon, but every minute we could spare for the next two days. I suggested that Sister Rosetta pick out the material belonging to 5-6 and 7-8 grade groups while I would handle the rest. Some of the items drew enthusiastic comment.

"Oh, here is something I wanted to see. The teachers followed our suggestion given in the monthly bulletin. Look at this response to: 'Draw something that reminds you of God Who is all-beautiful.' This little tyke drew some daisies in the field."

Sister Rosetta nodded. "I am sure that is some youngster living in the country. What are you going to do with it?"

"Put it on the bulletin board," I replied. "You know children love to see their work on display, particularly when a gold star is pasted on the paper." I flipped through more papers. "Here is another in response to: 'Find something God made that made you hold your breath.' Sure enough, it is marked Crater Lake."

Sister Rosetta put out her hand to get a look at Crater Lake. "I think the idea is perfect. Did you know that Crater Lake was, thousands of years ago, the site of Mount Mazarna? Yes, it was a volcano 12,000 feet high. The mountaintop collapsed, creating the caldron which now contains the Lake."

"I am glad that you like it. Here is another," I kept on. "Can you imagine a fourth grader doing this? It is supposed to show God's wisdom."

Sr. Rosetta looked at the drawing which I handed her. "If this isn't a cocoon from which a butterfly is emerging! That child has the idea, I think."

This was a type of work the children enjoyed; they liked to draw, although at times it took insight to know what they were trying to express. I was enjoying their efforts, but Sister Rosetta was becoming a little nervous. She remonstrated that if we took all the time exclaiming over their drawings, we would never get finished until doomsday. Picking up some books, she speculated, "What shall we do with these roll books?"

"Those should not take long. Note first whether they are up-to-date; how the attendance is; what grades the children are getting for their work. That will give us something definite on which to base our remarks to the teachers. We will meet them Saturday morning after class."

With the roll books lined up, my companion announced, "I am tackling the lesson plans next. We'll probably get these done by tonight."

This task meant concentration and time, for we wanted to check lesson plans on three points:

First, the aim of the lesson;
Second, how this aim was to be achieved; and
Third, how the pupils could live or put into practice what had been learned.

After a time, I interrupted my work. "I must have a stroll first, if it's only to see how the hamsters are doing in the lab." On my way there I was summoned for a phone call from Mrs. Murray who wanted an interview; we settled for 7:30 that evening.

Walking around, it struck me that while we had been at the Academy most of the day, we had had very little time so far with the Sisters. We had our meals with them and that was about all. Of course, they were busy teaching school, giving art lessons, conducting music and choral groups. When they were free from duty in the school, we were busy taking care of special problems. Thus it happened that evening when I was with the Sisters in the community living room, looking over some new acquisitions for the library, a visitor was announced for me.

As I expected, it was Mrs. Murray, and I looked forward to the conference. Mrs. Murray was graciousness personified. No matter what the topic for discussion, she was fair, considerate, and understanding. She smiled and began, "As usual, I have a few problems. What can we do to get a little continuity in the five-minute talks by Father, any Father, to the children when they come into church for singing? Too often the talk is omitted."

I listened and tried to weigh all sides to the question. "Sometimes the priest assigned to give the talk is away, possibly on a sick call or some other project, and he fails to get a substitute. Tell Father at the beginning of the year that you want the CCD children to know the priests of the parish, that this is one way the children come into contact with the priests, through the talks. If Father is hesitant to select a topic, suggest a few: for example, prayer; kinds of prayer; efficacy of prayer; etc. That does not sound too difficult, does it?" I asked.

"No, but the Fathers are busy and they think I can do that or one of the teachers. What do you think, Sister?"

"It would be better if one of the Fathers gave a little talk to all the children immediately after the opening prayer. If

90

Father Casey cannot convince them how eager the children are to hear from the priests, neither can I. Do the best you can, and don't worry," I counseled. "What do you do immediately after the talk?" I asked.

"Usually singing. I want the children to learn the hymns they hear at Mass and other services. That lasts at the most fifteen minutes. Then we go up to the Academy for classes. It's a break and the walk from the church does them good. Here's a list of questions that I would like you to discuss with the teachers," said Mrs. Murray with a twinkle in her eyes.

"CCD teachers recruited from parents of CCD children.

Co-operation of CCD and Academy staff.

Counseling for our CCD children.

Getting CCD children involved in parish activities."

I laughed as I scanned the list Mrs. Murray had handed me. "That ought to keep us busy for quite a while. We'll have the session here, Saturday morning, immediately after class, or Sunday afternoon at 2:30. But give the teachers a list, too. I don't want them to come to the meeting cold. What do you say, Mrs. Murray?"

"All the teachers helped to get that list together. Many feel very strongly about those questions," replied Mrs. Murray. "We want to make progress; we do not want to stand still. But I must hurry along. I have taken enough of your time."

"Our time is yours anytime. Goodnight. God bless you. Tell the children I asked about them, please." I watched her walk away and felt a deep satisfaction that the CCD program was so actively accepted. It was not something that was being imposed upon these people, but a vital activity in which they were interested and in the solution of whose problems they took initiative steps. They were people who thought, and quite openly and frankly stated their thoughts.

There was much to see and to do in Klamath; many of our activities here were like what we did elsewhere, but there was enough variation in the work and the people to add the spice of variety in this stay. Before we knew it, our week was up and we were due in Chiloquin, a small parish serving many of the Klamath Indians.

We enjoyed our ride along the winding stretches of Klamath Lake. Certainly, this was quite different country from northeastern Oregon. It was restful to look across the waters where numberless mud or reed ducks were gliding along. Mountains were on the opposite shore, with their jagged peaks gracing the crestline of the towering Cascades.

At Chiloquin, we went directly to Our Lady of Mt. Carmel church and rectory, where the Rev. Michael Ahearn was pastor. This place must be seen to be appreciated. When ground was broken for the church in 1926, a small frame house on the property was remodeled as a rectory. It was a small, low building, with a living room lined with books on makeshift shelves from floor to ceiling on one side and shelves above the desk on the other. There was a small bedroom, a bathroom, and a kitchen with a wood-stove and a table. Father ate in the kitchen; there was no dining room. That was forty-five years earlier; in 1950 it was replaced by a two-story building, put up by the Rev. John Phelan. The ceiling in the original rectory was so low that a stepladder was never needed; an average-sized person could touch the ceiling. All very homelike and cozy.

At the entrance to the rectory, on one side of the building, Father Ahearn and Mrs. Hans Anderson, a full-blooded Indian, awaited us. Father called out, "Leave your things in the car. You will be staying with the Courtwrights at the Klamath Agency."

With that, we were ushered into the kitchen. "Make yourselves at home. I am so glad you came. There is not much happening around here," Father went on.

"We are glad to be with you," both Sr. Rosetta and I assured him. "Tell us what you want us to do at the Klamath Agency."

"Mrs. Courtwright asked to have you as houseguests. You know her. She is like someone who has just stepped out of a Victorian novel, very proper and very gracious. She knows everyone at the Agency and on the reservation, and wields quite an influence with the Indian women," replied Father.

After luncheon of soup, sandwiches, and fruit, we went to the church basement to look over their Confraternity supplies and equipment. We trudged back to the Rectory where Father awaited us. He told us, "I can't get some of the kids to class. Would you go to school and round them up?"

"Of course; Sr. Rosetta will be happy to do that while I take stock. What happened to the large Biblical pictures?" I inquired.

"They are in a closet, stored away," murmured Father. "I thought we would get them out for the Sisters when they come for Religious Vacation School."

"A good idea, but don't keep them in camphor until then. Better get them out for the lay teachers to use during the year," I said.

"O.K.," was his answer, and we knew it would be done. Father was grateful for any suggestions and would follow them through to the letter.

Then he gave us instructions for going to the Agency. "Go north on the highway about six miles to the Agency. Huge radial signs, made from lumber cut out in the forest belonging to the Indians, stand at the entrance, bearing the legend 'Klamath Indian Agency.' Drive in; the first house to the right of a broad, well-kept road bears the sign 'Superintendent.' That's Courtwrights'. Mrs. Courtwright is waiting for you; she just phoned."

With these detailed directions we had no trouble finding Mrs. Courtwright; she was delighted to welcome us to her home. There was a large reception room where high tea was served. Afterward she took us through the house. There was a beautiful dining room with the table set for ten—our hostess, Sr. Rosetta and me, and seven prominent Catholic women from the reservation. Gleaming china and crystal with sterling plate graced the snowy linen: perfect, beautiful. We peeked into the kitchen where there was quite a stir of preparation for a banquet. Passing back through the living room and entry, Mrs. Courtwright pointed out, "This is Mr. Courtwright's den; here is your living room and this is your bedroom and bath. I'll have someone bring in your bags."

We both assured her that we were truly grateful for her overwhelming kindness. "Oh, I'll tell you a secret. I love to entertain and show visitors our home provided by the Federal Government. Because I want the Catholic Indian women to be at home with you, I've invited them to have dinner with us. Indians like to have recognition of their importance, you know."

"Is there anything in particular you want us to do?" I asked. "After all, this is the first time we are to live in a Superintendent's house."

"Pay no attention to me," our hostess said. "However, I'll try to give you a lead on what will make these women six feet tall. Dinner is set for 6 p.m.," she remarked, looking at a watch, "and I could have told it is almost six, for the women are coming up the walk now. They are courteously prompt."

Mrs. Courtwirght was charming in welcoming and introducing her guests. "Sisters, this is Mrs. Jerry Monks. Mr. Monks works with Mr. Courtwright. I am so glad you could come, Mrs. Hall and Mrs. Thompson." So it went until she came to the last one, Princess Mazama, a real true-to-life princess, beads and all.

Shortly, dinner was announced. Mrs. Courtwright presided at the oval table with Sister Rosetta and me at strategic points. The hostess managed to keep conversation in a continuous flow although the Indian ladies tended to listen quietly with an occasional smile and nod. Sister Rosetta's comments, questions, and anecdotes helped keep the talk going.

Bits of Indian lore were exchanged: how the coyote got his name; the meaning of the pictographs near Fort Rock; the heroes of the Modoc War; and tales of the Northwest. Indians are not talkative in company with strangers; they listen; they smile enigmatically; they listen some more. It seemed to me if you wanted an answer to a question, you supplied your own answer—a form of monologue.

The dinner was superb, delicious, and everything one would want. Coffee was served on low tables in the living room, where Sister Rosetta held sway on the things she learned from a faithful old Indian woman who helped around her home when she was growing up. I was kept busy listening.

After the pow-wow, we were glad to retire. The twin beds in our room were dressed in immaculate bed linens with appropriate coverings. No one needed to lull us to sleep. Again, Dawn came speedily, smiling through the window, with chirping birds and the goings on of busy little forest folks —squirrels, chipmunks, and grouse. We got up early and set out, a la Chevrolet, to Chiloquin for Mass. The morning air was crisp and invigorating, fresh with the perfume of pine, primroses, squaw-grass, and all the plants enriching the forest. Breakfast with Father Ahearn followed Holy Mass and prayers. The activities of today and tomorrow fell into the regularly irregular pattern of such visits.

Daytime was occupied with teacher meetings, interviews with individuals, and classes conducted for grade school children at the end of the school day. At night we had a session with the high school students. To our amazement, the young people came. After religion classes, we had some fun —cookies, lemonade, and candy, followed by night prayers improvised on the spot.

"Why don't you stay in Chiloquin a little while, a month or two?" they wanted to know. Certainly a heartening response; but we had to be content to tell them, "Look for us in the fall; we'll be back."

This was our final stopping place on the schedule of this tour. We packed up again to head back home through Bend, Arlington on the Columbia, and along highway 30 to Baker. Frankly, we were tired, and the long ride home, of some four hundred miles, would be wearying. At the same time we were encouraged and had had a lift, from having witnessed so much that had been accomplished and was in progress. Somewhere near Shaniko, Sister Rosetta roused me suddenly from my reveries, "Look, there's a rattler, I believe: I'm going to run over it. That will make certain that as a dead rattler he can't later injure some unsuspecting person."

In a moment she slowed and steered carefully to the side of the road, and stopped. I had averted my gaze when the car ran over the snake. She asked, "Want to get out and see?"

Without answering, I opened the door and gingerly alighted. She went to look and exclaimed, "Look, it's a big fellow with thirteen rattles!"

From reading and study I know that the rattlesnake is a viper, whose tail terminates in loose, horny shells that produce a warning sound that may be audible twenty feet away. As a Christian, I know that the rattler is a part of God's creation, inspiring awe. From a practical standpoint, I was not intent on getting too near, for its dying, spasmodic rattling was no assurance that he could do no harm!

When we got back into the car and were rolling along, I could look out at the rocky and sandy areas, and speculate again how much easier and safer were our journeyings than those of Ezra Meeker, pioneering with early settlers along the Oregon Trail. If there was a snake in Eden, then Oregon is a super-Eden. However, my thoughts went back to the people we had visited, and I could think of the country as Eden because of all the delightful Adams and Eves, and Abels and Seths, we had visited. I figured the snake was thrown in just to add variety as the spice of living, just to make that day a little different.

Chapter 6

Just At Home

Wartime may have made for a quiet celebration of June 17, 1943, Bunker Hill Day in Boston; but in Baker, it was decidedly a day for celebration. For Sisters Rosetta, Maurina, and myself, it meant another change. On that day, the Sisters of St. Francis of Philadelphia purchased through the western provincial, Mother Mary Mildred, the Rouse home, a dignified, spacious dwelling at 2337 Second Street, as our convent home. True, St. Elizabeth Hospital had given us office and convent accommodations for five years; but with the expanding CCD activities and the developing ministrations of the hospital, more space was needed, all around. The time had come for us, the Confraternity Sisters, to form our own community. It was great; it was fun; it was a thrilling adventure.

Much of July and August was spent in changing the house from a family home to a convent. The neighborhood was inviting and our immediate neighbors very much interested. They avidly watched the Sisters' comings and goings and doings. Carpenters, plumbers, and painters did their work unnoticed; but when we Sisters washed windows until they gleamed, and hung up new Queentex curtains at every window in the house, the neighbors were amazed, even inspired. Unsuspectedly, one fussy housekeeper was overheard saying to another, "We better get busy and wash our windows. Those Sisters are hustlers; their windows shine like the sun.''

Then there was shopping to do. We did not have a stick of furniture to our name. Wartime conditions prevailed. A Portland retail store had some very good pieces for a dining room and for a living room through a reputable second-hand dealer. These we bought at once. Beds, chairs, night tables, and bureaus came to us, brand-new, from one of our Superiors in the East, Sr. Regulata of St. Agnes Hospital in Philadelphia. By September, 2337 was definitely a convent, with a beautiful chapel on the second floor which was furnished by Bishop McGrath. On August 31, His Excellency blessed the Holy Family House, the name chosen by Reverend Mother Veronica, Superior General, who actually sponsored the new foundation. We were so anxious to live in the house that the evening of September first, the three of us slept there for the first time. I'll never forget it. We had no beds; only springs and mattresses had been delivered. We made these do; we would not have far to fall if we rolled out of bed, for the springs were on the floor.

I will not go into detail about our converting the house into a convent home, for it takes a lot of living to do that. Our fourth Sister, Sr. Lorena, came from the East on September second, accompanied by Sister Columba, our first guest. There was great jubilation with Sister Lorena's accession, since she was sister as well as Sister to Sister Maurina. Sister Columba stayed with us two days; then she went on to St. Joseph's Hospital, La Grande, her new assignment.

Confraternity activities, however, were not at a standstill during the establishment of the new center. The visiting of Huntington by Sr. Maurina and myself went forward; we set out September 6 with Father William Stone in charge. Two days later we left for Pendleton and Milton Freewater, the latter just about forty miles northeast from the round-up city and quite close to the Washington State border. Mrs. George Bishop, our hostess, was so happy about the setting up of Holy Family Confraternity House that she canned twenty quart jars of peaches for us to take home as a starter for our canned food storage closet in the cellar.

After a day at home, I again was on the road, this time with Sister Rosetta. We were headed for Heppner an inland town about sixty miles southeast of Pendleton, where the settlers, many of Irish origin, devoted their efforts mainly to sheep raising. I had just read the history of Catholicism in and around Heppner and learned to my amazement of the activity of the first priest to minister to the Catholics of Heppner —Father Louis Conrady, an intrepid missionary of high courage and unparalleled zeal. He was of Belgian stock and had come to America shortly after volunteering to do mission duty in eastern Oregon in 1874. Invariably he traveled on horseback. His missionary base was the Umatilla reservation where he devoted his time to the Indians. But he did not stay put there; he fanned out in all directions, visiting the Catholics of Pendleton and of all the settlements of Morrow, Wheeler and Gilliam counties.

His procedure was simple and effective. He would visit a Catholic Family, stay with the people two or three days. There he would celebrate Mass, hear confessions, instruct the children, and as need arose, administer Baptism or perform marriage ceremonies. When satisfied with his efforts in that area, he would move on to the next Catholic home. At that rate, he visited Heppner once or twice a year.

These thoughts stayed persistingly in my mind as we drove along toward St. Patrick's, Heppner. "And to think of it," I mused aloud to Sister Rosetta, "Father Conrady volunteered to go to Molokai to help Father Damien with his lepers."

"If you think that's the high point of his missionary hopes, you have another thought coming to you," said Sister Rosetta. "Father Conrady also served lepers in China. There were 800 of them near Canton. He not only nursed the lepers, but built barracks for them. He died in Hong Kong, I believe, and was buried there, as he wished, rolled in a mat and with lepers on either side of him."

I called on Father Conrady to bless our work; we were travelling in his footsteps seventy years later. If anyone could inspire us what to do while at Heppner, I somehow felt that he could. I placed our efforts under his special protection.

Our hopes at Heppner were not misplaced. The children came after school for the CCD directions for the coming year; the faculty of teachers was as one, anxious to learn all they could to make the scholastic year 1943-44 a success Confraternity-wise; and there was a huge crowd of parishioners who came to the Catechetical Day celebration and luncheon on Sunday. This day, proclaimed as a special day for celebrating the importance of religious instruction, was proudly held under the leadership of the pastor, the Rev. Francis McCormack. Whole families came, babies included. The spirit of community was evident at St. Patrick's.

A definite pattern was emerging for our CCD activities in the parishes outside Baker itself. Sister Maurina and I; Sister Rosetta and I; and Sister Maurina and Sister Rosetta: we thus formed three teams, each team taking a turn in visiting the outlying parishes. That meant that regularly a different Sister was at home with Sister Lorena to run the household and to perform countless Confraternity "homeworks" These projects were not only varied, but manifold. Among them was one that taxed our ingenuity to the nth degree—that of doing all possible to insure home-study by children in the grades and its supervision in the home by the parents.

To this end, the Sisters at the Confraternity House at Baker labored at constructing workbooks based on the texts used by the children. Every grade had its accompanying workbook focusing attention on both doctrine and Bible History. Each lesson had its own written exercise for the child. Certain rules were evolved in time to take care of snags. Some of the most important were the following:

1. No teacher may assign a lesson for home study that has not first been taught in class.

2. No written work was to be done without home study.

3. Parents were asked to set aside a regular time for the study of religion.

4. Children not able to attend regular classes were asked to do the written work under guidance of their parents.

5. Children were to bring their completed papers to their teachers each week for correction.

These workbooks, eight in all, 64 pages each, were first multigraphed at the Confraternity House for distribution throughout the diocese. Later on these books were printed by the Benedictine Press, Mt. Angel, Oregon, the Catholic Sentinel Press, Portland, and a local printing shop in Baker. We did usually 5,000 books of one kind at a time. Assembling them was a task that for years was done with the help of the pupils from St. Francis Academy in the basement of our home. That called for perseverance, lots of foresight, and management.

When that project was out of the way, we looked ahead to the Religious Vacation Schools. Illustrated books were devised to provide learning skills, to afford relaxation and pleasure during a day devoted to religious education, and to give some tangible evidence of achievement to the pupils. Some of the books devised were: *Fun in Color and Verse, Ten Wonder Hours, Avisiting with Our Lord, Living Our Faith*—all published in time by the Catechetical Guild of St. Paul, Minnesota. Sister Maurina and Sister Rosetta were constantly on the alert for apt illustrations to render attractive the various projects under way.

Honor rolls for use by the teachers were made by the hundreds at our convent home; so too were prayer cards, roll book slips, and various devices to attract and hold the attention of the children. It once happened that in visiting the Religious Vacation School at The Dalles, I noticed a child in the middle grades whom I had seen at the R.V.S. in Condon, Eunice Taylor. "Didn't I see you at Condon last week?" I inquired.

"Yes, Sister; I was there. I had so much fun, I thought I would come to The Dalles and repeat it."

Another time at La Grande, I found a boy in the class-room doing his handiwork while the rest of the class was out in the recess yard playing. That was most unusual; I asked, "Timmy, what are you doing here? You ought to be outside playing with the rest of the boys and girls."

Timmy looked at me quite frankly and said, "When the rest of my class are doing this, I am at altar boys' practice. I want to do this now, or I will not get it done." It is not often that you get such reactions. I was impressed by both Eunice and Timmy.

Confraternity "homework" was frequently interrupted for housework. Domestic activities at Holy Family were on a cooperative basis with Sister Kathleen, Sister Marie Brendan, and Sister St. Anne acting successively as principal house-keeper or "Martha." A spacious lawn surrounded Holy Family and during war years became mainly a victory garden where Sister Maurina and Sister Rosetta tried their skill with spade and hoe as a pleasant interlude from desk and file.

Our front door opened not only for Sisters going on the road, but to welcome visitors for various activities, or for just themselves. The junior high school group of Baker and the St. Francis de Sales Adult Discussion Club for young women held their sessions at Holy Family regularly for years under the di-rection of Sister Rosetta and Sister Maurina respectively. Con-fraternity children and their parents were always welcome there. In a diocese where two-thirds of the Catholic children were, mainly by force of circumstance, in the public school, Holy Family was the one convent that was expressly for them, particularly from 1943 to 1956.

The diocesan board on Catechetics met regularly at Holy Family during the episcopate of Bishop McGrath, or Bishop Fahey, and in the very early years of Bishop Leipzig. Priests from the various deaneries and the Sisters in the diocesan of-fice served on the board. Among the various functions of the diocesan board, the following are noteworthy:

1. Directs the activities of the Confraternity of Christian Doctrine by providing a yearly program of activities.

2. Sponsors annual deanery conferences of the Confraternity.

3. Maintains contact with parishes through monthly reports of local units to the diocesan office.

4. Provides service in organization and catechetics through annual visits to the parishes by various members of the board.

Notifications for these meetings were sent to every member of the board by the secretary, usually Sister Rosetta. This was only one of the many duties incumbent on the secretary. All correspondence, report forms from the teachers and for the parish units of the CCD were processed at Holy Family. It is worth noting that whenever the Sisters returned home after a visit to parishes and missions, they always brought much homework with them. Materials had to be sent away as requested or promised to teachers on the way. Records had to be kept up-to-date, for instance the number of hours recorded that the individual teachers attended training sessions.

It was a busy household: answering letters, instructing individual First Communicants, answering the doorbell, just being friendly. Our neighbors on Second Street were attracted to 2337 because we were different and they wanted to know what made us tick.

One neighbor, a middle-aged woman, who was not a Catholic, wanted us to know that she believed in going to church and in keeping the two commandments of the law. "I don't believe in the Ten Commandments," she confided. "That's too many; I could never keep ten, but I do love God and my neighbor." Then, wanting to know what I thought, she asked, "What is your thinking on the Ten Commandments?"

"Well," I started, "I believe that the Ten Commandments are an amplification of the Two Commandments that you prefer. When you respect your neighbor's property and do not steal or destroy it, that is one way of loving your neighbor. When you respect his life, and do not hurt him, that is another."

"Oh, I see what you mean," she agreed, "but I still think ten is too many." With that, she got up to go.

"Come back another time and we'll be happy to discuss our philosophy of life. Keep loving God and your neighbor. That's fine."

"Oh, I'll come back again. I want to know whether you believe in hell. God is good, you know; I don't believe He would send anyone to hell. I would stay longer, but I just put a cake in the oven, and it is time I looked after it."

With a nod and a smile, I let her out the front door; at the same time, another visitor was coming up the steps. This time it was Mary, a little girl of three with blonde hair, coming to see whether she could help us. Mary was our next-door neighbor. She lived there with her parents and baby sister, whom Mary found very annoying because she could not be loud while the baby was asleep. Mary was a delightful little girl.

She helped to stamp envelopes going out monthly to beginning teachers with lesson plans and general hints to make teaching more pleasant. She picked up papers from the floor when the Multigraph was in full operation. She even dusted all the curlycues in the altar upstairs in the chapel.

In describing the setting up of our "House," I mentioned that we had a chapel on the second floor. Here, twice a week, Holy Mass was celebrated by Bishop McGrath until sickness prevented him. Thus we were able to have the Blessed Sacrament reserved here in the chapel, a reality especially gratifying to us who were so frequently on the road in mission towns where not even in the church was the Blessed Sacrament reserved.

One day, seated on the platform, dusting the altar, Mary turned to Sister Maurina who was doing sacristy duty, and whispered, "Does Jesus know I am dusting His altar? Does He know I am here?"

Sometimes Mary stayed with us for the noon meal. Mary was very observant, noting in particular that we said grace before and after meals. One evening she recounted everything to her parents. The father was a little disturbed. Not long after, he saw me in the garden between our house and theirs. Without explanation, he began, "Make a good Catholic out of Mary, Sister, but please don't make a Sister out of her."

I assured him, "Don't worry; either Mary has it in her to be a Sister, or she doesn't. That comes from God. I could not make a Sister out of her if I wanted to. That depends on Someone else."

Today Mary is, I hope, happily married. I have not seen her for years. I hope her contact with the Sisters in her childhood helped, at least, to make her a good Catholic.

Holy Family Confraternity House saw lots of living; it was a happy home for many years. Children came to the house and rang the doorbell for "trick or treat" on Hallowe'en; we were serenaded at Christmas with well-wishers singing carols from sleighs with tinkling bells and chimes; inter-community celebrations with games, singing, and good cheer climaxed the New Year, with boxes of Christmas cookies, made by Sr. Maurina, serving as prizes coveted by all. In short, Holy Family was community living in miniature—with its comic moments interspersed with more serious ones, even dramatic ones. An incident that culminated happily makes me laugh even today.

During the last part of May 1944, my mind was not always on my homework, but strayed out toward Ontario where three Sisters were winding up the Religious Vacation School. These schools have been popular in the diocese for nearly fifty years. Generally they were held during the summer vacation for two or more weeks, so that the public school children could complete the work in Religion for the year. They were an ideal outlet for Confraternity work. Even the war in 1944, with its rationing of gas and with tire shortage, did not decrease the enthusiasm of the children for the R. V. S., as they were popularly dubbed.

Now, I am refreshing my memory of the period from the reports of the team that went to Ontario to fill out much of the detail. Summarized, the story reads as follows:

"Sister Maurina, Sister Rosetta, and Sister Agnes St.

Rose closed the Religious Vacation School May 29, 1944, with an enrollment of 163 children. All the children received Holy Communion in a body, thirty of whom were first Communicants. There was a delightful breakfast after Mass, at which the first Communicants had places of honor with their parents.''

Other details the travelers supplied. With the school session closed, the Sisters packed their belongings for the homeward trek. When everything was taken care of, they, with a final blast of the horn, were off for Holy Family House. They were too tired to talk, but talk they did. They enjoyed reliving some of their experiences, sharing incidents of which one or the other was not aware of.

"Wasn't little Jimmy cute this morning? He couldn't take his eyes off Father Gaire. He was darling.''

"I know. After he received Holy Communion, he came back to his place and prayed loud enough for those with ears to hear, 'Dear Jesus, I want to be a priest like Father Gaire.' I hushed him, but I hope not to the point of his not praying at all,'' said Sister Maurina.

At Holy Family, a warm welcome awaited the trio. I was glad to see them. You would have thought the Sisters had been away for months. However, this was the ordinary reaction even when any of the Sisters were absent for only a short time.

The Sisters were exuberant: all talking at once, bubbling over with excitement, trying to relay to me and my companion the satisfaction they experienced from the use of the Activity Books, which had been made by the Sisters themselves: *My Sacrifice and Yours* for seventh and eighth grades; *Living My Religion* for third and fourth grades; and *Sacraments Are Signs* for children in the fifth and sixth grades. All the books seemed to fit the capacity of the children for whom they were written. A great job that brought much deserved satisfaction.

And that is what the Sisters, who had just finished one Vacation School, thought as they trudged off to bed for the night. At least that was uppermost in their minds when they whispered their thanks to God in the chapel. But not for long! About 10:30 that night, while the Sisters were quietly preparing for bed, a shrill, piercing alarm at the front door brought the community back together with breathless, wondering expressions to question what the outcry was all about.

"Your house is on fire! Your house is in flames!" This from the Ladies' Auxiliary of the Episcopal Church. They were coming home from a meeting and, like good citizens everywhere, they sounded the alarm. In various stages and kinds of attire, all four Sisters went into action and reaction that is funny to relate *now*. There was a fire and things were aflame—but not at Holy Family. Dr. Ruckman's woodshed across the narrow alley from our back porch was on fire. It was too close for comfort. The fire department and approximately the entire population of Baker arrived at about the same time, together with its full complement of dogs and children. It was exciting; it was hectic.

We were grateful that Holy Family Confraternity House did not go up in smoke. We were grateful to the Ladies' Auxiliary for alerting us. We were also grateful that the back porch of Holy Family had a fine protecting lattice screen to hide our various degrees of attire from the so-called curious gaze of the world. At any rate we were a picture no artist could paint! The Ladies' Auxiliary could attest to the feminine styles in vogue among the nuns in the mid-1940s. The Ladies' Auxiliary of the Episcopal Church hugged and embraced the Sisters; the Sisters in turn hugged and embraced the Ladies in the utmost abandon of relief that the Holy Family House was not burning to the ground. It was a good feeling to know that our neighboring church wished us well. It was a sight that would have warmed the heart of good Pope John some years later.

"To relax," the annals record, "the Sisters listened to the late news, but not before going out to the Victory Garden with flash lights to examine the possible damage done by unwary feet of firemen and dogs. At last, to bed and rest!"

I believe that about that time there was a popular song: "I Don't Want To Set The World On Fire"; certainly, none of us

107

did. However, about a year after this fire scare, Sister Maurina was doing spring cleaning in the yard with the assistance of one of the boys from nearby St. Francis Academy. They raked and gathered old grass, dry leaves, and broken limbs from the trees and put them in a trash-can to burn.

After they had put in all the debris, Sister Maurina put a match to the contents of the can, which was located in the backyard and not visible from the front of the house. Immediately, a great cloud of dense smoke arose to the delight of the two gardeners. This had gone on for a little while when suddenly they could hear a great noise of fire engines and the clamor of grown-ups and children somewhere out in the street.

"I wonder where the fire is?"

"It must be quite near, Sister, because the fire engines are in front of your house. No; they are turning the corner now," Billy reported.

Sister Maurina looked aghast as a fireman jumped from his truck and came striding toward her. Sister asked him, "Where is the fire?"

The fireman looked at Sister and answered, "I believe that it is here, Sister."

"Why, we are only burning trash and dry leaves, and there is no fire," Sister stoutly replied.

"Sister, did you get permission to do this?" asked the fireman.

"Permission?" Sister exclaimed, "what for?"

"The next time you want to burn trash, just give us a ring and we'll know where the smoke is coming from. You know, Sister, where there is smoke, there is fire, and fire is our business."

"I'm sorry. I surely didn't know we had to have permission to burn trash, but I will do as you say. Thank you." And was Sister's face red!

In the next hour several phone calls came in from people wondering whether we had suffered much damage from the fire. Sr. Canice at St. Elizabeth Hospital called: "Pres, the radio says your house is on fire. What about it?"

"Nothing to it" I assured her. "Sister Maurina was burning some trash. There was so much smoke, someone sent in an alarm."

Again and again the phone rang; people all asked about the fire. I did not offer the information that this had been done without permission from the city. I hope we learned our lesson well: no fires without permission of the Fire Department.

Chapter 7

Howdy, Folks

Sister Maurina and I were enjoying the ride from Bend —locally known as the Gateway to the Cascades—to Chiloquin, an Indian town about forty miles from Klamath Falls. We passed Lava Butte about ten miles south of Bend. A paved, or rather surfaced, road spirals to the top of the butte, which is a cinder cone five hundred feet high, one of the many miniature volcanoes that hurled ashes and cinders over the fields within the last two thousand years—at about the time that Christ was born and that Caesar Augustus was emperor of the Roman empire. We were traveling a-la-Chevrolet and as neither of us cared to ride over a hundred miles without using the opportunity to do something Confraternity-wise, we pulled up and entered the first general store we spotted on our right as we entered town. We were naive enough to believe that the storekeeper could point out Catholic neighbors nearby.

"Howdy, folks!" was the greeting that boomed across the reaches of the store. The storekeeper was a swarthy individual, burly and proportioned like a Brahma bull. His "Howdy, folks" was friendly enough, but his stance in back of the counter suggested an attitude adamant and unquestionably on the alert.

"Good morning, sir. Can you tell us whether any Catholics live around here?"

"Around here" included stretches of beautiful forests with occasional huts or cabins far back among the trees on either side of the road. Here in the Cascades, we were so high that much of the snow that falls on them never melts. Mount Hood lords it over Oregon, and in Bend we could look out each day at Mount Jefferson and the three Sisters.

Our question brought the storekeeper out front from behind his bulwark of pickle barrels, molasses kegs, and sugar bins. He bristled visibly. Fastening his penetrating black eyes on us—by now mere slits—he scowled and rumbled, "R-r-r-r-roman Catholics?"

The prolonged trill of the r's in "Roman" all but rattled our teeth. There was disgust in his voice. No mistake about it. He was going to make short work of us. "Do you mean those people that believe in the Pope and all that stuff?"

"Yes, sir. I am sure we do," Sister Maurina bravely affirmed. "Do you know of any Roman Catholics in this area?"

With evident repugnance, he snorted, "I used to be one of those myself, but not any more. I am now an Old Catholic."

"Old Catholic." Where did I hear that before? What does that mean? It's surprising how my mind raced across the index of not too commonly used expressions and shortly triumphantly lighted on the identification. I recalled that after Vatican I, certain groups of people would not accept the definition of the Pope's primacy and infallibility. They separated themselves from the Church and designated themselves "Old Catholics" to denote their refusal to accept "new" teachings. This man was an Old Catholic, we realized, a man who certainly opposed the Pope and all he stood for.

Sensing a story, I countered, "Tell us what happened. Tell us about it."

It did not take him long to say what was on his mind. "Too much religion. Too many bishops in our family."

112

"Oh! I see. Who were some of the bishops in your family?" I asked.

Immediately, he mentioned two family names in a cascade of z's, v's, k's, and ck's, with some vowels appropriately interspersed—perhaps members of one of the Slavic peoples in southeastern Europe.

I must say I was interested. My immediate concern to find Catholics in the neighborhood was temporarily diverted. But listen to him now. "When I was a little boy, no more than six or seven years old, I was put into a monastery where two of my uncles were monks. They wanted to make a monk out of me. Too much study; no fun; too much hard work; not enough to eat; endless prayer, and no relaxation; no time for fishing in the lakes, or climbing the mountains all around us. Rocks and stones and boulders everywhere, with rivulets of clear, sparkling water flowing down the mountainsides, a perfect paradise for good healthy fun. Nix—nothing for me. However, it did not take me long to say I didn't like it, did not want to stay. The next time my father came to visit, I went home. He took me with him, a puny little boy who wanted nothing so much as to get away from the monastery, built high among the mountains where winds and storms prevailed."

I noted a tinge of bitterness in his voice; there was hatred in his heart, and revulsion for anything "Roman Catholic." We thanked him for giving us his time, and with a "Goodbye, sir," we made a hasty retreat.

A deep sigh escaped my lips. From the confinement of the store, we came out to the expanses along the highway where there was freedom from thoughts of oppression or from dislike generated by a dominating or domineering structure. "I feel sorry for that man," blurted out Sister Maurina. "If he was detained in a mountain fortress, he should not hold that against the Pope, nor against us."

It did strike me that we were Religious, up among the mountains, but confined not at all. We were as free as the bluejays winging their way among the treetops.

113

Back in the car, I suggested, "Let's get on our way. But please stop at the next little store or shop, and we'll try again. We can't afford to let one man discourage us."

"Well, it's all right with me, if you have time to waste. I hope that fellow won't take it out on his wife. You never know," commented Sister.

About fifteen miles farther on, we came upon a combination country store and butcher shop. An elderly woman was in charge. She was slatternly and apparently poor. A group of women of about fifty or sixty years were in lively discussion. They looked up inquiringly at us—attentive, shrewd speculation in their eyes as to what we wanted. Remember this was in the early forties and our habits enveloped us from head to toe. We were most likely the first Sisters to have set foot in this little accommodation set up along the highway for all and sundry. I could feel their gaze fitting us into the sundry class.

The same question as before. "We would like to visit or meet Catholics living around here. Can you help us out?"

A little bent old woman with a missing front tooth began, "Now let me see. Farther down the road you'll find a Catholic family." She was a picture, with one finger in her mouth, as if feeling for the words on the tip of her tongue. ´

All the while, the proprietress was nodding vigorously behind the little old woman and with bent finger, indicated her. In hushed voice, she whispered audibly, "She's one."

"What do you do in a case like this?" I thought, for I could hardly challenge her then and there, especially as she went on helpfully directing us to the post office across the way, intimating that if anyone could help us, the people in the post office could.

Directly across the highway we went. In front of a wooden one-room structure with a window on only one side, we stopped. This must be the post office; on a rough piece of lumber was lettered the legend: "La Pine Post Office." We unlatched the door and walked in. We found ourselves standing in a narrow passageway about three feet wide and some twenty feet long. Not a soul was in sight. Evidently the post office was closed through certain hours of the day. We looked—and looked some more. A window in the wall that seemed to separate the post office from living quarters was boarded. I rapped, rapped again, rapped a third time. A voice from within barked, "Who's there?"

With all the assurance of an ever-expanding hope,I answered, "Two Sisters." That worked.

Instantly, the door to the inner section opened and a woman stood in the doorway. She was middle-aged, belligerent; intently she looked us over. Hardly expecting the postman to be a woman, I still managed to say that we were looking for Catholics and would appreciate her helping us. As though by magic, her tongue loosened. A flood of words assailed us. She seemed hard and bitter. We let her talk.

"I was one of you in New Mexico—a Benedictine twenty years, teaching school. Never a let-up. Now I've given up everything except the rosary. I promised my mother to say that. Hope for me? I cannot say. My best years are gone. At any rate, ask the priest at Chiloquin how my marriage case is coming along."

"Well, it may help you to know that you are in Our Lady of Mt. Carmel parish, about forty miles or so south on the highway. We are going to Mt. Carmel, if we can ever make it before nightfall. We are 'fishing' for Catholics along the way."

A little bit more relaxed, she responded, "About a mile south from here are three or four cabins, a store and a boarding house. In the last of three houses to the left, you'll find a woman and her child. Both are supposed to be Catholics. Good luck. I am glad you stopped."

Out again in the car, we paused to take stock of our morning's work. Not much accomplished. It had been a gruelling, searching, probing trip. It had also been an exhilarating, refreshing, inspiring trip—depending on one's outlook. We started off again—our primary work lay ahead; if the people had been little responsive, we could still enjoy their country and watch the wayside.

115

Summer had been slow in reaching the upper levels of the Cascade Mountains. The warm, friendly sunshine filtered through the tall evergreens. Here and there a bluejay flashed across our path. Prairie dogs along the highway sat up in alarm at the sound of the car and charmed us with their quaint antics and quick dashes to safety. Yes, the trip south had much to offer tired nerves and drooping spirits.

At last we came to Gilchrist, publicized on large placards as The Dream City. This is a lumbering town with company houses provided for the employees. It beckons to weary travelers to stop and look around. Unlike other company towns of the thirties and forties, Gilchrist has rainbow and pastel-colored houses on wide-paved streets that wound in easy curves up the hill. There was a welcome shopping-center where a hot beverage or a cold drink along with sandwiches were available together with the regular supply of trinkets cherished by Chicagoans and other big city folks passing through the Dream City. Gilchrist, by the way, is the name of the family who built the town and lumber mill. The word comes from the Gaelic "Giodllo Chriost," meaning "the servant of Christ." How Gilchrist is today I do not know, but it was our favorite stopping place in going from Bend to Klamath. On this occasion we decided to stop at the school to find how many Catholic children we could interest in the CCD programs.

We found every room in the building in use. The principal offered to send the children to us in shifts of smaller groups according to grades. Pushing, pulling, crowding giggling, they came to see us in the lobby of the school. Children are alike everywhere. Some were bashful and hardly answered us loud enough for us to get their names, but their friends, not so backward, added all kinds of data—useful or otherwise, but generally colorful. "That's Tim; he's always bashful," or, "Everyone knows Shirley, she doesn't like peanut butter."

By the time we had interviewed them all, we had learned that the Coynes had a new baby; that the Conley twins had

116

new shoes; that Jerry Matt lived six miles in the woods where the lumber mill was located.

A boy about sixteen made a great impression on us. He waited until last. He stammered, stuttered, and almost tore his fingers off as his story stumbled from quavering lips. "I am not a Catholic, but I always wanted to be one. I don't know what to do. How do I go about it?"

We invited him to sit down with us outside the principal's office. Gradually we learned that "Bumps," the boy's grandfather, had died a Catholic at St. Charles Hospital, Bend. We did not attempt to probe why or how this event had aroused his wish; we looked to the practical side. We gave him the names of two priests, one in Bend, a Franciscan; the other, the pastor of Chiloquin. We assured Tom that either of the two priests would see that he got the instructions he needed.

Shortly afterwards, Father Ahearn from Chiloquin visited the boy and made arrangements with Mrs. Monks at the Klamath Agency to look after the boy. I wish I could report Tom's coming into the Church; I cannot. The next time we passed through Gilchrist, we asked for Tom; he was no longer there. He had moved with his family to California. That was a long time ago, but I often think of the day he said, "I would like to be a Catholic; what must I do?"

"Howdy folks" is a two-way street; often enough we howdied. That could be illustrated on a trip when Sister Rosetta and I were scouting for Catholic families between Klamath Falls and Lakeview. I think we developed a sixth sense for new avenues of contact in this work. As we jogged along in our ever-dependable Chevvy, suddenly we caught sight of a group of four children. Books swinging to the strap, lunch pails keeping time to the hop, skip, and jump of the children, their heads held high in song, they made an irresistible picture

"Pull up to the side, Sister, please. Maybe these children can direct us to some Catholics."

The children, two boys and two girls, stopped in their

tracks as the car pulled over and stopped. They looked at us inquiringly, smilingly—bashful after a greeting that was meant to break the ice.

"Hello there," I called. "Who are you?"

They answered, in turn, their eyes popping out of their heads. "My name's Angelo," said the twelve-year old.

"My name's Immaculata," ventured his sister. Not to be outdone by their older brother and sister, the two small ones, twins, volunteered, "Cruz" and "Annunciata."

We explained to the children who we were and our work. "We expect to have classes for boys and girls like you that will tell you all about God."

Nothing registered on their little faces. I went on, "Wouldn't you like to come and learn about God?"

"I don't know," answered Angelo, "Who is that?" This from a Mexican lad whose name was Angelo, and whose brother and sister had names that made up a litany!

We were anxious to meet the parents, so we simply asked the children to hop in the back of our car and to direct us to their home. It was not far down the road.

In 1915, Father Francis C. Kelley wrote a classic for the *Ecclesiastical Review* titled "Shanty in the West." I came across it in reproduction in the *Extension Magazine*. Now, often, the opening sentence of that article came to mind during our visits to some missions in the Baker diocese. At times on such trips, Bishop Kelley's "Shanty" became very meaningful, very realistic to us Sisters, when our night's lodging was the one or two rooms in the back of a little mission church, primarily for Father's stopover when he came every six or eight weeks to offer Mass. On some occasions, we listened at night to the "creaks and cracks" in a very simple house of one of the parishioners, far out from any city or town. Such lodgings had their drawbacks; but they had the virtue, in that we came to appreciate what for us was "departure" from regular convent living was the habitual factor in the living of so many we sought to serve.

When we came to the children's home, it matched the description of "Shanty in the West" to perfection. We stepped into the first room we came to, on both whose side walls were bunks, four in all double-decked, with a narrow passage between them. The next room was exactly the same. Beyond that, I imagine, was the kitchen.

The striking thing was that in every available space on the walls, above the bunks and between them, were pictures that surely marked the family as Catholic: pictures from calendars—of the Sacred Heart, of the Blessed Mother, of St. Michael, and of any and all the saints one has ever heard of. And yet, here was a boy who did not know what we were talking about when we asked, "Wouldn't you like to come to learn about God?"

The mother greeted us cordially, happily. Mamacita spoke English quite well. She had a big family. Two little ones were running back and forth in their birthday dress. She listened to our explanation of our work and our questions, attentively, eagerly. "Yes, yes, the children were baptized, but that was all."

Her eyes sparkled at the thought that the children would have an opportunity to learn what it meant to be a child of God through baptism. It was only a short time after that they were enrolled in classes held at Ivory Pine. I often think of Angelo and his home. Not all shanties in the West are rectories. Some mighty poor people are living in shanties, too.

What did we do with the information gathered on such tours? We were not sociologists gathering data for statistics; we were assembling data that would be of use to the pastors of these areas so that they could follow up the scattered members of their parishes. Usually after two or three days visiting homes in isolated rural districts, we would report to the pastor and give him the names of the families and the number of children in each, along with details of where they lived so that contact with these people could be maintained.

What good did it do to visit a family such as Angelo's as we passed through the area? First of all, it gave these people the understanding that the Church was not just a building some

two or three hours wagon-ride down a rough highway; but that
the Church was represented in a bishop eager to open doors on
a two-way basis. Secondly, it paved the way for the setting up
of instruction, either in class or within those same homes.
Thirdly, there was always the pleasurable possibility that continued contacts could deepen into acquaintance—a less likely
possibility since our tours took us over such a wide area.
These particular children I did not meet again until a year
later.

In outlining this visiting that was an integral part of our
work, I might give the impression that Oregon is just scattered
places where people lived in very varied circumstances. This
would be erroneous, for Oregon is decidedly a very beautiful
state. In traveling from one destination to another, we were not
unmindful of its many attractions. World-renowned Crater
Lake, Mount Hood, and Lake Wallawa rank among the best
and most scenic spots. State parks often lured us to picnic
along the way. Emigrant Springs Park between Pendleton and
La Grande invited us to eat breakfast under lofty pines; Chand-
ler Wayside boasted acres and acres of forested canyon to
those coming into Lakeview, while Ochoco Lake State Park,
seven miles from Prineville, afforded unexcelled opportunities
to enjoy mountains, streams, and other natural attractions.

Because we loved the great outdoors, we invariably
packed a lunch rather than that we should go into some stuffy
little restaurant for a cup of coffee, a ham sandwich, and some
fruit. I might add the note that packed lunches were cheaper
than picked-up ones. I do mention some of these natural attractions to give assurance that not all the long hours of traveling
were tedious. Living conditions in some areas were difficult,
even harsh; but we found the people alive and rugged enough
to enjoy their homeland.

Before leaving consideration of the Klamath-Merrill-
Chiloquin area for other parts, I may well mention our stop at
a little home that looked quite forbidding. It was rather square
and squat in appearance. There was a front door, quite blank;
all the windows, front and sides, had black paper on them.

You could not begin to get a glimpse inside to see what it might be like.

We rapped at the door; we waited. Eventually a little girl answered our knock. The family, like the one near Ivory Pine, was Mexican. We were invited to enter. The mother was sewing, but laid her handiwork aside while we were there. A chandelier with three straggling electric lights illuminated the interior.

We thanked the mother for letting us into her home. Then, following our regular procedure, we told her who we were, who sent us, what we hoped to do, and then asked the children's names and ages. She gladly went down the list, all clearly Mexican names, such as Domitilla, Lucia, Loretta.

"And the baby in the cradle, what is her name?" I quietly inquired.

"Her name is Phyllis," proudly answered the mother.

"Now, where did you get the name Phyllis, after all these names that are distinctly Mexican?" I asked.

The woman explained proudly, "Phyllis was born here in America."

With twitching lips, I noticed that to cap the climax the baby's little fingernails and toenails were crimson with nail polish—the last thing one would expect to find in a home marked by poverty, almost destitution. The baby was a darling, smiling coyly when I called her name. Often I have wondered what happened to the little "American-born" Phyllis. I noticed, too, that it was a picture of Our Lady of Guadalupe that added a little color to the dull, drab room. One thing we learned: Catholics are everywhere; not only in row houses and tenements and apartments in large urban centers, but also in log cabins along mountain highways and in hastily built structures on federal lands, opened to pioneer veterans for homesteading. We took nothing for granted. If we did not always meet Catholics, we did meet some fine people of all denominations or of none. Only once did we meet hostility in visiting a family.

We were in St. Francis parish, Bend, situated among the

foothills of the breathtaking Cascades. The pastor was energetic, zealous, untiring in his efforts to bring the Good News to all his parishioners, even those living in remote areas. In reviewing the needs of the parish, he said, "Our classes are coming along satisfactorily. However, there is one family causing me no end of worry, because of their indifference. I would like it if you would visit them. I'll go with you; their home is hard to find in the camp since there are no streets—only roads."

Visiting? At the word, Sister Maurina and I were alert and ready. Before long we were on our way, Father and the two Sisters. The home we were to visit was made of rough-hewn lumber with very high steps leading to the entrance. Most likely the lumber used in constructing this house had come from the lumber mill where the man of the house worked.

At the time of this visit, the lumber industry in the Northwest was over a century old. The first mill was built in 1826 near present-day Vancouver, Washington. It marked the opening of a new way of life, the beginning of the biggest industry of the Pacific Northwest, of which Oregon formed no mean portion. As time passed, sawmill after sawmill sprang up in the wilderness. Around the mills, little villages arose that later developed into towns and cities. The area in which we were visiting was by no means a city, not even a big town.

Father rapped on the door: No answer. He opened the door a crack and called in, "Nobody home?" At that, a tall, angular woman appeared. She patently knew Father and greeted him with a cold, defiant voice, "I told you Eric is not going to catechism class and that's that."

Father was hardly pleased. His rejoinder did not calm the woman, "But you are a Catholic and so is your husband. What's the idea?"

"We don't want Eric to have religion pushed down his throat the way we got religion in the old country. Morning, noon, and night—prayers, prayers, prayers. What good did it do us? We went to Mass often; sometimes every day. Now, tell me if you can, what good did all that church-going do us?"

"Be careful, woman, don't be blasphemous," Father said sternly.

With that, a man's voice was heard from an inner room above the grinding, scraping, splashing noises of the camp, "I told my wife we're done with religion. You might as well get out."

But Father was not abashed. "Where's your husband?"

The woman indicated that he was in the bedroom, sick in bed. Father quickly said, "I am going to see your husband."

He bolted into the room, which was really a sector partitioned off by curtains to insure some sort of privacy. The woman looked after Father with a quizzical grin. To no one in particular she muttered—possibly for our benefit, "Don't be too sure you can get my husband to change his mind. Only yesterday be threatened to use the shotgun if you'd ever come again."

There was some exchange of words in the bedroom. Nothing too drastic, but nothing too friendly either. In the meantime Sister and I surveyed the room in which we were—a sort of combination kitchen, dining room and sitting room in one. We sat on up-ended boxes. Still, on the windowsill, there were crimson blooming geraniums. They added a note of cheer and color to the otherwise gloomy atmosphere. After a few minutes, Father came out, saying, "Come on Sisters. We'll shake the dust of this place off our feet."

We got up, thanked the woman, said good-bye, and were off. Looking back furtively, I saw the woman laughing at us, hysterically, wildly, almost fiendishly, her head thrown back. Shortly she covered her face with her apron and partly stuffed it into her mouth. All three of us hurried down the steps to the car with, we hope, not too undignified haste. That was the only time I felt something like fear. I have always been allergic to a blast of a shotgun in the back.

Prospects of rough treatment did not always develop. At

one place, a young priest asked us to visit a certain home. He himself had gone to the woman's house and "She took the broom after me." With just a bit of trepidation, we went to pay a friendly call on her the same day. She invited us into her home; she was sociable, friendly, and even cooperative to the point of promising to send her two children to class. There was no broomstick in sight.

Such visits with favorable or less happy reception were not an end in themselves. As noted above, the aim was to establish classes where these children could get regular, systematic religious instruction in the fundamental truths of their Faith. Classes were effective where there would be the opportunity for the teachers to meet groups of children regularly. Such classes, however, in the isolated rural districts were limitedly few. As alternative, we Sisters then had no choice but to enlist the aid of parents to direct their children in home study of religion. For this, we offer no apology—parents are suitably fitted by nature and grace to be teachers; given a little specialized training, they usually did very well in teaching religion to their little ones. As an illustration of this type of activity in the home, I offer the work done in a mission attached to Cathedral parish, Baker.

Sisters Maurina and Rosetta formed the team on this occasion. They went to Huntington, a windy little place which demanded heroic efforts to prevent any Sisters from being prototypes of "The Flying Nun." At the mission church in Huntington, dedicated to St. Joachim, Mass was offered every two weeks. About fifty of the people were Catholic—this included a family or two from Lime and Rye Valley. Religion classes were held more or less sporadically. The Sisters carefully outlined their plan of action to interest parents in teaching religion to their children at home.

Mrs. Maude Hartwell invited the mothers to come to her home on the prescribed day at two o'clock. Children of preschool age also were invited, along with theirs mothers, and provision was made for their care. Mrs. Hartwell left nothing to chance. She was a real gem of a woman; she made the necessary contacts for the Sisters, called people on the phone, and went to see them. The Sisters never found out what method she used, but at that first meeting of parents in Huntington, twelve mothers came, mostly rather young, with six pre-schoolers in tow—three girls and three boys. The six little ones were shepherded by Sister Rosetta into the kitchen where she was in her element. Sister Maurina held sway in the living room where she saw to it that the mothers were comfortably relaxed and at ease. She got the session started with her broad smile.

"Sister Rosetta and I are happy to be with you. Sister has some games and story-books with colorful pictures for the little boys and girls who came with you. She will be happy to entertain them while you are at this talk on 'The Role of Parents as Teachers of Religion.' I am glad that Maude made this happy arrangement."

After a few minutes of introduction, Sister continued, "I will not tell you anything really new. You have heard it before, but it is something you should ever remember, continually recall. Every home is a school. In this school, that is the home, you are the teacher; the children are the pupils. Remember it is not an assignment that Father Lee or Father Walsh has given you; it is a God-given assignment that you assumed when you were married. No one can adequately replace you. Sisters and other teachers in school are delegated to supplement your work as teachers of religion—they can never supplant you."

Serious faces had their eyes on Sister as she went on. Momentarily, one mother was a little distracted when her little three-year-old boy peeped into the room, looking for her. He was quickly retrieved by Sister Rosetta, who had a handful of colored balloons. She marshalled her little band down the kitchen steps into the backyard where they were going to have a parade.

"Your ideals, attitudes, convictions, and opinions form the texts for you in teaching your children. Your ideals, attitudes, convictions, gestures, and actions are the textbooks from which your children study, learn, and read. This may

125

surprise you, but your children are your severest critics; they are sitting in judgment on you twenty-four hours a day. By their actions, they reveal you to the world. Children generally are carbon copies of you, their parents.''

From this, Sister continued, ''I hope you realize how important you are. Parents are important; you are important, whether you realize that or not.'' She went on to point out that children imbibe from their parents not only all sorts of questionable modes of action, but that parents are likewise influences for good. She challenged them to a short examen of conscience:

''What example do you as parents give?

''Have your children ever seen you pray? If not, why not?

''Do you take them with you to Mass and let yourself be seen greatly attentive and reverent?

''Are they too restless? Any teacher has to deal with restlessness daily.

''Have they seen the family on their knees for night prayers?

''Have they observed you use more time to read and talk of practical religious living than of events along the street?''

''Remember,'' she repeated, ''your children are carbon copies of yourselves. Little girls will arch their eyebrows just as you do. Little boys will march down the street with hands clasped behind their backs just as they have seen their fathers do.''

These parents seemed absorbed by Sister's words. They listened intently. In a clear voice, vibrant and warm, Sister Maurina went on. ''In the Gospel for the feast of the Holy Family, we read that the Christ child was subject to Mary and Jospeh. From this chapter children can learn plainly what God expects of them—if it is made known to them. Further on in the same Gospel we read that the Boy Christ grew in wisdom, in age, and in grace before God and man. Here parents are made aware of the triple responsibility that is theirs toward every child God entrusts to their care, namely: the physical, mental and moral formation of their children.''

By this time, the children were coming in from the yard and darted into the front room in search of their mothers. They served as good reminders that the talk was not about children—but about *these* children in particular, as individuals. After a five-minute break for the parents as well, Sister Rosetta coralled her preschoolers back into the kitchen for milk and cookies, provided by Maude Hartwell.

With the group settled again, Sister Maurina followed up the idea. "As a rule, parents accept quite readily the responsibility of providing for the physical and mental development of their children. Why, we must ask, are parents, Catholic parents, so fearful of doing everything possible related to the spiritual and moral formation of their children? The spiritual, moral development of a child should not lag, but should keep pace with the physical and mental development. It is a gross error to presume that parents can surrender this God-given right and duty to others. The paramount duty of parents to their children is: That they themselves provide their moral and spiritual training."

Sister went on with the development of her theme until she noted that silence from the kitchen was beginning to distract mothers, who knew lack of noise was not necessarily a sign of "good" children. Sister Maurina took a hurried, tip-toed glance into the kitchen and came back, beaming with the assurance that all the children were taking a nap around the kitchen table.

Realizing that her listeners had homes where work was to be done before the rest of the family returned, Sister began her summation, stressing again the irresponsible mimicry of children, their thousand eyes for the traits and acts of parents—especially for faults that to young as to older humans seem more attractive, their readiness in action to be severe reporters of all their parents do and say.

"Your attitudes, your ideals, your convictions are contagious. In a word," Sister was reaching for the punchline, "teaching is most effective when actually practiced by the teachers. Teach your child God's Ten Commandments by observing them yourselves. If you want your child to be truthful, to be honest, to have respect for authority, then you must show him or her the good example of practicing these virtues at home, on the freeway, at the supermarket.''

At this point, a mother ventured to interrupt, ''Parents can't be blamed for everything. Charles is ten years old. He never used slang until this year. Now, he says 'Everyone does that.' He also wants to wear outlandish clothes and to wear his hair like a Nez Percé. What can a mother do?.''

Sister Maurina looked at her watch. ''That's a really good question. I am glad that you asked it. However, time being what it is, suppose we defer the answer—if there is one—to our next session. I wish you would discuss as many angles in that question as possible. Talk it over with your husbands —fathers are parents, too; with your best friends and with your in-laws. Be open; be sincere and 'listen.' I have a feeling we will have a spirited discussion next time. Everyone satisfied?'' Grinning nods gave approval.

From the kitchen came the sound of three little girls snickering as sweaters and coats were appropriated for the homeward trek. Two little boys were struggling toward the living room. Sister Maurina wound up with a rollicking bon mot, ''A noted Jesuit educator put the role of parents in religious education of their children in this way: 'I learned the Hail Mary *at* my mother's knee, and the Ten Commandments *over* my father's knee.' ''

The laughter that followed brought the children into the room, happy with balloons and whirligigs, supplied by Mrs. Hartwell; they were weary now of play-teacher and ready for home basics. Above the babble of good-byes, the mothers were reminded to return to Maude's two weeks later for a session on ''Teaching Little Children to Pray'' and to bring along their answers to the tabled question. ''We'll be here,'' was the generous response, ''we'll be here with bells on.''

Chapter 8

Always Room For More

Holy Family Confraternity House on Second Street, Baker, was our home base for Confraternity activities in the diocese of Baker. Actually it was our home, our base of activities, and eventually our hostel. It provided adequate quarters for five Sisters. A beautiful chapel was located on the second floor. We have a convenient living room in the front of the house, which opened into a dining room and then into a pantry and kitchen. To the side of these accommodations was a spacious lobby that connected with a small private office opening into a larger office affording work space for three Sisters.

A pillared front porch graced the home, and a back porch was suitably screened against flies and mosquitoes. In the rear of the house was a small room with a small sink; this opened into a corridor leading to the back stairs. A full-size basement, with shower, concrete floor, and finished ceiling completed the house. Outside, lawns and flower beds tidily surrounded the four sides.

The living and dining rooms became work areas that could be suddenly and rapidly transformed into a reception room or a dining hall when visitors dropped in. Elasticity was an oustanding quality of the house, for we managed to offer hospitality to visiting Sisters without anyone really stepping on someone else's toes.

129

After the diocesan office of the Confraternity was established to include the Sisters engaged on a diocesan scale in its membership, visitors came to look over our set-up and to see exactly how we operated. Among the first visitors were two Sisters of the Atonement, Sister Roberta Daniel and Sister Jerome, who came early in the morning of October 14, 1945. Their visit was prompted by the express request of Archbishop Duke of Vancouver, B.C., where they were assigned to the archdiocesan office.

While peace had been declared August 14, 1945, war conditions still prevailed. After an overnight trip on the train, the Sisters were in need of a little rest. They had travelled practically all the eighteen hours from Vancouver to Baker, sitting up and without dining-car accommodation. They were a sorry-looking pair when we met them at the station, but their spirits were high. After a refreshing breakfast shared with the community, they were taken upstairs to Sister Maurina's room, which had two single beds, to relax and freshen up.

At the moment the Holy Family staff was busily engaged in getting things ready for the departure of two of our Sisters. However, the visitors' arrival seemed most timely since the inter-parochial rallies, scheduled to take place during the two weeks of October—15-25, would be an intensive and also extensive demonstration of the Confraternity in action, if they were ready for a bit more rugged travel.

With wartime conditions still in evidence, gasoline, tire and food shortages affected the post-war Conferences held in three strategic places in the diocese. Deanery conferences were all-day affairs; inter-parochial rallies were scheduled for half-day—from nine in the morning until the closing with dinner and entertainment by local talent at 12:30 p.m. The wartime restrictions brought about another change in procedure —instead of inviting the general public to participate in the rallies, we asked only all officers, teachers, and parents of children in the CCD classes to come. The rally points were Ontario October 15, Baker October 16, and Pendleton October 18; for the second week they were Hood River October 22,

130

Prineville October 23, and Lakeview October 25. The visitors could come along.

Sisters Roberta Daniel and Jerome found their way down the front stairs about 11:30, much refreshed and ready for worlds to conquer; they would come along on the tour. Dinner was at noon; that gave us about thirty minutes to get better acquainted with our guests. We learned in the course of the conversation that we had mutual friends at Catholic University and in Philadelphia. Dinner was informal—served for the six of us in the kitchen. After dinner we skirmished about for the things needed at Ontario, the first port of call and the rallying point for Burns, John Day, Vale, and Jordan Valley: registration slips, pencils, programs, and the rest to be placed in separate boxes for Ontario, Baker, and Pendleton; overnight bags for the two visitors and for Sister Maurina and me. We planned to leave for Ontario about mid-afternoon since it was on Mountain-time, an hour earlier than Baker.

We set out with Bishop McGrath in his car, with Sister Maurina at the wheel. Traveling time was less than two hours, but nonetheless it was 5 o'clock Ontario time when we pulled up at Blessed Sacrament rectory. Father Patrick Gaire, the recently appointed pastor, was awaiting us. Father, a rosy, plump man, was very enthusiastic about the rally that was to convene in the town's motion picture theater. He had made all arrangements for our overnight stay: the Bishop at the rectory, and the four Sisters with the Dominican Sisters at Holy Rosary Hospital, a few blocks from the parish church and the rectory.

Father Gaire, as always, was a most gracious host. He told us that dinner was being prepared by several Altar Society women, and that the Sisters at the hospital would not expect us until 7:30 or 8 o'clock. It was a delicious meal—Western pheasant just in season and all the trimmings, including yams, lima beans, a tossed salad, cornbread with honey, and the truly American dessert, apple pie a-la-mode. We were in good company and we might have stayed longer, but finally pulled ourselves away to seek our quarters for the night. Sister Stanislaus, the superior at the hospital, was expecting us. Two

131

rooms, each with two single beds, in the newly renovated maternity floor, were at our disposal. There were few patients on the floor and no new admissions were expected. Everything was in order for a good night's sleep; morning would dawn early enough with its demanding chores.

We four Sisters by 8 o'clock were in the Bishop's car, which we had used the night before. By 8:05 we were at the Ontario Motion Picture Theatre preparing for the incoming guests. Tables were set up in the lobby for registration (no, we didn't use the ticket booth), a small table was placed to the very front of the stage along with a podium, and several chairs set out for the presiding officers and speakers at the opening session at 9:30.

On time, the session got under way. The theme of the rallies was to be: "Religious Discussion Clubs Aim at Making Articulate Catholics." The agenda for this opening session included a welcome address by the mayor of Ontario directly after the opening prayer by Father Gaire. A priest-speaker followed with the keynote talk: "Making Catholics Articulate." Reports were offered by the secretaries of the local units represented at the rally, and the opening session culminated with short talks on the theme of the rally by members from the parishes assembled at Ontario. At 10:30, Father Delahunty, Board Member, conducted an open forum at which questions previously submitted to him were answered.

After a brief recess, the so-called Catechetical Session opened. Sister Maurina gave an inspiring talk on "Preparing the First Communicant in the Home"; I followed with a presentation of "The Role of the Recitation in the Classroom." Lay catechists added zest to the meeting by asking related questions. Then there was a summation talk ably presented by Father Delahunty and adjournment at 12:15.

Fifteen minutes was adequate time for everyone to be promptly at table for the dinner served by the parishioners. How they served such a good meal at a dollar a head is their secret. The host unit provided entertainment during the dinner hour, to top off the rally which had proved a success in

132

achievement and enthusiasm for continued zealous effort.

By 3 o'clock the car was repacked for the return to Baker where the next rally would be held for La Grande, Union, Enterprise, Joseph, and Baker. Our return home by 4:45 was just right; we could store away the reports and registration slips from Ontario until October 17 when there was no traveling to be done.

Next day our two visitors accompanied Sisters Rosetta and Maurina and me to the Eltrym Theatre, Baker, and starting at 8 o'clock, we followed through practically the same pattern as at Ontario until two that afternoon. By 3:30 we were home at Holy Family, reviewing the events of the past two days and making comparisons. Yes, we had every reason to be grateful to the host and the visiting units; they did themselves proud. It was a long day for visitors still cautioned to hold to thirty-five miles per hour to save wear on tires, and many had come quite a distance.

The following rally-less day was a day at home and gave us opportunity to show the visiting Sisters our files; teacher records giving periods of service in hours and years, the lectures they attended and the written assignments on tests satisfactorily taken, and explanation of the course of study. The visitors took notes, and were glad to get samples of teaching aids. During the morning, Bishop McGrath stopped at the house to see that the Sisters were comfortable and brought us some pheasants for dinner. His injunction to me was characteristic of him. "Be sure to share whatever you have in the CCD line with the Sisters; we are Catholic; they are poor; help them in any way you can." He left after reviewing our plans for the next day. We retired early for our schedule called for us to be rally-bound to Pendleton and to return to Baker the same day. Our timetable hopefully read:

Rise: 4.00 a.m.

Holy Mass: 4:45 a.m. offered by Bishop McGrath in our chapel.

Breakfast: 5:30 (strictly that—coffee and toast.)

Off to Pendleton: 6:00.

133

Registration at Vert Auditorium: 9:00.

Opening session: 9:30.

Return to Baker: 2:00 (approximately).

The outline for the rest of the day would be the same as at Ontario, but with new participants: Hermiston, Heppner, Milton, Freewater, and Umatilla Reservation. St. Joseph Academy, would provide the dinner.

Our work at Pendleton was over by 2 p.m. and we would have been willing to call it a day, staying overnight there. However, we decided to leave for Baker at once, hoping to get home in good time before 6 p.m. That decision was occasioned by the fact the Atonement Sisters had received a summons to return to Vancouver by the end of the week. So like the minutemen of early days, they decided on Friday night as their departure time. Since Thursday had been rather strenuous for them, we planned to make their last day with us less taxing.

All of us went to the 8 o'clock Mass at the cathedral. It was a good place to say thanks that half the rallies were finished with good weather, bright clear skies, and sunshine. The Atonement Sisters spent the morning with Sister Maurina indoctrinating them in Primary Methods and with Sister Rosetta finishing with Methods in Religion for the Elementary Grades. Then we gave them half an hour to pack. The afternoon was to be one of relaxation for them.

Sister Rosetta proposed that she and Sister Maurina, by way of diversion, should go pheasant hunting with the visitng Sisters to the McCullough Ranch. This ranch was situated about a third of the way to La Grande. I never learned what really happened. It was a sight, indeed, to see them on their return, straggling into the house with two pheasants and a chicken. Sister Rosetta brought up the rear, on her shoulder a .22 rifle that Bishop McGrath had given her. After some tall tales, they finally admitted that Rodney McCullough had been the marksman for the day.

The chicken was an added gift from his mother to provide ample supper for all of us before the Sisters left Baker on the

10:30 night train to Vancouver. We could hope we helped the Sisters a wee bit to adapt what they learned in one week in Baker, a small country town in Oregon, to the situations in a large coastal city of western Canada.

. Way back in early October 1952, The Most Reverend Joseph P. Dougherty, Bishop of Yakima (Washington), told us that he was expecting four Religious of Nazareth from France to come to his diocese to do Confraternity work. Then, simply and without ado, the Bishop added, "When they come, I'll send them to Baker to your Confraternity novitiate for help. I want them to do in Yakima what you are doing in Baker."

And so it happened. Early in January 1953, there was a phone call from Bishop Dougherty. The Sisters had arrived from France December 13, and were ready to leave for Baker January 6. Would we have room for three Sisters? Sister Bridget, to be their housekeeper, would await their return at Yakima. We assured the Bishop that the Sisters would be most welcome and that we would accommodate them.

The call was on Monday, January 5; they were arriving Wednesday morning, January 7. By rearranging the bedrooms and using a comfortable roll-away bed, we had sufficient facilities for seven Sisters: Sister Therese Marguerite—who replaced Sister Rosetta, hospitalized for spinal surgery; Sister Kathleen, the house mother; the three visitors, Sister Maurina, and me. The visitors arrived on time at the Baker station in a blinding blizzard blowing down from the north. We felt sorry for these Old World travelers. They had left Paris November 21; arrived in New York Thanksgiving eve: had Christmas in Yakima; and now on January 7, the day after Epiphany, were ushered into CCD work without many minutes' time to rest a bit from their all night trip. The Diocesan Board on Catechetics was scheduled to meet at 10 o'clock with his Excellency, the Most Reverend Francis P. Leipzig, successor to Bishop McGrath, presiding.

The Bishop was most gracious to our guests: grave-eyed, cordial Mother Damiens, the superior; vivacious, happy Mother Champanhac; tall, thin, but wiry Mother Poussin. It was a spirited meeting. The four priest members of the board were on hand for the meeting, plus our visitors and three of us, making eleven in all. The agenda were abundant; a chief item, the planning for the 1953 deanery conferences. Bishop included the Religious of Nazareth in the proceedings by explaining to them what Deanery Conferences were, why they were held, and who attended them. In fact, there was so much business at this meeting that when 12 o'clock rolled around, the bishop declared a recess until one, when the meeting was resumed after a brief snack.

During this time off from "business," we determined to become better acquainted with the Sisters. We were intrigued to learn that they were the first Religious to modernize their habit. Their new headdress consisted of a little white cap with a short veil, with ringlets or wisps of hair framing their faces. The hemline of their dress hung about eight inches from the floor. There was no further change in the basic style or pattern from their original habit.

They told how it happened that shortly after the change was effected, several of the Sisters in Rome accompanied a group of children from their school to an audience with the Holy Father, Pope Pius XII. His Holiness recognized the Sisters, and after the audience dispatched word to the convent that he would like to see several of the Sisters in their new habit and one in the old. When they arrived at the Vatican, His Holiness was greatly interested, had them turn this way and that, inquired as to the advantages of the new over the old. "Was it loose enough? Was it comfortable?" etc. One Sister had her veil-front over the forehead. "Push it back a bit," he said, "will you?" Then, nodding approval, His Holiness added, "There, that's better; that looks very intelligent."

As we learned more about them later, we found the Sisters tremendously interesting. At recreation and during snatches of free time, we had them tell us of their life and work. Mother Champanhac had us gasping with envy when we learned that she had been teaching eleven years in the Holy Land, both in Nazareth and Haifa. Mother explained that she could easily understand why the Apostles had been so terrified during the storm at sea.

"The Lake of Genesareth, or the Sea of Galilee, has not changed and is much the same today as it was in our Lord's day. Fishermen mend their nets along the shore just the same as they did then. The sea, or lake, is seven hundred feet below sea level. Quite often a storm comes up rather suddenly, usually about noon, lashing the sea into turbulent waves that threaten the fishing boats on the water. Sometimes the waves dash so high that the boat stands on its side, the fishermen trying with all their might to right it by standing on the ledge with one foot inside, the other on the outer rim of the struggling boat. The one sail is blown over by the wind so that there is no end of straining and tugging to set the boat aright.

"Friends ashore shout to the men in the boats: Do this; No, do that; or, Pull to the right—all of which is to no avail, for the howling of the wind drowns out all sound. But the Sea of Galilee abounds in a small, flat fish very good to eat. So, despite the storms that threaten the fishermen, out they go like true sons of Zebedee."

It is too bad that I cannot insert Mother Champanhac's gestures and activity as she helped right the boat during the account.

We learned that Mother Damiens had been born in London of French parents with a home in both countries. She went to school as a little girl to the Religious of Nazareth at Boulogne. She spoke a very precise and correct English, as did Mother Champanhac. True to tell, all three are accomplished linguists, with English, French, and Italian at their command.

Mother Damiens described for us some of their war days, telling how the convent at Boulogne, right across the English Channel, had fifty-eight large craters made by bombs in the grounds surrounding the convent. For days, she recounted, the nuns lived in the basement where they had the Blessed Sacrament with them. For months, too, their main food was black bread and rutabagas. They wore wooden shoes with pasteboard tops. To deaden the clap-clap of their walking, they managed to nail pieces of worn-out tires and inner tubes to the soles. We could appreciate how well these Sisters could adjust themselves to circumstances.

The third of our visitors, Mother Poussin, the burser of Nazareth in America, won all our hearts. She was a true Frenchwoman, with a heart as eager as a child's for America and its ways. She had a delightful way of saying, "Ah! Ah!" on a rising inflection when anything was said or shown to her that was new and strange. And then her eyes would grow big as she leaned forward with another "Ah!" But one day the tables were turned, for we learned that as a child, Mother Poussin had lived close to Lisieux and had had the same confessor as the Little Flower had. Then it was our turn to exclaim "ah!"

However, their fortnight in the Baker diocese was not all stories. We arranged meetings for them in several parishes and missions. At La Grande, fifty miles west of Baker, the Sisters attended a teachers' and officers' meeting as well as a parent-teacher meeting. We figured that if the Sisters could actually see the Confraternity in action and meet some of the people who did the work, it would mean more to them than mere lectures.

While in the La Grande parish, we went to the Elgin public school where we met not only the children belonging to our religion classes, but their mothers and Confraternity teachers as well. Here there was cooperation de luxe, with the principal apologizing that he had no other room available for us but the "Ag" room. Previously the mothers had gone to the principal and asked to have the children excused for an hour; he in turn not only excused the children, but provided a room for the session as well.

The Sisters accompanied us also to visit the Confraternity classes held in Ontario and in Vale. We made our headquarters with the Dominican Sisters at Holy Rosary Hospital, who always received us most graciously on our travels. After three days in these parts, we returned to Baker to coordinate the work for the Sisters.

At our home base they examined our files, bookcases,

closets, and records. They took copious notes on the sample workbooks, report forms, and Confraternity material, samples of all of which were given them. From our study and experience, we tried to find answers to their many questions. Then after two weeks the Sisters returned to Yakima, their first foundation in America.

To most Americans, Canada seems, if not exactly foreign, at least remote. We speedily came to accept the northwestern idea that it was a close neighbor. Thus, whenever any of the provinces in west Canada had a Confraternity Institute, several of us would attend. I recall registering for the CCD Institute at Calgary, conducted by Father John Hofinger, S.J., protagonist of Father Jungmann, author of *The Good News, Now and Forever*. We liked Father Hofinger immensely as a religious educator, but at the time never dreamed that we would have further contact with him.

April 19, 1954 was then a red-letter day for us; it was in fact a rare, privileged day. Father Hofinger, as Professor of Dogmatics and Catechetics in the seminary for (not in) Peiping, China, is rated as an expert. Our auditing of his talks at Calgary had made a deep impression on us. We were delightedly surprised when unexpectedly he stopped *off* at Holy Family to offer Mass. After his breakfast, he asked to see us about the Confraternity work in the diocese.

He told us that he had been in San Francisco to see Mother de La Cruz concerning catechetics in America. In speaking of Baker, she told him, "Sister Presentina is a Sister with initiative and catechetical know-how. If you need help, she and Sister Maurina will do what they can." He told us that he had inquired of Bishop Dougherty about our endeavors and that the bishop had substantiated Mother de la Cruz's observations. So, here he was, ready to give us the "once over."

During the course of the morning when Bishop Leipzig stopped in at Holy Family to see how Father was getting along, he aked, "What do you think of it?"

Father Hofinger's ready reply was, "Excellent."

At noon, Father went back to the hospital for dinner and a

siesta. On our part, we welcomed the break, for the busy morning we felt had been something of an oral examination by a one-man board of examiners. Still, by three, he returned to take up the discussion and querying. In great part, the afternoon session was a learning session for us Sisters. Father cued us in to the newer trends in catechetical work, not in Baker, not in New York, nor in Germany, but in the world. I have tried to remember what seemed his salient points.

1. He hoped for the spread of the catechetical renewal through the growing desire for cooperation manifested in countries throughout the world. For instance, it seemed to him that in mission countries the prejudice against modern textbooks as something of little or no value for the missions appeared gradually to be diminishing.

2. He stressed that the guiding principle for the first contact with any unbeliever is anthropocentric. Take the man as he is with his thought patterns, opinions, and the influences of his environment and culture. For our situation, that would mean taking the child as he is and building upon that.

3. He emphasized the need of presenting doctrines as motivating powers of living.

Four-thirty rolled round in no time; we could have relished a few more sessions with him, but his stopover was necessarily short. At the time, he was on his way to St. Mary's theologate in Kansas where he would study English intensively. "Then," he said, "I go to Notre Dame University where I will be guest professor for some summer courses in catechetics." Father went on, "Before going, I would like to encourage you and Sister Maurina to write articles on the Baker system for *Lumen Vitae* (an international magazine). Some missionary priest would like to adopt some of your ideas. Write to me when you get an article finished."

With all our crisscrossing of Oregon, we felt like stay-at-homes in comparison to Father Hofinger. He had been stationed in China for fifteen years and in the Philippines for five. After his stay in the United States, he was going to Formosa to build a seminary for Chinese priests. With regret we watched him leave. His parting words were, "Pray for me, please. I depend on your prayers."

From Canada, our neighbor to the north, there were quite a few more Sisters who found their way to Baker, and later, after August 1956, to Spokane when we were transferred there. One of these was Sister Rita MacLellan, a Sister of Service from Toronto. At the request of the Most Reverend Philip F. Pocock, Bishop of Saskatoon, and of the Reverend Gerard Provost, diocesan director of the CCD, Sister came to live with us for two months to observe and to learn the organization and method of training catechists.

Bishop Leipzig gave her a hearty welcome. She was a chubby little person whose main characteristic of cheerful acceptance of everything in stride made it pleasant to have her share our accommodations. Her living out of her community's motto, "I have come to serve," made it extremely easy to find her one of us. Her habit of somber gray was even then considered modernized, so much so that when Sister went to Ontario (Oregon, not Canada) to visit the Religious Vacation School, a little lad of about seven stopped short in his tracks and to Sister's surprise blurted out, "Where did you get that rig?"

Reaction of a different sort came from our little neighbor, Mary, who was quite taken up with Sister, although she found her different. Sister wore a sort of cap in the house, but a hat when she went outdoors. One day, Sister Rita decided to go down town on a shopping tour—mainly to Woolworth's. Mary saw Sister go out alone; she was dismayed. She came over to Confraternity House according to her casual fashion and asked in a very anxious tone of voice, "Shall we notify the p'lice?"

However, Mary was not the only one who was concerned over Sister's "doings." As Sister came out of one of the stores, a woman accosted her with the bold question, "Why are you alone?" In recounting this experience later, Sister was very much amused. Her explanation had satisfied the woman completely, "I am from Canada." Which explanation and its ready acceptance struck our delightful Sister as extremely funny and worthy of a cartoon.

But Sister was not left alone much during the two months with us, nor did she have much time just to sit around at Baker. She had come at a good time, for two activities of the Confraternity were in full swing. She went along to attend the Deanery Conferences of the CCD and to follow the preparation for Religious Vacation Schools to be held in every parish and mission of the Baker diocese. She certainly saw Confraternity activities and at the same time two-thirds of the state of Oregon and a good many of the people there.

I have been turning the pages of a diary of Holy Family House to refresh my memory of this tour. Under the date May 4, 1951 the entry reads: "Sisters Rosetta and MacLellan visited the Confraternity classes at Our Lady of the Valley, La Grande." La Grande, a beautiful little college town of about 9,500, is situated between the Blue and the Wallowa Mountains. The scenery alone would have justified Sister's visit, and would have given her a chance to compare the town with some similar Canadian town built up on the lumber and farm industries. La Grande offered Sister MacLellan the first opportunity to see a Confraternity class in action. She later remarked over and over again to us, "What splendid work the lay teachers are doing. Why, these Confraternity children are like products of Catholic schools."

On May 12-16, Sr. Maurina, Sr. MacLellan, and I visited the Hood River Confraternity. From our travels, we knew something of the beauty of Canadian scenery; in this area, we felt our guest was coming into a showplace. Hood River is an exceptionally beautiful spot at the junction of the Hood and the majestic Columbia Rivers. Mount Adams is about forty miles north and Mount Hood is twenty-six miles southeast of the city. Hood River is noted for its apple, pear, and cherry trees that form an unrivaled picture when the trees are in blossom.

Here, Sister MacLellan saw classes conducted by an efficient staff of lay catechists. She was also much impressed by

142

the way in which the Executive Officers ran their meeting, at which she was guest of honor.

A later entry in the diary reads: "Sister Rosetta and Sister MacLellan went to Ontario, a town lying within the spread of cattle country in eastern and central Oregon." Here they took part in a meeting of the Sisters and lay catechists, whose purpose was the arrangement of a schedule of classes for the summer. Sister MacLellan marveled at the discipline, the order, and the seriousness with which the children regarded Religious Vacation School. She summed up her observations in the remark to me, "This is the result of years of work following out a definite plan."

One of Sister MacLellan's experiences was in a sense a by-product of CCD work; however, it did illustrate for her that in our work we occasionally ran into strange obstacles. Sisters Raphael, Maurina, and MacLellan were driving to Burns, the seat of Oregon's largest county, to open Vacation School. Sister Raphael had been assigned to teach there; a co-worker was due to arrive a little later. The trip, while not as scenic as some others Sister Maclellan had made, was proving to be a pleasant and enjoyable one, until coming into Burns, the car burrowed into a cloud of salmon flies.

"Oh, what's all this?" exclaimed Sister.

"They're just salmon flies," Sister Maurina announced, squinting ahead and settling down over the wheel. "This is something to see if there is any visibility when they get done plastering the windshield."

In a matter of seconds, visibility was practically nil. Sister Maurina had the windshield wiper running full speed and power; even then it was most difficult to see the road. The two fellow travelers expressed some anxiety at the chances of getting to their destination. Sister MacLellan opined, "I know now what the plague of locusts must have been like for the Egyptians."

When they got home, they gave me a dramatic account of the whole thing: how they breathed in salmon flies with the air; how they nearly swallowed salmon flies alive. Natives of

143

Burns assure us that salmon fly floods last only three days until the wind changes and blows them away. Sister Maclellan did learn how the flies can plaster a car.

The lay catechists were anxiously awaiting the Sisters' arrival at the public school building where the Vacation School was to be held. Sister MacLellan was advancing from guest to cooperator, now that she had seen how we operated. She pitched in to help set up the rooms and to aid in the preliminaries of "setting up school." Later, when the Sisters faced the job of cleaning up the car—Burns did not have a convenient drive-through wash, and anyway it cost less to do-it-yourselves—Sister lent a capable hand, and her bubbling laughter made the experience seem even funny.

When finally Sister left Baker, she looked like the proverbial "Mrs. Buttermilk." Packages, teaching devices, and samples of correspondence increased her luggage multifold, so that along with her suitcase they challenged the number of her hands and arms. She looked at her baggage and laughingly remarked, "Thank you for all this. I have much more than all this in my head."

After her stay at Baker, Sister was to begin work as Supervisor of Catechetics in Saskatoon. Her first assignment was to be an address to a National Convention of the Catholic Women's League on the Confraternity as she had found it in operation in the Baker diocese. We could certainly wish for her all success in the work for which she showed such capacity and such delight.

Another incident dealing with our Canadian neighbors occurred in October 1954. Sister Maurina and I had hurried home after visiting parish units of the CCD in the southern deanery. Our desks in the office were piled sky-high with correspondence that needed attention. One letter from Kamloops, B. C., aroused our curiosity. Who would be writing us from Kamloops? What did they want? Was it a begging letter or was it just an ad? Perhaps to prove we were not too curious, we set the letter aside to tackle more routine correspondence from points in the Baker diocese.

I laid the letter still in its plain envelope on my desk for proper study in the morning. But that was not to be. At 11:30 p.m. that envelope began to gnaw at my conscience. So, putting on a kimono, I tiptoed down the stairs to retrieve the letter. Cautiously, I went up the squeaky stairs, protesting my stealthy goings on at every step. Past Sister Maurina's room I went without incident. Into my room I crept and closed the door noiselessly. I pulled down the shade, not so noiselessly, and turned on the lamp, a feminine affair with fluted shade. I slit open the envelope, and unfolded the sheet to read.

"This can't be so! This just can't be!" I groaned. The letter was from the Most Reverend M. A. Harrington, Bishop of Kamloops, up in Canada. A little mental acrobatics recalled that Kamloops featured extra fine trout in the lakes and streams of the surrounding countryside. There must be good skiing too, for the depot at Baker had an attractive poster from Kamloops extolling the beauty of Mount Tad with its double chairlift.

More mental gymnastics, and I realized that Bishop Harrington was not "up in Canada," for he and four of his priests were to visit us October 26—and already 10 minutes of October 26 were gone. It was exactly 12:10 of the new day.

I hastily re-read the letter, picking up the more important sentences: "We want to see what we can do to better our mailing set-up in Kamloops . . . So I, with four of my priests —half the diocese—plan to pay you a visit to see your set-up and to ask some questions . . ."

There was nothing to be done except to try to get some sleep and to wake early to get on the phone. We called the hospital, St. Elizabeth's (since it was operated also by Franciscans), thinking they might have gone there. We called the bishop's house—no, he had seen nothing of a bishop and four priests. We called the cathedral rectory—no, no one had come during the night. Baker is of a size that it would be hard for five clerics to get lost in!

So? With the shadow of an imminent eminence, we decided the only thing to do was to go about our ordinary duties, and then to fly into action at the last minute. Almost fourteen hours from the time I read the letter, the Canadian invasion occurred. Sister Maurina and I faced a barrage of questions through the afternoon and tried to give from our experience the information that the bishop and his priests sought regarding the CCD.

We gathered from their remarks that they had a Sister available for some work in the diocese and that they hoped to use her in some phase of the CCD that would be answering the great need in the diocese. I don't know how the plan worked out, ,but ever since the 1954 visit, Bishop Harrington has remembered us at Christmas with cordial greetings and wishes.

Toward the end of the afternoon, Bishop Leipzig stopped in to extend his best wishes and to learn what was being accomplished. Adroitly, he worked in the question as to where they were staying that night.

"At the Baker Hotel," came the quick reply. The visiting bishop was quite aware that the bishop's house in Baker was not a mansion.

Bishop Leipzig left, assuring our visitors that he would return about five to show them to their overnight accommodations. When later the visitors left with him for the evening, they expressed a wish to return to our office the next morning for further discussion.

Promptly at nine-thirty the next day, they came back, now to pin down the general outlines of CCD work to practical details and to their particular situations. Without wasting a minute, they posed a few sticklers. One I sharply recall: "We are only nine priests in the diocese. How can we possibly have regular, systematic religious instructions for all the children?"

From what we had seen happen in the Baker diocese, we offered the suggestion that they should organize some sort of correspondence course for all the children who could not attend classes. We proposed that since they had a Sister available, she could organize and supervise that work. All too soon luncheon hour came. However, the bishop and the priests shared the meal with us, so we were able to continue "talking CCD."

Finally, without much ado, the bishop said, "We will leave from here at 1:30. I will drive. I brought the priests; it is my responsibility to see that they get back safely. Thank you, Sisters. Instead of the States having been invaded by us, I believe you invaded our minds and hearts with your zeal and enthusiasm. Good-bye to one and all!"

There is a point I should like to make clear in closing up this account of our visitors. The Sisters at Holy Family Confraternity House received inspiration and encouragement from each and every visitor who shared our house. We hope we gave them help from our work and experience; but we learned from them, too. Their questions showed us that even though our explanations seemed perfectly clear to us, sometimes we took too much for granted, and that more examples and illustrations were called for to make the matter clear to others—a lesson that made us more careful, more precise in our dealings with children too.

Not just from other countries did our visitors come, either to study the CCD set-up or merely on casual stopover. While we were in Hood River for a deanery conference in April 1953, Father Martin Thielen, Superintendent of Schools in the Archdiocese of Portland (Oregon), broached the matter of a visitor to Holy Family. Sister Jean Marie of the Sisters of Social Service from Los Angeles had been appointed CCD Supervisor for the archdiocese. He said, "I hope Sr. Jean Marie can come to Baker to study Confraternity techniques as used in the Baker diocese."

One houseguest; that was easy. We asked Father to notify us well in advance of Sister's arrival, since June was a busy month when we would be frequently away from home. Finally on June 23, 1953 Sister came for a week's stay. Sister was really new at this work, but she was very capable and eager to learn. She was a convert to the Faith and had enthusiasm and zeal for any and everything dealing with the CCD.

We started her off with our Course of Study, which she perused studiously on the back porch. She is a true American, for she knows how to improvise and was not afraid to tackle any new task. Needless to say, we enjoyed Sr. Jean Marie immensely, with her unorthodox manner of expression, her giving vent to frustrations that came her way. Sister worked hard through the week, studying program objectives, reports, curricula, she took things in stride.

The last time we saw Sr. Jean Marie was in Spokane at the Provincial Congress of the CCD, where she represented the Paulist Press as the protagonist for the "Come to the Father" series of religion books. We are happy to note the favorable impression Sister made upon us. "Keep on keeping on, Sister; there are still more stars to reach."

In the fall of 1952, the Regional or Provincial Congress of the Confraternity convened at Great Falls, Montana, at which both Sister Maurina and I were program participants. While we were there, the Most Reverend Joseph P. Dougherty, Bishop of Yakima, looked us up and begged us to come to Yakima the following Saturday, October 11, 1952. "I need help to inaugurate the Confraternity in the Yakima diocese," he pleaded earnestly and eloquently. "I will be in this new diocese exactly one year on October 11, and would like to celebrate the occasion by doing something definite to advance the religious education of everyone not in the Catholic school system."

Such a plea could not be ignored, even though it meant the postponement to a later date of a trip already planned elsewhere. As a matter of fact, I think that visit to Yakima had much to do with the counter visit of the Religious of Nazareth, detailed earlier. Happily the day the bishop had chosen proved to be bright and clear, such a day as practically beckoned us to get up in the air. We drove to the airport at Baker; parked our roadrunner Chevvy there where it would be handy on our return that evening; and arranged a round-trip flight to Yakima via West Coast Airlines.

Mrs. Auvé met us at the airport outside Yakima, which is

often called the "Fruit Bowl of the Nation." Because it was harvest season, Yakima was pungent and aromatic with the delicious odors of pears and apples being packed along Produce Row. It was too early in the day to do any haggling over any of the fruit on display. In any case we could not stop since Bishop Dougherty had a full day's schedule arranged for us. He did not let us down; we had seven hours of talking, explaining, and demonstrating at Yakima that day. At the end of the day we were quite ready to return to Baker and to pick up the car we hoped was waiting for us there at the airport. This was our first venture at leaving the car behind us, and we could not but wonder whether it was safe.

But Bishop Dougherty had other thoughts. To show his appreciation of our coming to help him out, he gave a banquet to which all sisters as well as priests and laity were invited. Six o'clock dinner changed our plans; but this was something planned on the spur of the moment. Like many other events played by ear, it was a delightful affair and is treasured among our fondest memories. For the lay people, the Sisters and the priests of Yakima, we left with heartiest gratitude, appreciating all that they did for us. The run to the airport was simple —Mrs. Auvé again was our chauffeur.

It was a dark night, but flying conditions were good. We made good time, to arrive in Baker about 10 o'clock p.m. Against our forebodings and quite to our delight, the car was exactly as we had parked it that morning. In short minutes, we were in the car homeward bound. Along the country highway—and this was really open country—it was pitch dark.

Suddenly, about a thousand feet ahead of us, we saw two pinpoints of light determinedly flashing towards us. "Must be an accident," I suggested to Sister Maurina who had been humming to herself as she drove along. "Take it slowly so we can see what happened."

Not until we were well within thirty feet of the "accident" did we realize it was a roadblock, manned by two policemen who were stopping every car as it came along. We pulled to a stop, wondering "What?" There was no sign of a

149

wrecked car or cars. We did not have long to wonder. A policeman came over to flash his light into the car. I believe he was definitely surprised at the sight of two nuns' faces looking up questioningly. To our relief, he asked, perhaps a bit bewilderedly and perhaps feeling a little foolish, "You have no illegal deer?" At this time of the year, more than one hunter would return from the Blue Mountains with more than his allotted quota.

To satisfy his sense of duty and for our justification, another policeman gingerly accepted the keys and opened the trunk to check for himself. Finally with a wave of his flashlight, he told us to be on our way and bade us, "Good night."

It was close to 11 o'clock before we drove up to 2337 Second Street. To the perplexity of Sr. Kathleen, "our Martha" at Holy Family, we announced, "Here are your two dears without the deer some travelers are bringing to their campfires tonight. Night, now; pleasant dreams; we'll tell you all about Yakima tomorrow." Leaving her to lock up and to follow us in wonder at our sanity, we made our way to bed after a very busy day.

Chapter 9

Congresses Here, There, Everywhere

At its 1934 session, the Episcopal Committee on the Confraternity of Christian Doctrine, representative of the hierarchy in the United States, came to a decision to establish the following year a National Center for the Confraternity at the National Catholic Welfare Conference in Washington, D. C. The central committee was to serve as a unifying agency for all CCD organizations throughout the country. There was to be a priest director with several assistants, priests, and laity. This was to be a clearinghouse for CCD data to the diocesan directors. More than this, the Center was to promote or sponsor CCD National Congresses each year, starting in 1934 up to 1941. After that date, Provincial Congresses in various parts of the country were to be held, with National Congresses convening every five years.

St. Louis was host to the Third National Congress October 9-12 in 1937. It is this Congress that stands out preeminently in my mind.

I was new in the CCD field, but not new in the teaching profession. My name had been submitted to the National Center as Superior of Catechetics in the Baker diocese by the diocesan director, the Rev. John D. Lee. By the middle of September 1937, an invitation came from the Archbishop of

151

St. Louis asking me to participate in the Congress by acting as critic-teacher at a lesson to be taught through the use of pictures of any kind. I accepted. At Mother Casimir's request, Sr. Rigoberta accompanied me to St. Louis. Sister was a veteran teacher at St. Francis Academy, Baker. During our absence, her classes were taken over by Sr. Emmanúel Mary.

Both Sister Rigoberta and I were like babes in the woods in St. Louis. Our first faux pas was made when we were looking for the Library of St. Louis University. We used the trial and error method of locating the Library. "This must be it," Sister exclaimed, as we came to an imposing structure with many, many steps leading to a portico with many fluted columns.

No sooner said than done. Up the steps we climbed to be met by a portly gentleman of grave countenance and mien. Pointing across the boulevard, he said, "There it is." No wonder he was so forbiddingly adamant in directing us elsewhere. We were seeking admission to the Masonic Temple where members of the lodge were in an official conclave. An enterprising young man with a camera handed us a printed card stating: "Your picture was just taken by . . ." as we reached the pavement.

I do not recall much of the sessions at the St. Louis University Library; however, the sessions at Rosati-Kain High School were unforgettable. We arrived at the high school an hour before time. A dense crowd was clamoring for admission; we wedged our way into the midst of the crowd. I whispered to my companion, "I believe every Catholic Archdiocese is here to observe these 'demonstrations'; there are about twenty of them to go on simultaneously. Will we ever get in?" Inch by inch, we made our way to the entrance, only to find the hallway so congested that one simply moved with the crowd.

It was impossible to see signs on the room doors. I was looking for "6B." Temporarily giving up the search, my next move was to locate the stage where I was to make my report as critic-teacher—on the demonstration transacting in the undiscovered "6B"—to the mass of interested auditors from the demonstrations. My plea to different people in the corridors of the high school, "Pardon me, will you please tell me how to get on the stage in the school auditorium," met with a response, invariably the same, "I'm sorry; I do not know."

How I got there, I, too, do not know. A man ushered me to the bottom of some dark stairs with the direction, "Go up these stairs; turn to the left; open the slide; and there you are." I did as I had been told; my quest was at an end. As I opened the door, I stood on the side of the stage, in the wings, seeing all, but unseen myself. I stepped out onto the stage, just as I heard the presiding officer, a priest, say, "Is Sr. Presentina from Baker, Oregon, in the audience?" I bowed slightly; the audience tittered a bit. "Will someone please direct Sr. Presentina to the stage. We know she is here at the Congress. She registered." I bowed some more and walked up front toward him. He expected me to come up from the front, not from in back of him. Everyone in the audience enjoyed the situation with rippling laughter. That laughter broke the ice. I was not nervous. The show had to go on. I took the seat he pointed out.

The presiding officer called on one after another of the class critics of Grade VI for their comments. Each demonstrator in the Grade had used a different teaching method. The outline method, the open book method, the picture method, story, and historical methods were illustrated. When my name was called, I advanced to the podium. I looked first at the presiding officer, then out at the audience. I began, "Reverend Father Chairman, esteemed Sisters, and dear good teachers. I have a confession to make. I was caught in the general melée on the first floor of Rosati-Kain High School and never made it to the room where '6B' had its class. It was to be a demonstration of the use of pictures in teaching. I cannot comment on the method used an hour ago, but if your Chairman consents, I will say something about the picture method in the ten minutes allotted to me." Father graciously approved; I went on.

"A child of three or four can enumerate objects in a picture. 'How many people do you see? Count the trees in this garden.'

"A child of six or seven can tell the story of a picture. 'This is a picture that shows Jesus as a boy. His mother and His foster-father are with him.'

"A child of nine or ten can describe a picture. 'This picture shows a child saying her night prayers at her mother's knee. I know it is night because the moon and stars are out. The little girl is very devout. Her hands are folded nicely. The mother has her head bowed.'

"A child of twelve or thirteen can interpret a picture; in this type of work, we gain insight into the student's thinking. For example, the picture of Washington Crossing the Delaware might inspire a child to write these few lines: 'Washington has great courage and faith; he is fearless in the face of difficulties. He stands upright in the boat to give his men courage. If the Hessians should see the approaching Federalists, Washington would be the real target. You can tell that Washington is no sailor. A sailor would not stand up in the boat.'

"Pictures are used to illustrate truths in a striking manner; to arrest the attention and to hold the interest of the children; to add pleasure to the teaching and the learning of religion and to add variety. One picture, the Chinese say, is worth a thousand words."

With that, the gong sounded and I stopped at once. The chairman told me I had another minute after the gong. "Thank you very much. I did not see the demonstration. I do not think I'll use the extra minute you have offered me. Thank you."

St. Louis was grand to us. I enjoyed the crowds; I enjoyed the speakers; I enjoyed the visits to historical spots. In short, both Sister Rigoberta and I loved the excitement, the inspiration, and the encouragement St. Louis gave us. I thought of the song "Meet me at St. Louis, Louis, Meet me at the Fair," and was humming it softly as we boarded the Union Pacific homeward bound.

We were back at our respective posts in Baker just about a week when a letter from the Rev. Aloysius J. Heeg, S.J., of the *Queen's Work* reached me. Among other things that he wrote was the information that he had heard me speak at the Congress in St. Louis and asked that I kindly send him a copy of my comments on the use of pictures in the teaching of any subject, particularly religion. That was like sending coal to Newcastle, but I acquiesced. Father Heeg was a recognized authority in the teaching of religion. He taught literally thousands of Sisters how to put life into their religion classes. What he was particularly interested in was the ability of children at the various age levels to learn by means of pictures and other illustrations. To this day, I often refer to Father Heeg's books; he wrote classics all catechists should know.

Towards the end of May 1938, an invitation came to me from the Bishop of Hartford, the Most Rev. Maurice F. McAuliffe, to participate in the Fourth National CCD Congress, to be held that year October 1-4, by addressing the assembled delegates on Institutes for Rural Teachers. The diocesan board on catechetics voted that Sister Rosetta and I should attend the Congress. It was the first time that I had addressed so many as were in attendance for my presentation.

In my address I stressed three main points to be kept in mind in conducting such institutes:

1. The objective to be attained;
2. The procedure to be followed in preparing teachers of religion, including parents; and,
3. The compensating results qualifying the success of a rural institute: a renewed interest in things Catholic; a leavening by a deep faith in Confraternity activities; and a more willing spirit of sacrifice in spreading the Kingdom of God on earth.

The thing that stands out most vividly in connection with the Hartford Congress is the vast devastation and ruin evidenced by thousands of uprooted noble trees and unroofed houses throughout Connecticut, eastern Massachusetts, and northern New York as a result of the 1938 hurricane that swept the northeastern States. Train travel from New York to Hartford was practically nil. At last we got there in a long-abandoned train that had been resting in the railroad yard; but get there we did, and were happy that the people of the diocese of Hartford decided to go through with the Congress despite the obstacles.

At the solemn High Mass, celebrated at the opening of the Congress, 80 bishops with their chaplains were in the procession. I shall not forget that line, for when Father Joseph Schmidt, chaplain to Bishop George L. Leech, Bishop of Harrisburg, passed where I was standing, he boomed out in his loud voice, "Look, Bishop, there is Sister Presentina, a Lancaster girl, from our diocese." There were so many Sisters in the area that it was difficult to tell whom Father Schmidt was indicating. I was relieved.

On October 26, 1938, the Most Rev. Edwin C V. O'Hara, chairman of the Episcopal Committee of the CCD wrote a letter in which he thanked me for my contribution to the Catechetical Congress at Hartford. Among other things, he recognized the part of our Community in the Congress. He wrote:

> In expressing appreciation to you for your part in the success of the Congress, we are not unmindful of the debt of gratitude which we owe to your Mother Superior and your Community. We realize that your participation in the program necessitated many sacrifices from your own community, but it is the glory of our teaching Sisterhoods that they have been generous in extending the knowledge, love and practice of Christian Doctrine among our Catholic children.

The next Congress was held in Cincinnati November 4-7, 1939. Many activities in the Baker diocese demanded my presence there; in particular, the 17th Annual Convention of the National Rural Life Conference was to meet in Spokane, Washington, the week of October 13, and I was expected to participate in that meeting. In his letter asking me to speak on Religious Vacation Schools, the Rev. William Mulloy, Chairman of the Rural Life Committee wrote:

> His Excellency, the Most Rev. Edwin V. O'Hara, D.D., Bishop of Kansas City, has given me the information that

156

it would be most pleasing to him to have you accept an assignment on this program. . . .

The topic which we would like to have you discuss is, "The Program of the Religious Vacation School." I would like you to deal with the topic in a very practical way, showing how the program itself can be adapted to almost any type of Religious Vacation School. . . . .

I accepted the assignment. Sister Rosetta went with me to Spokane, a neighboring diocese of Baker. We enjoyed every minute of the convention, particularly the personal meeting with Peter Maurin, the apostle of the laborer and a moving spirit of the *Daily Worker*. The best part of conventions and congresses, according to my thinking, is the encounter one has with men and women who do not know the meaning of, "Let's quit; we're discouraged."

In 1940 the Sixth National Congress of the CCD was held at Los Angeles in the Ambassador Hotel October 12-15. The Most Rev. John J. Cantwell, Archbishop of Los Angeles, asked me to address the delegates in a meeting devoted to "Meeting the New Needs of the Human Race" on the topic "Teaching Religion to Public School Children." Sister Maurina had come to the West to assist in the training of teachers just about six weeks before the congress; she was a natural to be my companion to the City of Angels. We were completely captivated by this city with its surrounding orange and lemon groves, with its ravishing display of color in the climbing red and purple bougainvillea, to say nothing ot its golden-yellow poppies blooming everywhere. Los Angeles was beautiful; Los Angeles was excitingly splendid.

In his letter inviting me to participate, Archbishop Cantwell had added the observation:

In conjunction with the Congress, we are celebrating the centenary of the founding of the first diocese in California. The first Bishop of California was the Most Rev. Francisco Garcia Diego y Moreno, O.F.M., 1840-1846.

According to the Archbishop, Bishop Moreno had his residence in San Diego and sleeps his last sleep in Santa Barbara.

157

In his day, one hundred years ago, he was the pioneer of the Confraternity of Christian Doctrine.

Californians were leaving no stone unturned to attract thousands to the Congress. At the railroad station, as we walked with other Sister delegates to the terminal, we saw several photographers with their cameras and other equipment looking intently at the mass of people coming through the concourse. "Look at those photographers, ready to take pictures. I wonder who is coming in that they are going to shoot?" wondered Sister Maurina aloud.

"Some movie star, I imagine," was my guess. "They are alert to anything that is news."

With that, one of the men stepped forward and gave orders for us to line up for pictures. A sister demurred. He quickly won his point by stating, "This is by orders of the Archbishop."

That did the trick. Seven Sisters from four different Communities formed ranks: two Mission Helpers of the Sacred Heart from Towson, Maryland; one Sister of St. Joseph from Cleveland, Ohio; two Franciscan Sisters from Baker, Oregon; and two Felicians from Chicago, Illinois. It was truly a picture of convergence—all coming together to study, to discuss, and to evaluate various methods of teaching the faith, particularly to children of Mexican origin living in the southern part of the state. For the Spanish-speaking group, there were special sessions, so that their particular needs were well taken care of.

"Teaching Religion to Catholic Children Attending Public Schools" was scheduled for Sunday afternoon October 13, 1940, at the Ambassador Hotel in the Coconut Grove Nightclub. Palm trees with climbing monkeys and shiny electric-light eyes were the main decorations. Archbishop Glennon was the honorary chairman at this session which was well attended by over a thousand delegates.

When Philadelphia offered to be the host city to the National Congress for the seventh congress, Bishop McGrath wrote, in a letter addressed to Redmond, Oregon, where we were giving a course in methods to prospective teachers:

"Now, I don't suppose you expect me to be a killjoy and prevent you two from revisiting the scenes of your birth. We gladly give our permission to accept the invitation to the Confraternity in Philadelphia."

In due time, then, Sister Maurina and I attended the Philadelphia Congress, where I spoke to a packed house of Sisters in the auditorium of Little Flower High School for Girls. Bishop Edward J. Kelly of Boise, Idaho, was the honorary chairman at this session devoted to teaching projects. A few points or highlights of my talk were these:

1. The content of the course of study should be used to effect a real transformation in the child.

2. Much of our religion teaching is ineffective because we neither have nor give *clear* ideas.

3. Sisters function most efficiently in the Confraternity program when they duplicate themselves by training lay catechists to teach.

4. Make a Christocrat of self in order the better to form Christ in others.

At the Philadelphia Congress, several far-reaching resolutions were passed. One had to do with the frequency of the congresses. In order to bring the CCD to many more people in a given year than could attend a national congress, it was resolved to convene nationally every five years, with Boston to be host in 1946.

The resolution provided for provincial congresses to be held in the intervening years, so that as many as eight or ten or twelve provincial congresses could be held in any one given year, not specified for the national conclave. In 1941 when the resolution was formed, the Archdiocese of Portland (Oregon) embraced the dioceses of Baker, Boise in Idaho, Great Falls in Montana, Helena in Montana, Seattle, Spokane, and Yakima in Washington, together with the Vicariate of Alaska. Each year a different suffragan see would be host to a provincial congress.

Philadelphia was the site of a stirring Congress. For Sister and me, it had sidelights. We met many boys—now young

159

men, some of them priests—whom we had taught. One usher at the Bellevue Stratford asked us, "How come the taxicab driver knows you both, way back when? And that priest, too?" Our registration tags pointed us out from the far country.

"Well," piped up Sister Maurina, "we'd expect someone to know us. We both taught in Philadelphia from ten to fifteen years."

In 1946, Archbishop Cushing was most gracious in asking me to participate in the Eighth National Congress to be held in Boston. Sister Maurina was invited to act as a consultant or advisor on Confraternity matters at an information desk. The Congress committee had outlined a comprehensive program, offering excellent presentation of the Confraternity objectives and techniques. The Archbishop proposed that I address a special session, entitled "Religious Instruction of Elementary School Children, Rural" on "Teacher Preparation and Grade Grouping," which would be followed by a discussion period. Both Sister Maurina and I were happy to co-operate. Both of us had taught in Boston before going into Confraternity work. Sister Maurina, in fact, had come directly from Boston in 1940, and I had taught there in my early years from 1913-1919. Boston, for this reason, had a special attraction for us; both of us were glad to get back.

There was an air of festivity about the Copley Plaza Hotel, headquarters for the Congress. Staid Bostonians raised eyebrows and looked askance at Sisters sipping ice-cream sodas or eating a hearty hamburger in the coffee shop. When some staid matron with sedate and serious mien broached the matter to Miss Mirian Marks, Executive Secretary from the National Office, she replied, "You've seen nothing yet. Wait till the Sisters pour in here from all over the United States. Then you may see something worthwhile." I wondered what she really meant.

One day, as we were going from one meeting to another, a bishop accosted us, saying, "You do not know me; but I know you. I am Bishop Johnson of Nelson, B C. Every bishop in the United States knows about your work. I am sending a priest to you, Father Joseph Barnes. I want you both to tell him how you operate in Baker. Nelson is very rural with few Catholics. Help him all you can.''

In a few minutes Father Barnes found us in the exhibition room. We looked for a secluded spot where we could have some privacy. Sr. Maurina cued Father Barnes in on teaching methods and techniques, and I tried to outline the organizational structure and its functions. We enjoyed Father Barnes and hope he went back to Nelson with its mountains traversing the diocese, confident that he could steer the course of the CCD safely and well.

Among those who came forward after my talk was a priest, young and full of life. He stammered a bit and then asked, "What Community do you belong to?"

"Sisters of St. Francis, Philadelphia Foundation," came my reply.

"I think you have a beautiful habit," he continued.

"Thank you very much, Father," I replied with a smile and felt like a little girl when someone compliments her on new shoes or a pretty hair-ribbon. And my heart was singing because of that young priest's remark

The most spectacular Congress that I ever attended was under the auspices of Cardinal Samuel Stritch of Chicago, November 7-11, 1951, with headquarters at the Sheraton Hotel. Sister Maurina and I were asked to conduct a seminar on rural confraternities. We worked as a twosome during a two-hour session before directors and Sisters from all over the country: Birmingham, Alabama; Burlington, Vermont; Cheyenne, Wyoming; Savannah, Georgia; Grand Island,Nebraska; Beaumont, Texas. Many a visitor stopped at the door to see what the hilarity was about. We enjoyed the experiences of dyed-in-the-wool stories with Southern Baptists or Yankee adherents to the dicta of early settlers of New England—all reviewed in, with, and by the charity of Christ. Under the laughter there was a seriousness that only full commitment to the CCD could bring forth. In fact, one member of the seminar

161

decided that CCD stood for Commitment, Consecration, and Devotion to the cause of Christ.

While the sessions in Chicago were the very best, the weather was not. The city was treating us to one of its wildest, coldest, iciest blizzards; the waves on Lake Michigan were towering, lashing, and thundering destruction with its winds and freezing blasts. However, Sister Maurina and I had only one day of battling the elements. Bishop Leipzig intervened; he made arrangements for us to stay at the Sheraton. This set-up greatly added to our general convenience. Attendance at the general sessions held at night was simplified; we reserved seats by way of squatter's rights.

These meetings were not only colorful, they were inspiring. I'll never forget the night Clare Boothe Luce, playwright, editor, lecturer, public official, addressed the House. It was a night that had airlines and traffic in general at a standstill. Her entrance was dramatic. At 8 o'clock sharp, a side door at the back of the hall opened and Clare Boothe Luce entered the ballroom, which accommodated 5,000, escorted by eight policemen. Four of the police officers came first, then Mrs. Luce, followed by four more officers. Clare herself was a picture, attired in an evening gown of red velvet. No one could miss Clare Boothe Luce; she stood out vividly for all to see. At the same time, Fulton Oursler, noted editor, author, lecturer and convert in 1943, held his audience spellbound in the second ballroom. At 9 o'clock, Mr. Oursler and Mrs. Luce exchanged *platforms* so that all of us had the double treat in one night.

Clare Boothe Luce needs no paeans of joyous song from me to convince anyone that she is a powerful lecturer. Experience in Congress was most evident. Her topic was "Spreading the Faith Everywhere." She felt that cradle-Catholics let untold opportunities of speaking about one's faith go unheeded. "Yesterday morning as I arrived in Chicago by air, I was a little surprised at the effects of the blizzard, with the wind then blowing at about thirty miles an hour. The taxicab driver from the airport to the hotel was quiet, fully aware of the grave conditions. Finally I broke the silence, 'It behooves us to be in the state of grace.'

"The driver sensed I was saying something important for he answered, 'State of grace? This is Illinois, or were you alluding to something else?'

"That was just what I wanted; one more man was giving serious thought to the state of his soul, occasioned by the weather." The speaker made no apologies for bringing in religion; she, like Oursler, is a convert and very zealous in spreading the faith.

Exactly at 9:10, Mr. Oursler came on; it took that long to get from one ballroom to the other. His topic was "Why Don't Converts Come into the Church Sooner?" He gave incident after incident to show how the indifference of good Catholics toward non-Catholics is frequently the cause of non-conversion. "My own case is typical. One day a friend asked, 'Why aren't you a Catholic?' My answer to that was deflating. 'No one ever asked me to be a Catholic.' " According to Oursler, all he needed was someone to say to him, "Why aren't you a Catholic?"

It should be clear why I think to this day that the Chicago Congress was the best. There is only one more gathering at Chicago that I want to mention. It was the closing at the Chicago Arena which accommodated 50,000 people. The singing by this vast congregation was truly tremendous. There was a play of "The Story of Catholic Education," and the Liturgy in which everyone participated. The Most Rev. Fulton J. Sheen had the sermon, in which he contrasted the use of the terms "down" and "up." Instead of saying, "Down with this" or "Down with that," Bishop Sheen exhorted us to "Look up to God; look up to heaven. Up with courage. Lift up your hearts." He was magnificent; he was dramatic; he was overpowering, and as usual, magnetic.

The bus driver who took us back to the hotel couldn't refrain from saying to his busload of delegates, "Did you hear that man? I had my loud-speaker on and heard every word. I wanted to shout, 'Give it to 'em, Boy.' That's the way to talk.'' Then, noticing that all in his classroom-bus nodded assent, he set the machinery in motion and we were on our way.

Regional or Provincial Congresses of the CCD were held as early as 1939 in six provinces under the auspices of a bishop within the province. Since then regionals have been held with ever-increasing number. In the archdiocese of Portland (Oregon) provincial congresses were held in Seattle—before 1951 when it became the seat of an archdiocese for the state of Washington; in Portland; at Pendleton in the Baker diocese; in Spokane; in Great Falls; at Butte in the Helena diocese and at Helena; and in Boise. Participants came from Montana, Idaho, Washington and Oregon to the regionals, held in the years between the national congresses.

Sister Maurina addressed general and special sessions at Seattle, and Butte, Kalispel, Boise, and Great Falls in the Big Sky State. We also took active part in regionals at Calgary in Alberta and at Vancouver, British Columbia. The regional at Calgary brought both Sister Maurina and me no end of satisfaction and joy. It was our first venture into Canada with its wide expanses of golden wheat ranches and its towering mountains of living glaciers and tumbling avalanches. It's a trip I'll never forget.

Toward the middle of August 1954 there was an urgent letter from Calgary, inviting Sister Maurina and me to come to Calgary for the Fourth Regional Congress September 10-13 of that year. Our bishop, Bishop Leipzig, was not in Baker at the time. I gave what I thought was a tentative answer, accepting responsibility for two sessions each for Sister Maurina and me. When Bishop Leipzig came home, I immediately informed him of my provisional acceptance. To my great surprise, he demurred, ''You are taxing yourselves; I do not think you should go.''

A telegram was sent at once to Calgary, stating, ''Sorry; cannot accept speaking engagements; best of luck.''

A phone call from Father Le Fort, director of the CCD in Calgary, came the same day: ''Sister, you cannot get out of commitments to the CCD from western Canada. We have published your and Sister Maurina's coming in every paper. It is impossible that you do not come. Our program is built upon you and Sister Maurina. We must have you!"

Here I was in another dilemma. I simply could not accept, I made it clear, without our bishop's approval. Father Le Fort said he knew our bishop would approve. The matter seemed urgent, and neither one of us thought we were overtaxing ourselves. Again I accepted with the proviso that we would go with our bishop's approval.

A few days later Bishop Leipzig consented. "I am glad that you can manage. Go in God's name."

With word of the approval came plane tickets for two from Baker to Calgary. And away we went. Several stops were made along the way at Walla Walla, Spokane and Great Falls; and finally at Lethbridge, the Canadian Customs site, there were some "firsts"for us. It was the first time our baggage was inspected; it was the first time that we were asked why we were coming to Canada and how long we intended to stay, checking our immigrant or visitor status. It was all very official and terse, no smiles for any of us. I had no tobacco, cigars, or alcohol stored away, but a strange feeling came over me as the customs official expertly put his outspread hands under our clothes and shook them a bit to see whether somewhere among these belongings some contraband might be found. A light heart was ours as the official declared us free to proceed on our way.

It was a lovely trip from Lethbridge to Calgary over vast prairie land rich in wheat and oil. We arrived at Calgary International Airport at 10 p.m., where a committee of the Knights of Columbus awaited us. They welcomed us and saw that we were properly escorted by motorcycle police, fore and aft —shades of Clare Boothe Luce. We were promptly taken to the Sacred Heart Convent, conducted by the Faithful Companions of Jesus, a Community founded in France, but with their Motherhouse in England.

When we arrived and alighted at the convent, another del-

165

egation was there to welcome us in the name of the women in Calgary. Really they went all out to make us feel at home. One well-intentioned matron exclaimed, "Really, you are most welcome. A police escort, just like Queen Elizabeth!" Mother Madeleine, the Superior at Sacred Heart, welcomed us most graciously, even though it was after 11 o'clock.

Today one can get a direct flight on the West Coast from Calgary to Baker, and vice versa; but on this trip it took us ten hours for a flight that normally takes only two. It is the understatement of the year to say we were ready to retire. Mother Madeleine suggested a long sleep, a suggestion we gladly followed. But a word about our room. We were intrigued by our bedroom. It was under the eaves and had poverty, worthy of a St. Francis, stamped all over it. However, it was meticulously neat and clean, with china pitchers and basins for our ablutions.

We slept well; morning came too soon. After putting ourselves and the room assigned to us in good order, we went with the lay Sister to the dining room. A substantial breakfast fortified us for the onslaughts of the day. But first Mother Madeleine showed us the convent grounds where a colony of beavers were busily engaged in gnawing incisively with sharp teeth at the trees lining the bank of a stream that flowed through the grounds. The flowers in the garden were colorful and bright; the weather was delightful and everything that one might expect, even though the calendar said September.

We left shortly for the cathedral, close to the convent, where a Pontifical Mass opened the Fourth Regional Northwest Congress in Canada. Saturday afternoon was devoted to the actual teaching of religion. When Sister Maurina was introduced as the speaker on "Methods of Teaching Religion," the chairman noted that this was a very important subject since few, if any, teachers in Canada had had any opportunity of studying methods of religion teaching. Afterwards, when at other meetings Sister Maurina was recognized by teaching Sisters from Canada, she was shooed into some secluded corner where a group of teachers would submit questions to Sister for her opinion. All in all, it was a glorious time for Sister Maurina. Fourteen bishops and archbishops were in attendance at this session.

There was another Pontifical Mass on Sunday at which Bishop Johnson of Nelson, B. C., preached a magnificent sermon. In the afternoon there were demonstration classes and skits to illustrate various methods and techniques used in teaching religion to Grades from 1 up to 12. Later there was a high school rally at which a Ukranian choir was featured. They were dressed in colorful native costume and sang several folk songs extolling special Ukranian customs observed for feasts and holidays.

Monday was the day devoted to promoting the Confraternity idea among the clergy. I spoke on "The Manner of Training Lay Catechists" to the priests and bishops. They were alert and keenly interested. All kinds of questions followed. In the second row was one distinguished-looking clergyman. He rose to pose a ticklish question. He began, "No one but an archbishop would dare to ask this question! Where does the money come from to conduct this program?"

I thought fast and furiously, and then ventured a response, "In the United States there are:

"1. The American Board of Catholic Missions, an arm of the National Conference of Catholic Bishops, established to render financial aid when necessary to mission dioceses.

"2. The Propagation of the Faith subsidizes needy parishes for the building of churches with multi-purpose halls, used for CCD and other activities.

"3. In the 'Provido Sane Consilio' of January 12, 1935, the Sacred Congregation of the Council states: 'A collection may be taken up for the promotion of catechetical works' (on Catechetical Day).

"4. Associate members help defray the expenses of the parish CCD unit. (Confer Manual—Associate membership).

"5. The Treasurer plans, with the cooperation and approval of the entire board, for raising needed additional funds when a parish fund is unavailable, or when funds collected from associate members are insufficient.

"These are the means commonly used. I am sure your own fertile minds are suggesting such things as cake sales, bingo games—where legal—and such like activities." These suggestions evoked some other posers common to many church organizations in need of funds.

After this session, Sister Maurina and I participated in a panel conducted by the diocesan director of Northwestern Canada. After the panel session, Bishop Carroll looked about cautiously to make sure that no one heard him say to us, "Sisters, we could never have put on such a successful clergy session without you. We have been trying for years to put across this program. You have helped us no end."

On our part, we found the clergy very responsive and cooperative; and we were convinced that it was just a matter of time when the CCD would have a strong hold in the diocese of Northwestern Canada.

After the clergy session, Father Le Fort met with us to express his appreciation and that of the diocese for our coming to the congress. We returned to Baker by train, coming from Yahk in Canada to Spokane on a train making its last run. While the train may have made its last run, the good-byes said in Calgary were not the last word. On September 19, the Most Rev. Francis P. Carroll wrote among other things:

I have been to Edmonton since the Congress. Here, there, and everywhere, I hear words of praise for the part taken by the Sisters from Baker. It is quite safe to say that your participation "made" the Congress, and you have the satisfaction of knowing that you had a very substantial part in doing the good which the gathering accomplished.

I think, too, that every bishop present is now anxious to establish a Catechetical Bureau such as you conduct in the Baker diocese. Unfortunately for them, they all want Sisters Presentina and Maurina.

There is one more type of institute that I like to recall. Under the sponsorship of the Most. Rev. Edward D. Howard, D.D.,

168

the archbishop of Portland (Oregon), and the Most Rev. Francis P. Leipzig, D.D., bishop of Baker, two institutes for priests were conducted at Milwaukee (Oregon) March 22 and 23, and at Eugene (Oregon) March 25 and 26, 1954. Committees from both the archdiocese and the diocese took care of housing, transportation, arrangements for Masses, and hospitality under the General Co-Chairman, the Rev. Martin Thielen of Portland and the Rev. William Stone of Chiloquin.

The two days were packed with lectures, discussions, and panels from 9:15 a.m., after the opening Mass, to 12:30, when one hour was allowed for lunch. After the refreshing break, there was a period of serious delving into the topics: "A Course of Study for the Elementary School of Religion," "A Course of Study for the High School of Religion," and "The Improving of the Religious Vacation School," until 4:30 p.m. Both Sister Maurina and I were on the platform as discussants at all these sessions.

There followed an Open House for the clergy—in Milwaukee, at St. John's Parish and Hall. Dinner was scheduled for 6:30 p.m., after which there was an evening session on "The Use of Released Time in Oregon Schools" and "The Apostolate of Good Will." We Sisters were again acting as consultants; we were indeed happy when 9 p.m. rolled around for an adjournment to the next day.

The sessions that occupied the following day were a continuation of the same type of work with an ongoing list of topics: "The Training of the Laity for Parish Visiting," "Using the Legion of Mary in the CCD," "The Religious Discussion Club," and "The Inquiry Class for Non-Catholics." Father Thielen gave a summary of the institute, which was brought to a close with Pontifical Benediction of the Most Blessed Sacrament at 4:15 p.m. with the archbishop as celebrant.

It is an understatement to say we enjoyed the institute. The priests were marvellous to work with; they were open, very cooperative and magnanimous in every way. They were very eager to put the CCD on a recognized basis as a religious educational force in the Northwest. We are happy to say that today the CCD has come into its own. Very few people in the Northwest can truthfully say, "What is the CCD? I never heard of it before." They are knowledgeable and very competent in providing leadership in the various developments of the CCD. Our two days in Milwaukee were well-spent.

The next day, March 24, we went with Sister Jean Marie, supervisor in the archdiocesan office to Eugene for the institute scheduled at St. Mary's parish. The program was a repetition of the institute at Milwaukee, excepting that the Committee for the Marian Year requested a Holy Hour for priests. That request indicates the caliber of the priests we worked with —dedicated, conscientious priests serving their fellowmen for the love of God. They were idealistic, yet practical; they were convinced of the necessity of the CCD in their parishes, but not to the neglect of other pastoral duties; they were men patterned after the Heart of Christ.

Sounds as though the Sisters of the Confraternity Office spent a great deal of time traveling. We kept a log of our journeys, particularly from 1943 to 1956, the period of thirteen years from the time we acquired the Rouse home as a Confraternity center to 1956 when both Sister Maurina and I were transferred to the diocesan office in Spokane. We traveled by bus, by train, by plane, by private cars, and afterwards by the Confraternity car wherever we went—in and out of the diocese, to Canada and to a lot of points in the States. We averaged 25,000 to 30,000 miles a year; in time, that totaled about 390,000 miles of travel, equivalent to 15 times around the earth. No wonder we say "And away we Go" when recalling our days in the diocese of Baker. No wonder we wonder at the unusual tasks that we encountered and that we accomplished only because of the unfailing encouragement of Sisters, priests, and laity everywhere. They were a brave, courageous group whom we remember fondly. They were our support at all times; without them, we could have accomplished very, very little.

Chapter 10

The Soul of The Baker CCD

I can never think of our efforts in CCD work in the Diocese of Baker without thinking of the one person who motivated it, actuated it, and encouraged us to promote it at all times. He guided us, counselled us, and stimulated us. This dominant personality was the Most Reverend Joseph P. McGrath, D.D., Bishop of Baker for thirty-one years. Both Sister Maurina and I saw in this kindly bishop on every occasion a direct successor of the Apostles who labored with and for Christ two thousand years ago. However, Bishop McGrath regarded himself a little depreciatingly, always seeking the last place and never looking for honors.

A vivid instance of this trait springs to mind. It occurred in October 1938, just shortly after Cardinal Hayes had died in New York. At that time I had just been appointed to the five-member Diocesan Board on Catechetics for the promotion of religious education and was attending for the first time a meeting of the board. Bishop McGrath was the presiding officer; with me, in attendance were Fathers Curran, Lee, and Delahunty. I was not accustomed to the free and easy way of addressing the bishop with simply that title. When asked an opinion on a subject, I used the formal "Your Excellency" in answering. He bore with me patiently the first time I used the

171

title of address. The second time he faced me squarely, "Whom do you think you're talking to? That dead Cardinal back in New York?"

That set me straight then and there. However, I fear that on another occasion I may have disturbed him even more. The faithful—the bishops, priests, laity, and Religious from Oregon, Washington, Montana, and Idaho were in session at the Regional Congress of the CCD held in Boise, Idaho. The bishops had a place along with the presiding officer and speakers on a special platform. There were three of us on a panel: Sister Amalberga, S.N.J.M., from Marylhurst, Oregon; Sister Bernice, F.S.P.A., from Marycliff, Spokane; and myself. When the presiding officer introduced me, he spoke of me as the soul of the Confraternity in the Baker diocese.

Then it was my turn to speak. "Your Excellencies, Reverend Fathers, esteemed Sisters, and dear members of the laity," I began. "Before going on to my assigned topic, I would like to make a little correction. I am not the soul of the Confraternity in the Diocese of Baker. The soul of the Confraternity of Christian Doctrine is our Bishop, the Most Reverend Joseph F. McGrath."

With that, there was a groan, a moan, and a general rattling of papers from the Episcopal section. Bishop McGrath was scowling darkly, head down, eyes averted from the ensuing applause and approbation. I knew, as far as Bishop McGrath was concerned, that I had made a faux pas, but that did not worry me. Bishop McGrath was the soul of the CCD in Baker, and every bishop present knew it; in fact, every bishop west of the Mississippi knew it.

He was my inspiration in this arduous task as CCD supervisor. Many of his epigrams are indelibly etched in my mind. When efforts seemed fruitless and frustrating, he would say, "No effort in this direction is ever lost"; and I held to that concept firmly, consistently, unwaveringly.

Again, he would remind me, "If there were no cross in the work, in what you are doing, I would be worried. The cross is the autograph of Christ. Where the cross is, there is

172

Christ." Or, he would say, "If the work is of God, it will endure, it will prosper."

When questions of various difficulties involving theological differences—the logical result of speculative theology—came up, he gave one answer, "I take my cue from Rome. What does Rome say about this matter?" That settled it for Bishop McGrath. His loyalty to Rome was outstanding; his love for the Holy See, faithful and true.

Bishop McGrath gave us his unfailing support at all times. He made no secret of his zeal for the Confraternity. Sisters Rosetta and Maurina—the two longest associated with me in the work—as well as other Sisters who worked there for periods of time were unanimous in their appreciation of Bishop McGrath's understanding and wholesale support.

Devotedly conscious of the profound obligations of his office, he never let his appreciation of the dignity of that office hem in his genuine personality; he was offhand in his contacts with us—as with every human he met. Once when I was alone in the Confraternity office, the telephone rang. It was the bishop.

"Did I see your sidekick driving a car down Second Street with a State policeman in attendance?"

"Yes, Bishop," came my reply. "Sister Maurina is learning to drive."

Silence on the other end; then, "Aren't you afraid to risk your life with her?"

"Not at all," I assured him; "but how about coming over here to talk it over?"

"Fine; I'll be over in about five minutes."

In the meantime, Sister Maurina came in from her lesson, very happy and content. I told her that the bishop had seen her and that he would be over. Her reply, "Ummhmmm. Well, I'll be back in the packing room if the bishop really wants me."

He arrived shortly. After seating himself, he began, "Tell me all about it. What will your Community say? I do not want anything done that would hurt the Confraternity.''

This was the fall of 1942 when it was not usual for Sisters to drive cars. I gathered my wits and answered, "I am sure we can get permission to drive a car. The School Supervisor drives a car for Mother Provincial and herself.''

"Call Sister Maurina, please. I want to talk to her," he directed quietly.

A hurried call to the packing room brought Sister Maurina into the main office with her cheerful, "Good afternoon, Bishop.''

Bishop McGrath was in a mood to tease. "What's this I hear about your needing a car? Well, you will have to do three things to get one. Go out and shoot: a pheasant, a rattlesnake, and a coyote; and bring them to me.''

Sister Maurina proceeded to argue her case. "I am in earnest, Bishop. Last year we were going over Quartz Mountain with the pastor from Lakeview at the wheel. He fell asleep and zigzagged across the road. I told Sister Presentina to continue to talk to Father to keep him awake. Had I known how to drive, I could have relieved Father at the wheel and forestalled any danger of accident.

"Then again, last spring the assistant pastor at Bend took us in his car to one of the missions near the crest of the Cascade Mountains. He did not fall asleep, but the muffler of the car broke and we were stranded. Father accepted the offer of a passing motorist to take him into town for help. We sat patiently in the car until after more than an hour, we saw the pastor of St. Francis of Assisi, Bend, and his very fine young curate coming to our rescue in the parish car.

"After hitching the assistant's disabled car to the sedate parish car, we proceeded—the pastor driving his car, the assistant steering the disabled car. Had we known how to drive, I could have done the steering and saved the pastor a thirty-mile trip to where we were parked. At any rate, I am learning to drive. Uhmm, I didn't expect you to see me driving down Second Street with Officer Colbert.''

Sister Maurina had presented her case ably to the bishop.

After more probing by him about other experiences we had had on the road, he asked, "What kind of car do you want? I had no idea you needed a car." The bishop was apologetic. Once more he asked, "What kind, what make of car would you say?"

Sister Maurina was equally as profuse as the bishop. "I have no idea what kind of car we can use. I was not really angling for a car; all I wanted was to know how to drive. Coming back to the idea of a car, I think it should be heavy enough to stand the kind of driving we'll have to do."

"All right; we'll see what we can do," said the bishop in parting.

About two or three weeks later while we were working in Burns, Mrs. Ira Walker, the chairman of teachers, greeted us heartily, "I was in Baker yesterday and saw the Nile green car you have. Aren't you excited?"

Sister Maurina and I could hardly wait to get home. Just like the bishop, to buy a car for our use. What a godsend. Public transportation had always offered us problems in getting all our equipment to the place we were going; transportation by friends' cars, often kindly offered, had always the hazards of delayed departures and late arrivals, and inconvenience to the driver waiting on us.

One of his characteristics that brightened many a heavy moment, or cut formality down to size, was the fact that we never knew what Bishop would do or say. Once when Sister Rosetta attempted to kiss his ring, he said, "For pity's sake, Sister, get up. Your nose is as cold as a block of ice."

For all his offhandedness, he was deeply concerned for those who worked with him or for whom he worked. During World War II, Bishop was concerned that our car would always be in good shape. Because of rationing, we were forced to practice economy. This was particularly true in the use of gas, oil, and tires. Several times he met us leaving town for Confraternity activities. He invariably hailed us to stop. "How are you for gas? How are the tires holding up?"

Sister Maurina explained, "We have enough gas to take

175

us to Hermiston; but our tires are a little thin.''

With that, the bishop circled the car, blessing each tire. "Go, now, that blessing takes care of you. There will be no trouble," assured the good bishop who had extended his blessing in the middle of a busy highway. And there was no trouble. The blessing took. He was unique; he was our bishop.

He did the same thing on Holy Saturday following a tragedy that happened outside our house on Ash Wednesday. An unknown assailant had shot a woman as she was returning from work at Western Union about 9:30 p.m. The Bishop came to the house with a bottle of newly blessed Easter water. "I would like to bless your house," he announced when I answered the doorbell.

"Fine, come in, Bishop. We are grateful," I managed to say. "I'll call the Sisters to accompany you."

Up the front stairs we went; stopping at each room, he blessed it and sprinkled it with Easter water. All through the second floor including the Confraternity storage closets. Then down the back stairs, praying all the while. We made the rounds on the first floor from the lobby to the kitchen. Our black cat, Nickie, was on a cushioned chair, looking out the window. He looked up at the procession moving into the kitchen just as the bishop gave him a dash of holy water as he said, "And for the cat, too." That kindly act of our bishop in blessing our house did much to allay any fears we had; for we were not accustomed to having a murder on our front lawn every day.

Lest anyone get the impression that Bishop was all for prayer and devotions, I hasten to add that he also enjoyed his moments of relaxation and fun. He loved picnics or a fishing trip with a group of priests, for which trips he provided the fried chicken and gingerbread. One of his favorite spots was Wallowa Lake where he enjoyed hiking, rowing, and fishing.

Wallowa Lake lies below steep, forested mountains, an area that is rich in Indian history and legend. By the lake's north end is the impressive monument of Chief Joseph, leader of the Nez Perces. Terminal and lateral moraines formed during the last glacial period may be seen here. At its southern tip lies the rugged Eagle Cap country along with such other peaks as Sacajawea and Sentinel. Recreational facilities at Wallowa are varied and numerous. No wonder Bishop McGrath never tired of spending a few hours at this lake.

He also enjoyed playing cards—pinochle to be exact —with the priests who came to his home. Once in writing to us while we were at Merrill, he added, "I hope you have no trouble with the new tires. I won ten cents at a pinochle game last night. That shows I still have some gumption left."

If the bishop rejoiced in pocketing ten cents from a pinochle game, he was equally pleased when he could be lavish with others. When our Community bought Holy Family Confraternity House for us Sisters, he furnished the chapel completely—altar, priedieux, chairs, vestments, draperies, etc. Best of all, he gave us his gold chalice from New Zealand sent to him on the occasion of his silver jubilee in the priesthood by his friend, the Rev. E. P. Murphy. Today that chalice is in the Provincialate of the Sisters of St. Francis on Palatine Hill, Portland. When bishop presented the chalice to us, he said, "I want someone to have it who will take good care of it."

When Mr. Braasch, an artist from abroad, was working in some of the parishes of the diocese, Bishop McGrath commissioned him to paint the four windows in our chapel with liturgical symbols. After Mr. Braasch was finished with the windows, he invited the community to pass judgment. He accepted the gasps of delight and admiration with a quiet grace. Finally he said, "If they were my windows, I would make them look old; but Sisters, no! Everything must have a clean, scrubbed look." The painting of the windows of the chapel in the spring of 1945 was a gift of our good bishop. He was unique. He was happy to win a penny; he was happy to spend a substantial sum for anyone but himself.

No occasion seemed to come for which he did not have a word of wit and wisdom. When Sister Emmanuel Mary and I were in Pendleton at St. Mary's parish in 1938, the Bishop learned from Father McKenna, S. J., the pastor, about our activities in his parish. By way of encouragement, the bishop wrote a little note to me in which he said, "I mind the innocent way you doubled your audience Tuesday evening. There is an old Irish saying in the west of that country which Sister Emmanuel Mary can translate into better English than this: 'No harm to let you out.' It means something to the effect that, like the proverbial Kerry Cow 'You can thrive where others starve.' "

Similarly, in September 1938, Sister Rosetta accompanied me to the East for the Congress at Hartford. I had had no time to outline my talk on "Institutes for Rural Teachers" before I left Baker. While at the Motherhouse in Glen Riddle, I wrote it out in full, as I felt I wanted the bishop's approval first. I always believed that I could not go far wrong as long as I did that. In answering the paper, he wrote September 26, 1938, "Our censor deputatus scrutinized with his eagle eye the matter and form of your *opus magnum* for the Congress at Hartford and found everything orthodox. So I can say go ahead and God bless you."

Further on in the same letter, he added in a light vein, "Regarding your week at Catholic University, Washington, will say that if they know anything you do not, by all means stay as long as necessary, with one proviso, however, which I think is necessary—do not be beguiled by those politicians around Washington to accept a permanent position at the headquarters of the Confraternity there."

His letters always had a light touch. About the middle of October 1939 we were in the Southern Deanery. Bishop was ever conscious of the needs of his diocese and never failed to alert us to new situations. He wrote to us about the Legion:

> Miss Mary Duffy, official organizer for the Legion of Mary will be in Klamath Falls, Saturday, Nov. 4th, if she hears favorably from Father Casey. I suggest that she contact you by phone in Lakeview or Paisley, if she gets there. You may be able to advise her if Lakeview would consider the Legion.
>
> Kindly order the books you suggested for the mothers;

the enclosed check is for that purpose.

As it is difficult to guess your whereabouts and where this letter may reach you, I shall close this brief note, fearing it may fall into the hands of some bigoted censor.

In 1941 Sister Maurina and I both attended the CCD National Congress in Philadelphia. On November 22, a letter reached us at Georgetown University Hospital, our home away from home while in Washington, D. C. "The home guard of the Baker Board of the Confraternity of Christian Doctrine is pleased to hear that the Better Half has survived the ordeal of mingling with the intelligentsia of the effete East in matters anent Confraternity lore."

Always the bishop was intensely interested in every phase of Confraternity work. The summer or Religious Vacation Schools always aroused his keenest interest. One summer we agreed to board three boys from Richland to attend the Baker Vacation School. We set up three cots in our basement as sleeping quarters where there was a shower and other bathing facilities. Sister Kathleen felt personally responsible for their welfare, calling them in the mornings, seeing that they were properly fed and clothed and in time for school. She set a table for them on our back porch next to the kitchen. All in all, it was a satisfactory arrangement, and the boys loved to go up our back stairs to the chapel, which they promptly christened the Sisters' little church. The bishop did not fail to note the enlarged menage. One day he arrived at the back door with a huge sack of potatoes. "I hope this will help you out since you have those three boys staying with you."

While earlier I wrote against an impression that the bishop was all for prayer and devotions, I wish to stress that he was a man of prayer and frequently asked for prayers, especially in the last years of his life. Hours spent before the Blessed Sacrament gave him the Christian courage to face death unflinchingly. We visited him at the hospitals to which he had gone as often as possible.

Even in his extremity, he thought of others. Once when I entered his sick room at St. Elizabeth's Hospital, Baker, he

179

beckoned me and said, "I die happy. You made it possible for every Catholic child to receive instructions in the faith. I would have been ashamed to meet Our Lord if this had not been done. I thank you."

Sister Maurina and I went to Portland to the Provincialate to get Religious Vacation School assignments for the Sisters of St. Francis. On our return the next day, Sister Rosetta met us at the station. She was subdued, solemn, and looked into space. She didn't say a thing; she didn't have to. We knew our bishop was dead; we knew our bishop had gone home.

Those were sad days, indeed, for priests, Sisters, and laity of the diocese, since Bishop Fahey, coadjutor with the right of succession to Bishop McGrath, had died suddenly March 31, 1950, just twelve days before Bishop McGrath. He had served less than two years; in that short time he had made a lasting and very favorable impression through his colorful and happy personality. As his funeral cortege was leaving the cemetery at Bay St. Louis, Mississippi, word was received there that Bishop McGrath had died that day.

A week or two after Bishop McGrath's death, I received from the Rev. Albert Bauman, O.S.B., Editor of *St. Joseph's Magazine*, a letter, requesting me to write a tribute to Bishop McGrath for the next issue of that family paper. I wrote from my heart. I append it here. There is a danger that an item written shortly after a death may be emotionally biased in favor of the dead. After twenty years of reflection and of learning more of the man from others, I would not cut a word of tribute; rather I would extend and deepen our expression of appreciation of this man. I present it as written!

* * *

Some years ago, a noted speaker in a sermon on All Souls' Day included a paraphrase of Job: "Man's life can be briefly summed up in a few words: He is born, he lives a little while; he suffers; he dies; he is forgotten." That can be a disturbing thought, but no one has ever agreed readily with this

180

noted speaker more than our recently deceased bishop, The Most Rev. Joseph F. McGrath, D.D., who died in the episcopal city of Baker on April 12, 1950. Frequently the bishop was heard to say, "No one but a bishop is sooner forgotten after death than a priest. A priest is forgotten soon; a bishop, sooner." This little appraisal then of our good Bishop McGrath is written with the hope that the bishop lives not only in our hearts and prayers, but also in the ideals he so beautifully exemplified during his 31 years as chief shepherd in the diocese of Baker City.

Have you ever heard it said that the truly great are humble? Bishop McGrath was truly great. Ever and anon he would counsel the Sisters engaged in the diocesan office of the Confraternity of Christian Doctrine: "Remember that it is the will of God that the work of the Diocese of Baker City remain humble. The very geography of the diocese tells us that we are never meant to blaze the trail. While we have sagebrush and jack-rabbits to spare, the diocese of Baker City is one of the smallest in the United States." In 1949, there were only 14,000 Catholics in an area of 68,000 square miles.

Yet at Bishop McGrath's obsequies, His Excellency, the Most. Rev. Charles D. White, Bishop of Spokane, in the funeral sermon spoke of Bishop McGrath as "Blazing the trail for his brother bishops in a diocese with difficulties similar, but greater than theirs."

Even with all his humility in regard to himself, Bishop McGrath was ever generously Catholic in thought and deed when it was a matter of his resources. "If anyone asks you to share Confraternity plans and successes with them, remember we belong to the Catholic Church. Send them material; be generous in time and effort to give them what they want. It is not Catholic to refuse anyone coming to us for information regarding ways and means we have found to work in our diocese." So today the records of the Confraternity of Christian Doctrine show that Bishop McGrath's program for the religious education of Catholic children and of adulsts in a preeminently missionary diocese was shared with bishops, priests,

Sisters, and lay people all over the United States and Canada. Truly remarkable, when we remember that the bishop did not consider publicity and advertising as being in keeping with the diocese he shepherded so well.

It is difficult to give an appraisal of the spiritual character of Bishop McGrath that will do him justice. He was a courageous leader of his flock. No matter how unpromising an effort may have been to bring the truth of Christ to some child or family, his inevitable comment, cheering the faltering heart to further action, would be, "No effort in that direction is ever lost. In God's good time, there will be results. Let's pray and see what that does."

Forgetfulness of self; a kindly, paternal love for children, here, there, and everywhere; a gently understanding heart for everybody; a deep charity for the poor: all were so much part of Bishop McGrath, that these qualities delineate him in the memory of those who knew him well. Along the streets of Baker, Bishop McGrath was a well-known figure. On his way from his residence to the Chancery Office, little children were often seen on a morning to run out for a cheery word and a smile. Every child knew that the bishop would stop and talk to anyone of them. No wonder that in late years, little four-and five-year-olds would visit him on his porch, or help him rid the lawn of dandelions on a fair summer's day. In his comments on children, he often said, "It is easy to make a good child laugh."

Bishop McGrath had a responsive heart for the "poor," who, as in our Lord's day, "are ever with us." For years, around Christmastime, Bishop would commission the Sisters to remember the poor throughout the diocese with gifts of clothing, books and toys. What a pleasure for Bishop McGrath to visit the Confraternity House two weeks before Christmas to view the multi-colored array of sweaters, jackets, stockings, caps and woolen suits destined for the little Marys and not so little Williams in some faraway mission of the diocese. Yet Bishop McGrath took good care that his name was never connected with blessings from the Christ Child. We hope it is all

182

right to speak of this charity now. In characteristic style, Bishop McGrath would say, "At Christmas time, all of us should dig into our jeans and pull out a penny to help the poor."

Needless to say, Bishop McGrath's penny was multiplied ten thousand times and more. And that, from a man who had taken no salary during his thirty-one long years as bishop, and who often said his own clothing was the gift of friends.

About four weeks before his death, the Sisters visited him before leaving on a Confraternity trip. Quite casually the bishop said in bidding them good-bye, "By the time you get back, I might be in the realm above." And Bishop displayed the same easy manner the day before he died. "I am going home," he would say to the Sisters in attendance at the hospital. "I am going home." Death held no terrors for the bishop. He was simply tired; he was going home.

We could go on and on reminiscing about our good bishop. However, no sketch would be complete without touching on his spirit of prayer. His life was one long, well-ordered day, with many an hour set aside for prayer and meditation. Through the many years of his priestly episcopal life, our Blessed Mother was ever his guiding star and light. Emblazoned on his coat of arms is the motto "Cum Maria"—With Mary. Bishop McGrath loved souls to the point of heroic unselfishness. No wonder His Excellency Bishop White, in his funeral sermon, used Bishop McGrath's own words as a perfect picture of himself. The citation was from an address to the students at St. John's Seminary; in it, Bishop McGrath summed up in a few words the character of the priests who had done the work of the Lord in the Baker City diocese:

There are conditions to cope with which require an ardent love of labor for the salvation of souls. Only men of God, men whose model is Jesus Christ; true priestly men, men forgetful of selves and of public opinion; men willing to make whatever sacrifices would be demanded of them; they alone can persevere and succeed amid difficulties as discouraging as they are tremendous. (*The*

Guardian, Little Rock, March 3, 1923)

That Bishop McGrath loved and esteemed his priests is a point without question. He realized the difficulties they often met with, so he endeavored to lighten the burden by a sympathetic understanding that was gemmed with Christ-like love. He often praised the beautiful spirit of fraternal charity that is characteristic of the priests of the Baker City diocese. He prayed for them, suffered with them, labored with them, and encouraged them always. Is it surprising then to learn that Bishop McGrath spoke of his priests as bearers of grace whose steps sanctify the ground on which they walk?

Thirty years or more of faithful service, in what Bishop O'Brien of the Catholic Extension Society calls "A Forgotten Mission Diocese," was not unheeded by Rome. Mindful of Bishop McGrath's quiet, but efficient administration of the diocese and of his untold labors in this difficult portion of the Lord's Vineyard, His Holiness Pope Pius XII conferred on him in October 1949 the signal honor of Assistant at the Pontifical Throne. It was Bishop McGrath's wish that this recognition by the Holy See be kept in his own heart during his life. He did not say that word of this distinction was not to be shared with others after his death. Friend, Counsellor, Father, Chief Shepherd of Souls, Joseph Francis McGrath! Your spirit is with us in the diocese of Baker City. Your kindly, unswerving fidelity in the dutiful discharge of the manifold obligations that were yours in a far flung diocese of the Northwest, despite your own prediction, will not soon be forgotten. Our bishop lives on in our hearts and prayers; his works are fruitful; they are not dead.

* * *

On May 10, 1950 I received a letter from the Most Rev. Edward J. Kelly, Bishop of Boise and former Chancellor of Baker for eight years under Bishop McGrath. He wrote:

I can see that you had a very true and deep appreciation of the soul of Bishop McGrath. As you so well said, forgetfulness of self and thoughtfulness of others was ever the characteristic of this truly apostolic bishop. He never sought to escape from this very poor diocese as he had many opportunities to do; on the contrary he adjusted himself and made himself perfectly happy in exerting himself with his whole heart, his whole soul, and his whole mind for God's glory, the good of souls, and particularly that of children in the appointed portion of the vineyard.

To depict in detail a giant in a miniature defies possibility. Bishop McGrath was a man of keen observation; he had facility of expression, though he preferred blunt, down-to-earth communication with his people, whereby they could readily grasp his ideas, his ideals. He could have been a writer; he could have outlined great thoughts for a wide audience. He chose deliberately to work with the limited number of faithful consigned to his care through his episcopal office. He could have written an autobiography that would have been delightful reading; but he chose to let his biography be written in the lives of his people, and in those of others who would indirectly incorporate in themselves the love of God and the following of Christ from contact with those whose lives were deeply influenced, guided, and stabilized through his everyday work.

He loved poetry; he found in it an uplift from beauty in the midst of humdrum. His verve in thought and in life influenced others to reach for high thought to brighten dull, daily patterns.

Practically, he saw the CCD as the direct means of influencing individuals in their everyday comprehension and practice of religious principles. Certainly, he never slighted or minimized any of the functional practices of the Church; but the CCD, with a minimal stress on organization for organization's sake and with all-out pressure toward its functional effect, was his prime means toward truly uniting his people to serve a loving God and to find peace in living.

If in this book I may have seemed to stress the work that I and the other Sisters accomplished, I have failed my objective. My aim was to bring out how this man of driving force could inspire us to see the goal as important even while there were so many obstacles, difficulties, problems, disappointments in working thereto. It was his spirit, his gentle urgency, his offhand encouragement, and his prayerful assuredness of accomplishment that gave us a lift, that buoyed us to tackle the next problem, to be confident that all the hardships and weariness were worthwhile. In this book, I have tried to outline the development of the CCD in the Baker diocese; if the detail of activities and happenings are foremost and obvious, Bishop McGrath was the source and soul of them.

Chapter 11

Ins and Outs on the Road

Just as a pomander—a ball with perforations in its rounded surface and filled with dried rose petals and aromatic spices —emits a fragrance like the attar of roses enriched by cloves, so the ventures and adventures recalled in this chapter may diffuse the varying moods and sentiments that touched us, and may add color, hues, and tints to the general picture of our work in Baker. Some of the incidents brought smiles; some, a hardly-withheld tear; they constitute a collection of recollections of the little and of the occasionally not-so-little items that make up the matrix of actual living.

I readily admit that I am referring to the annals of Holy Family Confraternity House to prompt my memory. A short item from under date of 20 April 1944 vividly stimulates my feelings and thought as of that time:

At 6:30 Sr. Presentina and Sr. Rosetta left by car for Portland, Oregon, to arrange with the Provincial for Sisters to teach the Religious Vacation Schools. Going over Cabbage Hill, they were caught with sixty or seventy other drivers in a blinding snowstorm. They returned from Portland by way of Hermiston where they spent several days in catechetical activities.

To the uninitiated, this account may seem innocent enough,

187

with notice paid only to the inconvenience of the snowstorm. The full picture is a bit different. From Baker to La Grande the trip was uneventful. La Grande, with an altitude of 2,784 feet, lies close to the Blue and Wallawa Mountains. It is in the center of the Grande Ronde Valley, picturesque at all times. Pendleton is about fifty miles from La Grande, farther west over the magnificent Blue Mountains. April 20 was a beautiful day with no forecast of what was to come. A few deer were at the riverbrink along the road, drinking their fill. We passed Kamela, a high point on the road, with no sign of snow. Six miles farther west was Meacham. Near the crest of the mountains and closest to Deadman's Pass, the storm was raging furiously. In a few minutes the snow was swirling about us from all directions, blotting out our surroundings, whirling in a sort of frenzied confusion.

"This can't last long," muttered my companion.

"Looks like a blizzard to me," I answered, trying to catch my breath.

We were in the mountain pass, with forests of evergreen on both sides already collecting mantles of white. It looked like a page from fairyland until we saw two cars and a truck in the ditch. A little farther on, about half a mile from Meacham, we came upon a regular bottleneck, formed by about eight trucks—big, unwieldy things—and about a dozen cars standing crosswise, lengthwise, and otherwise. I thought, "We had had our snowtires removed just a few days before." Two State policemen were trying to unravel the traffic snarl. A very narrow path had been cleared to the left. "Keep moving," they advised, "but take it easy!" To those congesting the highway, the traffic officers urged, "Go back to Pendleton; you'll never make it to La Grande without chains."

We were closer to Pendleton than to La Grande. We were at that point where I was sure that Henry Hudson and his crew played ninepins when the Catskill Mountains were the site for other adventurers. Always this was a tremendously beautiful site. Sister Rosetta regularly stopped there on our trips to let my imagination roam afar. Today, we took a sidelong glance only. There were cars and trucks of every description in trouble. We did not want to join their company, for we were due in Portland.

Slowly, cautiously, prayerfully, we nudged our way out of the confusion. It took us two hours to go down Cabbage Hill with its eight cutbacks and its eight hairpin turns; the drop from the plateau to the lower level is about one thousand feet which is negotiated by about a mile and a half actual forward progress back and forth down the side of the one hill.

Every bend in the road revealed to us new stragglers, struggling with the snow. When finally we got to the bottom with its straight run of about ten miles into Pendleton, we came upon newspaper reporters with cameras to take pictures of the mountain and its unhappy wayfarers in the ditches. By that time, at least seventy vehicles were stranded.

"How did you get through?" the reporters wanted to know. "Is there anyone up there with wrecking equipment?"

They did not wait for an answer; they were trying to make time while they could. It does seem unbelievable, but the sun was shining on our last stretch into Pendleton! Our hot coffee and roast beef sandwiches had been a slight consolation while we waited for clearance coming down the mountain. After we struck Highway 30, we followed the Oregon Trail, made famous by Marcus Whitman, Henry Spalding, and countless other pioneers, trudging, working, suffering, blazing their way across the continent—a contrast in mode of travel, but the same hazards.

Our trip that day also reminded me of Ezra Meeker, a pioneer who wrote his travels in the book called *Ox-team Days on the Oregon Trail*. This book may well be styled "Confraternity Days on the Oregon Trail." For the early pioneers coming from Missouri to Astoria or other Pacific sites, crossing the Blue Mountains was the toughest passage of all. Their ox-teams were unable to hold back the heavy wagons on the downward journey. Long chains were tied to the rear wheels and wrapped around tree trunks to keep the wagons from crashing down the steep mountains. The chains were released a few feet at a time until the wagon reached the bottom of the slope. For a hundred years, trees bore the deep chain scars. These scars tell the story very graphically of the crossing of the mountains by the early pioneers.

Did we reach Portland that blizzardy day? Yes, about five hours late, but we made it. Like the United States mail service, Confraternity work must go on.

There were other hazards of the road that we met on our journeyings. One such was a sandstorm that threatened us while coming from Arlington on the Columbia River to Pendleton. It was springtime; farmers and ranchers had just finished plowing; a few had sown the wheat and other grains. Sister Maurina was with me. We enjoyed the cheery greetings of the meadowlark perched high on a fence-post as we sped along. As we came close to Boardman, about twenty miles from Umatilla, I remarked, "Something is wrong ahead of us. I wonder whether we can circumvent it."

I had no idea what the something was that lay ahead. Great, billowing clouds were making visibility practically nil. It grew dark and threatening. Suddenly we were aware we were riding into the eye of a duststorm. Snowstorms are bad; but sandstorms seem worse. You breathe dust, and it creeps or rather penetrates the very warp and woof of your garments. Here, too, cars, many of them, were in the ditch. We could not stop the car and wait out the fury of the storm; travelers coming behind us would have run into us. While Sister Maurina gave all attention to the driving on what she could see of the road, I opened the car door a little to see how close we were to the edge. "To the right, a little more; you have six inches." Or, "Take it slowly; the traffic in front of us is at a standstill."

Once when we waited for the traffic to move, a man with a bleeding cut on his forehead clambered up out of the ditch and came up almost on top of us. He reached in the car, opened the backdoor, climbed into the backseat, saying, "Take me to Pendleton, please. My car is in the ditch. Have you any idea where the Templeton Hotel is?"

190

"Yes, we do," I assured him. "And we will take you there as soon as we can move."

To reassure us, he added, "Don't be afraid. I belong to All Saints' parish, Portland. I will not do you any harm."

The story has a satisfactory ending. We delivered the man within a square of his destination. Then we proceeded to St. Joseph Academy. I shall observe that if I had my choice, I would prefer a snowstorm everytime. And Sister Rosetta, Sister Maurina, and I have weathered some treacherous snowstorms.

Not all threats along the road came from overhead. Some came from the ground, from the type of territory we were traversing. Our visits to the various parishes took us through many places of interest and beauty: national forests and parks, mountain ranges and streams, canyons and deep rivers, desert land and rural areas. We would often get out of the car for a short respite to enjoy the grandeur and beauty of God's creation. We drove through canyons that were breathtaking and over mountain ranges whose peaks soared high into the heavens, through desert lands that were more or less tiring. Sometimes other motives than those of the scenic attractions caused us to stop.

On one of our visits to the Southern Deanery, both Sister Maurina and I expressed the desire to visit the grave of Father Donovan who was buried in Mt. Calvary cemetery. We would pass the cemetery which was located some few miles from Klamath on the way to Lakeview—our next stop. As we came near the cemetery, Sister remarked about the high weeds that covered most of the area.

"Do you think that we can drive right into the cemetery?" she asked anxiously.

"I think so; and then we do not need to walk so far in this heat," I replied encouragingly.

"This place surely needs some attention," commented Sister. "I wonder whether we can find Father's grave with all these weeds covering the stones."

She drove ahead into the cemetery; both of us alighted

and began our search for the grave. We walked down one side and up the other. It took close scrutiny to see the names on the various stones, but we kept looking.

"Here it is," I called to Sister Maurina who was a little distance from me.

She came over to where I was standing. We looked carefully at the stone and there was the evidence wanted:

REVEREND JOHN DONOVAN
Born August 14, 1912   Died February 14, 1948

Father Donovan had been one of our favorites. He was keenly interested in the CCD and gave all the cooperation any one could expect. More than that, he gave us many a good laugh. He would correct the children's homework exercises; after they were corrected, he would throw them on the floor to indicate north, south, east, or west sections of his parish. He would then pick them up and deliver them according to location when he was visiting homes. He was a hard worker, a good priest. These, along with more prayerful thoughts, went through our minds as we stood by his grave.

Suddenly I said, "I think we had better go at once, Sister."

Sister Maurina turned quickly and answered. "Yes, let's go right now."

We left the grave immediately and went directly to the car without looking right or left. Seated in the car, we looked at each other. Then Sister said to me, "Did you hear what I heard?"

"Yes, I heard it; that is why I said, 'Let's go at once.' "

"It gives me the shivers when I think what could have happened. How near do you think it was?" she asked.

"I don't know, but it was quite near because he gave us a warning that he would strike," I replied. I, too, was quite disturbed because I am not fond of rattlers. We have often seen them crossing the highway, and occasionally we ran over one. When that happened, we would cautiously leave the car to count the rattles. However, God is good; He took care of us. Both of us should have known better.

All the conditions were there to arouse a rattlesnake. It was hot; the weeds were high and tangled with underbrush; it was forbidding. Our coming into the cemetery invading his premises caused vibrations and radiations which alerted the rattler to our presence. The noise he produced with his rattles was sinister, ominous. Buz-z-z-z-z it went. We did not see the rattler, but the warning was there. It was unmistakable. Buz-z-z-z-z-z, it went again. The *warning* was adequate. We had left in a hurry. Instinctively we got the message and heeded it. We went as we came, in a hurry, without fanfare, glad to let the rattler unseen, unwept, unloved, and too close for our comfort.

Once when we were at Chief Joseph's Dam on the Columbia River in Washington, we came close to rattlers. There at the lookout platform for visitors was a high wire fence to keep anyone from overstepping the bounds. A large sign warned people not to disturb the stones on the incline leading down to the dam: Rattlers were there. Instinctively I moved back from the thick wire fence when I read the sign. We were too close to rattlers for comfort; I wanted no part of them.

Not all hazards were directly from the road; some came from directions. Once, when Sister Maurina and I were in Freewater, we inquired of a boy the way to a certain house. He was very obliging, but his directions left much to be desired. "You go to Freewater along the main street until you come to a place where they sell sneezing powder and your pictures taken while you wait. They live in back."

Another day, out in the open country, we asked a lad weeding in a field how to get to Jerry Murphy's ranch near Adel. "Go out the highway about five or six miles; cross the bridge; go over the cattleguard; that's it."

On occasion, finding place and people did not fully solve the problem. It happened one day that Sister Rosetta and I were in Enterprise, the Switzerland of America. Our objective was to meet two boys, born of Catholic parents, but who seldom came to Mass or to Religion Class. They lived out on a ranch, but no one was home when we arrived at the farm-house.

We scanned the surrounding fields and noticed some activity off near the barns and sheds. Nothing to do, but to take ourselves off to that place—perhaps the boys were there. Now we saw what was going on. The sheepherders had brought a band of some hundreds of sheep down from the mountains with the aid of their sheepdogs, hurrying about, nuzzling stray sheep into a more or less compact body. There was much frantic baaing and crying as the lambs or yearlings were anxiously looking for their mothers. At the head of the band of sheep was a man gesticulating vehemently to us. He did not wait to see what we wanted. Instead, he shouted to me, "Stand here and count, ten, eleven, twelve, and so forth. Let the sheep in this gate one at a time!"

They were not going "into green pastures," but into a large vat filled with sheep-dip, disinfectant. Of course, there was much struggling among the sheep to get to the other side where there was an opening into a field. Here he stationed Sister Rosetta to count once more. In the meantime he was busy prodding the stragglers through the dip.

It was a great lesson in sheep husbandry. The man who set us to counting sheep never did find out what we really wanted. He directed us back to the house where the Missus would take care of us. I do not remember what explanations were given for the boys' absence. I do remember that many, many sheep went through the dip. By getting the exact count of the sheep, the owner could tell what the net increase was from the previous year. I can only hope that my CCD was developing as extensively as my education in farm and cattle and sheep economics. I have found that the system works this way:

A herder takes ten thousand dollars worth of property into the hills on open range, and the owner does not see the sheep again for months. Whether the year shows a profit or a loss depends greatly upon the herder, upon his judgment and loyalty, his competence, his ability to find water, and his alertness to act in an emergency. He must be a good veterinarian

194

and must be on the lookout, day and night, for bobcats, coyotes and, in the mountains, bears. Men with these qualities are rare.

I have never forgotten the experience of counting sheep on a ranch close to the Wallowa Mountains. It was a great day! It was fun! And incidentally we did get the two youngsters lined up for better attendance at Mass and at class. Where there are sheep, there's a way.

As has been indicated earlier, this visiting of the homes of children who absented themselves from class without leave or license was part of our regular procedure in rural districts. In Union, a small town about fourteen miles east of La Grande, we had organized a small primary class of about six children who were to meet for a lesson every Saturday morning at the Ranger Station. Week after week, a certain "Tony" was absent. We knew where Tony lived and decided to pay the family a visit. Sometimes all kinds of reasons keep a child from class: at times the family is not sure of the meeting time; at other times, the child has a fear of untried, unfamiliar experiences. It takes less courage to stay away than to attend. In Tony's case, we simply did not know.

We arrived at the ranch-home in a hollow, but hesitated to leave the car. A three-legged, growling dog snarled viciously at us. Finally, a character, who seemed odd to us, came from the back of the house and passed the car without as much as seeing us. Something had to be done. With an eye on the dog, circling the car and sniffing and snarling all the while, Sister Rosetta called to the man, "Is this the Harmon place?"

The man stopped, looked thoughtful for a moment—his eyes focused at a point far beyond us—then drawled a slow, long, drawnout, "Y-e-s." (The name Harmon, by the way, is fictitious; otherwise the story holds to the facts.)

"Is Mrs. Harmon home?" Sister pursued.

"Y-e-s," came the reluctant reply.

Obviously we were not too welcome here. "Are you Mr. Harmon?" Sister Rosetta continued.

The man, unkempt beyond description and in the process

of becoming more wary as the interrogation continued, thought for some time before the reluctant, "Y-e-s," was forthcoming.

"Well, you are the man we came to see," I chimed in cheerfully. Then I explained our mission.

Mr. Harmon was very unresponsive, so I ventured further, "May we see Mrs. Harmon, please? She is home, I believe."

The man was a study. He pondered for a few moments, then said, "She's sick."

"Oh, I am very sorry. But we visit the sick. We'll be glad to go to see her. Perhaps we can do something for her. What do you think?"

Mr. Harmon answered gravely, "I'd be ashamed for you to see our house. It is in a terrible condition, dirty and messed up."

My heart was touched. "Really, we did not come to see your house. We came to see you and your family. We are interested in you as a family group, not your house."

That seemed to do it; Mr. Harmon led the way to the house, Sister Rosetta bringing up the rear with the dog sniffing at her heels. Mrs. Harmon was in a morris chair in a reclining position, very sick. We did not stay long, only long enough to see what she needed most—some warm clothing and some nourishing food. The Harmons were nearly destitute; we could appreciate the father's reluctance in not wanting us to see the plight they were in.

Our House annals report: "We notified the Visiting Nurse to call on Mrs. H." The visit bore fruit for on Saturday morning little Tony Harmon, very happy and respectably clean, attended the class. We had sent warm coats, underwear and shoes for all three, along with potatoes, carrots, canned soup, and vegetables to last them ten days. Friends of ours had given us many a thing we needed for people like the Harmons. God was good to us always—the dog, despite his manifold growlings and sniffings, did not hurt us. If Aeneas could brave the three-headed Cerberus to get into hell, for heaven's sake—and

196

for that only—we could brave, a bit timorously, a three-legged dog.

Sometimes there were quite unexpected results from the Sisters' visits to homes in search of children on their list, but conspicuously absent from anything Catholic. It took us two trips to Keating—a station of the Cathedral parish—to visit the listed homes, since some of the parents were shopping in town. One man inadvertently gave information that Sister Rosetta and I acted upon at once. He mentioned that his sister had graduated from St. Francis Academy in Baker, and was living near the Powder River bridge on the Keating Road. We asked her name; we knew at once it was a stranger to our list. Immediately we went to the house and found the father, not a Catholic, at home, but the woman herself was absent. The man was cordial and frank; he thought that possibly the eleven-year old girl was baptized, but he added, "I am sure our seven-year old son and younger girl have not been baptized. However," he added, "I have no objections to religion, but I leave everything in that line to my wife." At that moment the wife arrived home, visibly confused for a moment-at seeing us. She was friendly and invited us into the living room to discuss Religious Vacation School.

"Tell us first, please, are any of the children baptized?" I began.

"It's like this. We never got around to it. I often wished that the children would be baptized, but never went through with it." She went on that she was quite willing for the older girl to come to summer school, but was very doubtful about the boy. When the boy was questioned what he wanted to do, he expressed himself as very willing to attend.

Errands like this one brought us intimately into contact with the results of indifference and neglect in regard to religion on the part of those entrusted by God with the religious education of children. I am happy to relate that these two children became children of God by partaking of His love and His life through Baptism, after two weeks in the School of Religion.

197

They were enthusiastic, they liked the R.V.S.; we had little difficulty in bringing about their attendance at the year-round classes.

There were some odd quirks to some stops along the roadside. In November 1946, Sisters Maurina and Rosetta had spent three weeks in the southern deanery on Confraternity activities. In time they returned to Holy Family House like homing pigeons, happy to be home, filled with enthusiasm over their visits, and brimming with anecdotes of every kind of incident—amusing, gratifying, heartbreaking, and soul-stirring. I recall one episode in particular that had a light touch.

While they were in Merrill, Father O'Connor hoped they would find time to visit a certain family with a Celtic name, where the father was Catholic, but the mother belonged to no church. Father encouraged the Sisters to find the reason why the children attended classes sporadically. Once they were on the way, a gas-station attendant directed them to a tin house so many miles down the highway. "Ah! here it is," exclaimed Sister Maurina.

To their amazement, the house turned out to be a garage. A few yards away from the "tin" house was a small frame building that invited investigation. They rapped, walked around the building, and ventured to open the door and to call in. No answer. Rather than dismiss this visit as a "Nobody home," the Sisters inquired at the next-door neighbor's, a good city block from the tin structure. They knocked; they waited. Just as they were getting ready to leave, a man answered the door. He looked surprised for the moment, but said definitely, "No; the family has gone to Longrell Valley for the day." So that was rather final, until further developments the next day.

That day the Sisters visited the Malin school and to their surprise discovered the children of the family they had sought. Sister Maurina said to the little girl, "We were at your house yesterday, but all of you were away."

"Yes; Daddy said you were there and he told you nobody was home." With that, the little girl put her hand to her

198

mouth, to keep from revealing other secrets. However, she added, "That was our garage you went to first. And the house you walked around is our home. When you found Daddy, he was at grandma's house."

After leaving the school, the Sisters went back to the house. The father was much confused and contrite that the Sisters came back a second time. The mother of the family came to his defense with, "Sisters, he should be ashamed of himself, but he was in shock when you came yesterday. He had been shingling the roof, and he fell off the house on his head. He is a good man." The Sisters sensed a certain solidarity in the family expressed proudly when mother and children proclaimed of the head of the house, "He is a good man."

Not all our contacts were difficult or discouraging. Many of them on recollection still bring smiles. I select a few that still make me chuckle. Sister Maurina and I were at Bend, visiting the parents of pre-school children. One home in particular stands out. The mother, with an engaging boy of three and his brown-eyed sister of five, is home.

"Yes, indeed, we have family prayer, but I am not sure whether I am teaching them right. You see, I am not even baptized, but I want to live up to my marriage promises and to bring up the children Catholic. Come, Ronnie, and show the Sisters how you fold your hands to pray. And now, Mary, say the Hail Mary for the Sisters."

"Good for Ronnie and Mary! And very good for Ronnie's and Mary's mother." An instruction followed. We told Ronnie and Mary the story of the Hail Mary. They listened wide-eyed, sitting on the edge of their chairs, drinking in every word. Interruptions occur in the narrative as Ronnie hastens to explain that God is upstairs. Mary likes the idea of saying the same prayer as an angel did. The mother is all attention during this period; she, too, is learning why Catholics love Mary; why Catholics love to greet Mary with the angel's, "Hail."

Before leaving, we gave the mother the Parent-Educator leaflets, published by the Confraternity of Christian Doctrine in Baker City diocese, about the sign of the cross, the Hail Mary, and the Our Father. A cheery "Good-bye" and a "God bless you" bring this visit to a happy end.

Next we visited Mrs. Crane. "Run-Abouts," leaflet #23 in the series "At Home from Three to Six" catches Mrs. Crane's interest. "That's right. I have two myself: Jean, three and a half, and Michael, nearly six." She chuckled over the idea of visiting with the children while doing the dishes after meals. Then Mrs. Crane grows communicative. "Children are a delight. They are precious. Rose Marie, the older one who is only in grade one, startled her father during dinner the other night by blandly, but suddenly announcing, 'Daddy, someone is standing in back of you!'

"Quickly her father turned to see who had entered the kitchen unannounced, 'What? Who?'

"Quite satisfied with herself, Rose Marie softly announced, 'Your guardian angel.'

"Then there are Michael's everlasting questions such as 'If I came from heaven, why did I have to come here when I must go back to heaven again? Does my Guardian Angel like ice cream? Why must I say my prayers out loud? God knows what I am saying, doesn't He?'"

We explained then the Parent-Educator series of leaflets for parents of pre-schoolers. She smiles gratefully as we list her name and address so that she will receive the literature. Mrs. Crane, like many another parent, needs and wants all the aids the CCD has to offer parents. We are grateful; so is Mrs. Crane. It always gives us a happy feeling to meet so many wonderful parents, all in the one day.

We moved along to another stop. Mrs. Edstrom welcomed us Bohemian fashion into a tiny room heavy with incense. "No, I am not a Catholic, but I want my little boy to be a Catholic. He goes to the Catholic Church twice on Sundays; he likes the Fathers so much."

Further questioning was encouraging. "I do not object; if Freddy wants to be a Catholic, that is O.K. by me. He has books from which he studies. It is nice to have the Sisters come to see me. I am not like my father in Texas. He is a minister down there. I will not tell him Fred is going to the Catholic Church. You see, I am broad-minded and do not care."

A question about the boy's father brought quite a barrage of rapid-fire statements. We learned that Fred's father had no religion; he was in and out of jails no matter where he went. He was not interested in Freddy at all; he was a fly-by-night. As far as Mrs. Edstrom knew, he was in Alaska at the moment.

We enjoyed visiting with Mrs. Edstrom. She had interesting antiques and souvenirs from China, India, Greece. Had we been so inclined, she would have entertained us all day.

There was oriental atmosphere in that little incense-saturated room. We were glad to get out into the bracing air of this central-Oregon city, boasting a western skyline with a mile of snow-capped peaks of the towering Cascades. We breathed deeply of the crisp chill air. We left the results of these visits to the providence of God.

Across the street of the Edstrom home is a mother with a problem. She has a crippled child, spastic, one who will never run and play like other children. Ruth is now seven and very intelligent, but definitely handicapped. Only one course of action is open to us. We promise to arrange special instructions for Ruth. A catechist would come to the home at least once a week to instruct Ruth and to prepare her for first Holy Communion.

The mother was delighted when I told her that I knew a teacher who would gladly help her daughter. "She is a professional teacher and understands little children. In a day or two, Miss Joyce will visit you and make all arrangements."

It might seem that the obvious thing was that we should suggest the mother herself do the teaching; there was good reason for our course of action. The mother was ill and was not a Catholic; the father worked in the woods as a lumberman. Since the mother hoped some day to be a Catholic, I can only look back now and speculate whether Miss Joyce may well have given instructions to both.

After a cheery good-bye, sealed with a wet kiss from Ruth, we bade them both the day's blessing. There's a song in my heart: I am happy for little Ruth. There is no question but that these visits consumed a lot of our time, but in the long run they had worthwhile results and they made the families realize that we were interested enough in them to go out of our way to bring the CCD and its values to them. I can add that these visits never became routine; each had its own character.

I will never forget our visit to the Apodacas. Sister Maurina and I were visiting a newly-formed parish in Nyssa, Oregon. The parish was canonically erected by Bishop Leipzig in January 1951. Earlier, it had been a mission of Ontario, about eighteen miles from the parent church.

Our visit to the new parish was in response to a call from the newly-appointed pastor, Father Rembert Ahles, OFM. He thought he had about 60 grade school children and about nine or ten high schoolers for CCD classes. After we had visited the public schools, he was surprised to learn that there were nearly 200 grade school children and about 30 high school students in the Nyssa parish. The problem now was how to get all these children to come to class. There was an added phase to the problem in that many of the families in this area were Mexican. After sizing up the situation, we thought it best to visit as many of the Mexican families as we could and to encourage the children to come to the religion classes.

We set out for the home of the Apodacas, a mere shack of two rooms. We stopped a little while; then Sister Maurina took over at the Apodacas, and I went down the road to visit another family. As faithfully as possible, I give Sister's account of her visit.

"Eight children greeted me and they laughed heartily as I walked into what might have served for a living room, kitchen and dining room all in one. The adjoining room was a bedroom, with triple bunks on each side of the room and a large bed in the middle. All over the wall there were nails to hang up any clothes they had; one window was in the rear.

"Two of the children were of pre-school age, three in the

primary grades, and three of middle school age, about fourth to sixth grade. A large wood stove served to cook the meals as well as to heat the place.

"I greeted the children with a big smile. The ones of school age soon found room on a long bench back of a large table. They knew why we were visiting them; they had seen us at school a few days before. When I began to ask questions, they were in the giggly stage, and everything I said seemed to tickle their fancy. After a short time they settled down, but just when I thought I had their attention, out flies a rooster from under the stove. It was surprising to me, but extremely funny to them. There was a short span of attention while I was trying to get their names, ages and the grades in which they were in school. It was comparatively quiet and orderly, but not for long. From under the stove, a scraggy dog ambled out to see what was going on. The children were more hilarious than before, due—I think—to the expression on my face. I thought I would get rid of any further disturbance by asking, 'Any more livestock under that stove?'

"Laughingly they answered, 'Yes, the cat has kittens in a box under the stove.'

"Well, we got rid of the rooster by putting him out in the yard, and the dog made his way down the road; but we decided the cat and her kittens could stay. There's hardly a woman alive who would put a mother and her offspring out into the cold, even if a cat is the mother.

"Innocently I asked, 'You have books for your religion class? Let me see them, will you please.'

"Instantly there was a wild scramble in all directions into the bedroom to retrieve their books from a large box under the bed. For a minute I thought I had lost my class. Miraculous to relate, every child of school age had his or her book. Now class began in earnest.

"After a short session with the children when we reviewed fundamentals, I took leave of them, lost in the same hearty laughter with which I had been greeted. 'Good-bye, Sister; come again' could be heard as I walked down the road, marvelling at these happy children from Mexico. They were, indeed, precious."

We visited thirteen Mexican families in Nyssa—all trying hard to adjust to life in the States. Later we concluded that our problem was to find some good Mexican woman, well-enough instructed in the faith to teach these children according to their capacity and background and to meet their particular needs. That was always the challenge, finding competent teachers for the children everywhere—in parishes of long-standing as well as in newly-created ones like St. Bridget's at Nyssa.

It would be impossible to recount every incident on our travels in CCD work and when working in the various parishes. All were most interesting, some very funny, a few unusual and hair-raising, but all were necessary to keep alive fond hopes for the work in this part of the Lord's vineyard. Sometimes, tired and weary, we failed to see the funny side of the incident at the time, but when recalling the happenings on our return home, we found many things that evoked laughter and lively discussion. Many a recreation period was spent at Holy Family, recalling some of the experiences of our Sisters out on the road. We laughed at the telling of the one little boy, greatly delighted with the story of the Prodigal Son. To dramatize the story seemed to him the perfect climax to a good lesson; he began, "The father was so glad to see his boy he nearly popped his buttons. He said, 'Servant, bring him a Coke.' But when his brother saw the goings-on and the dancing girls, he threw up his hands and cried, so everyone could hear him, 'I'm gypped.' "

Little children have a way of translating Gospel stories under influence of events they have seen at home and on TV, which may have been on the novel side. At least they have gotten the idea.

One gem we had to piece together from the various participants in the event. Father McCormack, pastor of St. Francis church at Heppner, was exact and conscientious. Even the grade school boys knew that. One day one of the lads excused himself from attending religious instructions. Immediately

Father McCormack checked the attendance by calling the mother of the absentee. The hired man was summoned to take the errant lad to class. On the way back, Bobby muttered and murmured to himself, "That Father McCormack is so holy it's pitiful."

One important feature of a round-up on a range is the separation of brands; range-wars have started from one rancher ignoring signs. Sister Maurina and I tried to contact the parents of some children of the Cathedral Confraternity at Baker. Only one mother was at home, a non-Catholic; the others were out. We were frustrated, but not to the point of inaction. "Let's go to the Tiedeman School and see whether we can find any of the children themselves," suggested Sister Maurina. Visiting public schools to find Catholic children taxed our ingenuity to the utmost. There are no brands to show who belongs where.

The secretary to the principal was most cooperative. "Wait here until I can make the rounds of the lower grades."

When she returned with five wondering-what-this-is-all-about children, she put us in the little library. "Is this all right?" she asked.

I noticed one little boy who came in with the group. Since both his name and face were strange to me, I asked him, "Are you a Catholic?"

Unhesitatingly the boy answered, "Well, I'm kind of one."

On further inquiry, it was discovered that the boy was not Catholic, but had attended St. Francis Academy for a year. His mother did not approve of his attending the CCD classes; the family was Mormon.

This incident was not unlike the time we stopped at the Bly School to visit children. The principal hustled about and brought about twenty assorted children to us in the lunchroom. One stranger stood out among the rest.

"Are you a Catholic?" came my question.

"Yes," he nodded, "I am a Catholic."

"Since when?" I kept on.

"Since last night," came the reply.

"You are a very nice little boy, but it takes longer than that to become a Catholic. For now, you had better go back to your classroom."

Truth to tell, this little fellow just wanted to see where his classmates were going and why. As a matter of fact, we did have a filmstrip on the Mass that day, but the youngster was back in class doing his "sums" and reciting his ABC's.

Not all events took place along the road and the byways; I like to recall the words of Father William Morris' summary observation after he had visited our chapel at Holy Family House. In June 1946 Bishop McGrath brought him, when he was on a visit from St. Edward's Seminary near Seattle, to look over the Confraternity House. We were honored to have Father come to see what we were doing along the Confraternity line. It was a delight to show what we had, particularly since Father Morris was so enthusiastic. I recall that the picture file intrigued him no end.

"Where did you get all the pictures?" he wanted to know.

"We bought a few to complete a particular series. The most are from calendars, from Catholic magazines, and from friends," Sister Maurina answered. "Of course, we trimmed the edges and mounted them."

Bishop suggested that we outline our instruction courses and show Father the diploma we awarded the registered catechists. He was greatly impressed by the rigorous course of training for the catechists. Sister Maurina and I were on schedule to go to Enterprise High in the Wallowa Mountains, but Sister Rosetta remained capably to do the honors for the rest of Father's visit.

When she took him to our chapel on the second floor, both prayed silently for some minutes. Then Father Morris, who had helped to train countless numbers of young men for the priesthood, whispered to Sister Rosetta, "This is a lovely little chapel. Christ is here. But remember this: He is not only here for you and the other three Sisters in this household, He is here for the whole diocese. From this chapel He urges and prods and animates Bishop McGrath. He is reaching out from the secluded tabernacle to every child in the diocese, to every parent, to every priest. He is eager to touch them, to establish Himself in their hearts. You three Sisters are His tangible hands; your voice teaching the little ones, urging and encouraging the parents is really His. This is Christ's powerhouse in the diocese."

Is it any wonder we could say, "No sacrifice is too demanding, no labor too hard, no traveling too much," when Sister Maurina, Sister Rosetta, and I had such ideals set before us, not only by Father Morris, but by innumerable priests and parents of the diocese? We felt the immensity of the task before us, but we were not dismayed; we loved it.

One last word for the road. Little children have a way of being disarmingly frank. Sister Maurina tells that while at Pilot Rock her Religious Vacation School companion, Sister Falconieri was getting into the car when a little child called after her, "Hey, lady, wait."

Sister waited until the child came up to her; then asked, "Did you want something?"

"No," answered the child, "I just wanted to look you over."

When something like that occurs, you are lost for an answer, excepting that you stand long enough for the child to look you over. You can only hope and pray that the symbolism will lead her on to the Reality symbolized.

Chapter 12

The Bishop Rises To The Occasions

The early morning of September 11th gave promise of a bracingly clear day, and for us, a sort of holiday. Sister Maurina, Sister Rosetta, and I were stowing our overnight bags in the trunk of our car. We had a long trip ahead of us to reach Portland, the metropolitan see of the Province, 320 miles to the west. We were intent on assisting at the consecration of the Very Reverend Francis P. Leipzig, pastor of St. Mary's parish in Eugene, Oregon. We were happy that Father Leipzig had been named as the third bishop of Baker City, our bishop. We were happy.

The ride over the Blue Mountains was magnificent. Emigrant Springs Park, about 20 miles east of Pendleton, was our first stopping place. A very refreshing spring there had been used in the early days as a campsite by emigrants following the old Oregon Trail. We appreciated the welcome shade that the tall trees afforded by the cool, sparkling water and a chance to stretch after the confinement of the car. Sister Maurina used a few minutes to find a rare woodland bloom; Sister Rosetta noted the tracks of rabbits, deer and other forest creatures that visited the springs; I contented myself with relaxing and listening to the varied sounds about us.

We did not stop again until we were well on our way

along the Columbia River highway. Today was a gala day for us; no Confraternity activities awaited us at the end of the day. Today was a day we could take our time and revel in the wonderful scenes nature so lavishly provided.

"Look," cried Sister Rosetta as we came rolling into Arlington, "Isn't it glorious?"

"Keep your eye on the road," counselled Sister Maurina. "We can't afford to lose too much time. Let's keep going to Celilo Falls. Then I'll relieve you at the wheel."

Celilo Falls, an ancient Indian fishing grounds up to the 1970s, is now completely submerged under water backed up by the Dalles Dam. I always liked Celilo. It was like stepping from the 20th century into the days when the original inhabitants of America found sustenance in the river and in the mountains nearby. Occasionally a squaw would be seen gathering herbs or curing salmon. Celilo Falls had been the happy fishing grounds of the Indians of the Northwest. The story is still told about an early spring morning when the Indian men and boys were fishing there, standing on the craggy and protruding rocks in the middle of the Columbia River, the mighty, magic stream of the Northwest. Every man and boy was poised there with spear, eyes alert for salmon. Suddenly one of the smaller boys, excited by the prospects of a grand catch, teetered on his narrow rocky ledge and fell headlong into the swirling waters churning high with foam. Instantly the wire basket, intended to pick up the speared salmon, was deftly and adroitly maneuvered into the violently agitated waters and neatly picked up the flailing boy. High above the waters and all of the perilous rocks he was raised, then unceremoniously dropped to a rock to resume his efforts with his forebears at fishing. Little did he realize that he was the biggest fish dramatically caught that day.

Celilo, as we stood there enjoying the scene, called to mind other times, other persons. Here it was on one occasion that Father DeSmet, the intrepid missionary of the Northwest lost some brave men and a couple of boats—bateaux—at this dangerous and rough point where the Columbia plunges

210

through the Cascades. Much to think of, but we could tarry no longer. After a drink of cool water we hurried on through The Dalles to Hood River, an exceptionally beautiful spot at the junction of the Hood River with the Columbia.

Hood River lies in an extremely fertile valley devoted to lumber and fruit production. Apple, cherry, and pear trees bloom in April and make Hood River a veritable paradise. Besides processing fruit to go to the markets of the world, Hood River has a vodka distillery of satisfactory proportions. Here at Hood River we had our lunch, tempting and appetizing, brought at one of the inviting cafes that dotted the highway.

On this trip, with no planning for catechetical endeavors the next day, I could let myself enjoy the recollections that so many spots suggested. The Mt. Hood road brought to mind the A. A. Mohr family. They had a fruit orchard with the home set well back from the road. We had often stayed with them, one, two, three days, or a week. They had a commodious farmhouse fashioned to take care of many. Now Mr. and Mrs. Mohr lived there with only their son Jerry and Patricia their youngest. All of them loved animals, flowers, and the great outdoors. Mrs. Mohr generally gave us a large bedroom on the second floor. It was a good place to sleep. Nothing broke the stillness except the occasional hooting of an owl or the whispering of the pines. One night after a game of pinochle, we trudged upstairs. Sister Maurina and I were just ready to turn in when we heard a steady plodding from the stairway to our door. A cautious peep through a crack revealed Jerry leading his pet racoon to us to say, "Good night."

Another time Sister Rosetta was with me. As always she was a very light sleeper. This time she could not sleep at all. Her thought, "I believe I'll go down to the kitchen and make a cup of hot milk. Perhaps that will quiet me."

So cautiously down the stairs she crept to avoid disturbing anyone, went silently through the living room to the kitchen. No sooner had she entered the kitchen and opened the frigidaire when a voice, guttural but sharp, demanded, "What's the matter? What's the matter?"

211

Sister stopped in her tracks. Then suddenly she chuckled, realizing that it was Polly, a large green parrot, keeping watch through the night.

Yes, Hood River tugged at our heart strings. The parish had a very active CCD with both men and women energetic in the work. It was a luxury to reminisce here, but the road to Portland beckoned. We drove on past Cascade Locks, the last of little towns along the Columbia River situated in the diocese of Baker City. Shortly we were in Multnomah County with its breathtaking, awe-inspiring Falls.

The first time I ever glimpsed Multnomah Falls was from a train. I was all eyes to behold this scenic splendor. One moment we were there; the next, the Union Pacific had sped towards Portland. When the conductor came round to see that all was well, I took courage and voiced my disappointment. "Doesn't the train stop at Multnomah Falls? Oh, what a pity!" I kept on after the negative shake of his iron-gray head. "If the Union Pacific officials at Omaha realized how much tourists and other travelers anticipate a few minutes at Mult-nomah, they would surely order the train to go at snails' pace when it came to this magnificent waterfall. I think it would pay to make a few minutes stop. What do you think?"

The genial conductor had amplified, "Vista House and Multnomah Falls are just twenty miles from Portland. The Vista House is a roadside observatory set 725 feet above the Columbia. You can see 30 miles up or down the river on a clear day."

On this trip, we were held to no railed schedule, and I had been looking forward to a stopoff at these spectacular Falls, named after an Indian chief. Presently we arrived and pulled into the parking area at the Falls where a food-concession takes care of traveler's needs. The Falls drew me like a magnet. The water leaps out over a high cliff, then drops in long, feathery streamers of mist and spray. It strikes a mountain ledge and forms a large, limpid pool; then falls again for a total of 626 feet.

I could not get enough of the view. Slowly I walked up

the winding trail leading to the pool. There is a rustic wooden bridge that leads across the pool to the other side of this beautifully splendored thing. I was about to cross when the peremptory voice of our driver reached me, "Don't cross. Come back at once. We are leaving." I had wanted to say David's Psalm VIII at this spot. I recited it back in the car, for nothing is so fitting as to join the psalmist in praising the God of creation as the invitatory: "O Lord, our God, how glorious is your name over all the earth."

As we pushed along, the thought of Bishop McGrath's comment upon one of our chance stops along the way came to mind. He had been traveling with Sister Maurina and me when we were going to Portland to attend a provincial congress of the CCD at which we both were scheduled speakers. We had pulled up to look out at Shepherd's Glen when we noticed three goats and a few lambs frolicking on the wooded hillside nearby. Their antics were so funny that Sister and I laughed to see them skip and jump in such cavorting and kitten-like behavior. The bishop was patient and tolerant with us. When Sister Maurina resumed driving, he chortled to himself, "In Ireland there's a saying that pronounces to all who listen, 'It doesn't take much to make a good child laugh.' "

The run in from the Falls into Portland didn't take long and we established ourselves at our Franciscan provincialate to be ready for the ceremonies of the next day, the 12th. For Bishop Leipzig's consecration in St. Mary's Cathedral on the feast of the Holy Name of Mary, many dignitaries had assembled. The Most Reverend Edward D. Howard, D.D., Archbishop of Portland, was consecrator; Bishop Edwin V. O'Hara, Bishop of Kansas City—and Bishop Leipzig's predecessor as pastor at Eugene—and Bishop Edward Kelly, Bishop of Boise, were co-consecrators. I don't mean to put us Sisters among the dignitaries, but we felt we had a proprietary right at the consecration since this was our bishop.

We were quite aware that we three Sisters were only "among those present" in the large group of clergy and laity from all over the archdiocese—many journeying over there from Baker—who followed with pleasure the ecclesiastical and civic events attendant upon the consecration. However, we were already looking forward to the welcome he would receive into St. Francis de Sales cathedral in Baker ten days later when he would be formally installed by Archbishop Howard. We looked forward to his coming, but we didn't anticipate Bishop Leipzig's understanding and love for the work in which we were engaged.

Two days after the bishop's installation, we had just cleaned up after the evening meal and were in the community room, enjoying the Hi-Fi. We liked "Montovani, Music for Listening," "Music for Relaxation," "Music for Studying" in particular. Suddenly the sweet strains of music were pierced by the ringing of the doorbell. Although the porch light and a small light in the lobby were lit, we couldn't catch sight of the visitor; all eyes exchanged the question, "Who is it?" What a surprise and delight to welcome our new bishop to our home!

The community room exploded when our guest was ushered in. The bishop was dignified, but affable and quite at home. He had many questions, but he listened a lot also. We rejoiced to find that he knew Confraternity, both from personal experience and from his pastoral concern in Eugene, where he had been pastor since 1929. He assured us, "Don't worry. I know your work. Have you many children who study at home and cannot come to regular classes?"

I replied, "About 16% of the grade school children are on Directed Home Study, but considering all the circumstances they are doing well."

"Fine," the bishop commented. "You knew when I was little, my family lived in Chilton, Wisconsin. We were miles and miles from church. We got to Holy Mass only twice a year, one of the times being the Assumption. The winters in Wisconsin are hard and long; the snow is deep and fence high. No, we did not get to church often."

"You must have had something to keep the faith. It must have been something like Ireland," observed Sister Marie Brendan, our current homemaker.

Bishop Leipzig smiled his assent. "Yes; we did have something to nurture the faith. Every Sunday the family gathered in the front room where father led us in the prayers of the Mass. Then came instructions from the Baltimore catechism. My father saw to it that we knew our faith and practiced it."

This revelation gave us much heart. Our bishop had first-hand experience of the work of the CCD and understood the area in which we were working.

In the course of the discussion, Sister Marie Brendan, prompted by Sister Rosetta, brought us a cup of tea. The bishop went on with his reminiscences, "I remember how father would hitch up a team of horses to our farm wagon to take the whole family to Mass. We thought that was the way it had to be. Mother would take care of us younger ones, putting on our good clothes to go to the parish church quite some miles distant."

"Did you never go even to a Catholic high school?" ventured Sister Rosetta. "Sounds an awful lot like the Baker diocese."

"My first formal religious education began at St. Francis Seminary, Milwaukee, Wisconsin where I enrolled for the Baker diocese in 1911. My parents had moved here in that year. Seems coincidental that the Baker diocese had a connection with my youth. Now I am back as a bishop, but if I remember rightly, Baker has not changed much. The mountains are still in their place as usual."

"Do you really remember Baker?" asked someone, I believe Sister Rosetta.

"Of course; you cannot forget the sagebrush and the mountains."

No wonder Bishop Leipzig delighted us; in the course of the evening we felt we were coming to know him. He recalled his endeavors in the founding of St. Alice's church, Springfield, Oregon, before his appointment to the parish in Eugene. With this account, the pleasant visit was brought to an end. As

215

he left, he gave us assurance that he would be there in case we needed him.

That this was no casual, formal expression became very clear from the wholehearted interest he showed in the CCD. He attended the meetings of the Diocesan Board of Catechetics held at Holy Family or elsewhere at various schools and halls throughout the diocese. He captivated the interest of the priests by naming one priest from each deanery to the Board; he made their terms of office one or two years to bring many into action, and at times tapped for office the least expected to contribute to the good of the whole.

Bishop Leipzig likewise attended every Confraternity regional congress, where he met many of the laity in the diocese. Indeed, this was no small thing—to travel hundreds and hundreds of miles from one part of the diocese to the other. The congresses in 1955 were held at Pendleton, Condon, Burns, Lakeview, and Redmond. To attend each and every congress required traveling some 3,000 miles and more under conditions that were not always the best.

I might illustrate this last statement. Burns sounds as though it might be a hot place, but Monday morning, April 25, ushered in a day that looked like Christmas. Before leaving for Mass from Mrs. Ira Walker's, where we had stayed overnight, Sister Maurina and I cleared the car of snow before we could proceed to the church. Delegates from Ontario, Vale and Nyssa attending the Conference reported sliding all over the road at Stinking Water Mountain. Weather or no, immediately after finishing at Burns, we took off for Lakeview about 131 miles southward. Our schedule called for no lost time getting from one Conference to another.

Lakeview might sound as though it might be a summer resort; sometimes it might be. Bishop Leipzig and Father Beard, diocesan youth director, drove with us on this segment of our trip. Everything appeared to go well. Father Beard was at the wheel and the bishop was with him in the front seat. Sister Mary Alice, our missionary friend from Alabama, Sister Maurina and I were in the back of the car. Abruptly as we neared Valley Falls we noticed how dark it had become; a

216

storm was brewing nearby! At Valley Falls itself we were hailed by a blinding snowstorm that simply presaged the worst blizzard of the season. Snow was swirling thick and fast in all directions, a high gale blowing. It was hard to keep the car on the road. Silence reigned within the car as all passengers strained eyes to see what lay before us. Silent prayers were not wanting. Sister Maurina opened her door a bit, the better to see.

"To the left a little more," she told Father Beard, "unless you want to get into the ditch." Between gusts, she continued to act as navigator.

The highway was slick all the way from Valley Falls to Lakeview. Father put on the fog lights, not that we could see anything on the road, but to warn others that we were coming. If we had landed in the irrigation trough that would have been freezingly hard luck. But the bishop was with us; the threatened spill did not take place. When we arrived at the rectory at about 7:30 p.m. Father O'Connor, the pastor, was just about ready to go out on the road to see what had happened to us. Afterwards the bishop asked, "Did you realize the danger you were in?"

Our pale faces gave answer only too well.

"What would you have done, Sister Maurina, if you had been at the wheel?" Bishop asked.

"I think I would have done the same as Father Beard, just kept on," Sister answered.

The last Conference was in Redmond on April 27. Bishop went with us to Klamath, but then went on to Redmond with the Klamath Falls priests. Father Beard stayed along with us at Klamath. On the way to the Conference site, we joined Sister Alice in looking for deer. To our delight we saw not only one lone deer, but several groups of deer, about fifty in all, grazing quite close to the highway. Arriving at Redmond about 4 p.m., we were greeted by the bishop who wanted to know what had delayed us.

"Shooting deer," was Father Beard's response, "for the gal from Alabama."

Conferences might come under the heading of major

217

events for which the bishop would go out of his way to make time, but he also visited Confraternity classes when the opportunity presented itself. Once while the Religious Vacation School was in session at Baker, he visited the children. He asked, "How is your Vacation School? Do you like it?"

A manly little boy of seven answered, head high, shoulders squared, unhesitatingly, "It's fine and dandy, Bishop," What better answer could one expect? It *was* fine and dandy.

Of his devotion to Mary, our heavenly Queen, Bishop Leipzig, from the very outstart of his episcopate, made no secret. He made it a point to teach to everyone he met the little prayer he had learned many years before as a student at Mt. Angel Seminary, St. Benedict, Oregon:

Mary, take care of me,
Father, mother, brother, sister, friends.

To Mary, he dedicated his diocese, and as his motto on the episcopal coat-of-arms, he adopted the phrase, "Maria me custodiat." Bishop Leipzig delighted children with the finger-play connected with his short Marian prayer. Pointing with the index finger of his right hand to the thumb of his left hand and then to each finger, one word to a digit he intoned the prayer, "Mary take care of me." Then reversing the process, he continued, pointing to the thumb of his right hand and touching each finger in order, saying, "Father, mother, brother, sister, friends."

The first Sunday at his Mass in the Baker cathedral, Bishop used that prayer as the springboard for his sermon, asking everyone present to recite the prayer with appropriate gestures. It was a lesson involving everyone present. Not only we in the Confraternity work were aware of Bishop Leipzig's love of Mary as the dominant influence in his spiritual life.

Another quality that commanded attention was his love for children. He was affectionate with them and they responded in kind. They liked to see him when he came to visit a parish and to study its needs. His love for them was effective and practical. He was quick to see that facilities were provided for the Schools of Religion. Multi-purpose halls were soon built, with classroom space for at least five distinct rooms formed by sliding walls. Usually there was a large hall in the center with the rooms on both sides. What a difference it made. Instead of holding class in a choir loft, in a sacristy, or in a dark basement, lessons now were dignified with a special place for each grade or combination of grades. The teachers were delighted; it made for order and discipline.

Another trait I happily and gratefully remember. Bishop Leipzig took it for granted that the Confraternity Sisters would share with him in playing host to visitors when circumstances called for it. An incident in November 1950 illustrates the point.

We were enjoying a quiet Sunday afternoon when the doorbell rang. There stood Bishop Leipzig and two Holy Cross Sisters. Bishop explained, "I found these two Sisters about to spend the afternoon in the depot until the evening train. I know you will be good to them."

Our whole house went into action. First priority went to the Sister visitor tormented by a thumping toothache. I found oil of cloves and some other remedy in the medicine chest. Then we urged her to go to bed to get what rest she could. Sister Kathleen prepared an excellent dinner of ham, string beans, and potatoes flavored with ham. A tomato-juice cocktail was on hand to whet everyone's appetite, and the favorite American dessert, apple-pie a la mode, to top off the meal. Sister Rosetta set the table with our best Haviland china and silverware; when Sister Philip sat down to dinner, she exclaimed with gracious good humor, "I must be a bishop; no, perhaps a cardinal!"

The unexpected visit turned out to be a most enjoyable occasion. Our visitors, Sisters Philip and Consolata, from the College of St. Mary's of the Wasatch, Salt Lake City, brought us new ideas and outlooks as well as a harmony in basic thought. The evening train was late so there was time after dinner for a very pleasant exchange of experiences and convent incidents before Bishop Leipzig returned to take the Sisters to the depot.

It appeared that Bishop welcomed occasions that called for celebration with a gathering of people together. He knew the secret of turning ordinary days, characterized by daily strivings, into days of gracious living and loving design, On April 7, 1952 the diocese observed the 50th anniversary of its founding. From among the clerical visitors gathered for the occasion, four bishops and three priests offered Mass at Holy Family House.

Three years later, on April 15, 1955 Bishop Leipzig celebrated a Solemn Pontifical Mass in the cathedral in honor of the centenary of the founding of our Community, the Sisters of St. Francis of Philadelphia. He seemed to find satisfaction in the thought that Baker had its centennial Mass before the Community at the Mother-house at Glen Riddle, Pennsylvania.

Bishop Leipzig seemed clearly to recognize his crozier in its original character—the shepherd's staff. He was intent on caring for his flock. He had become keenly suspicious that the Holy Family Confraternity House was operating on a rather low budget. About three or four months after his installation as bishop of Baker, he paid me a somewhat formal visit. Quite unexpectedly he said, "Sister, as your bishop I would like to see your books, giving the income and expenses of this house. Your work is too important to have your mind burdened unnecessarily with financial problems."

I gave the bishop the books and he went away with them, saying, "I will return them tomorrow."

He brought the books back the next day and offered this counsel, "You are operating on a very low income. I will increase your allotment so that your balance each month is more than you have now. What would you do in case of an emergency? You simply must have more on hand than you do now."

Another instance of his interested observation and practical solution of problems comes to mind. Sister Maurina and I went to the Ninth National Congress of the CCD at Chicago in November 1951. We were to act as Chairman and Co-Chairman of a special Workgroup on Rural Confraternities. As would be expected, Bishop Leipzig was in attendance as a participant in the Congress. The first morning, he met us in the lobby of the Sheraton Hotel, the Congress headquarters. "Where are you staying?" he asked. When he learned we were housed with Sisters about three miles from the Sheraton, he went into action. "Come with me," he directed. "You should be here at the Sheraton. All the sessions are here and you will get proper rest."

Forthwith, he accompanied us to the registration desk and saw to it that we were duly taken care of. To say that we were grateful is putting it mildly. As I mentioned earlier, Chicago at that time was treating visitors to the worst blizzard in thirty-nine years. We did not have to brave the elements that week, and we could enjoy the renowned speakers scheduled for the night sessions. I am eternally grateful to Bishop Leipzig for making it possible for us to hear them. That is what it means to have a great man at the helm.

These qualities and traits, the instances, and incidents are not a summary, but a sampling of the bishop's character and actions during the years we worked with him up to 1956; and reports assure us that Baker has continued to be blessed in its bishop.

An amusing happening gives sharp evidence of the bishop's aplomb. On the evening of January 25, 1956, the investiture of Father Michael McMahon as Monsignor, took place in St. Peter's Church, The Dalles. Sister Maurina, Sister Claire Inez and I wanted to attend it. Since the highway from Baker to Pendleton was icy in spots, we left the day before; that was a good decision. We stayed that night at St. Joseph's Academy, Pendleton, and took off for the Dalles about nine in the morning. We arrived at St. Mary's Academy in The Dalles in good time for the ceremony. The three of us, accompanied by many Sisters of the Holy Name, wended our way to the church.

At the ceremony, Bishop Leipzig presided. Father Crotty preached the occasional sermon, paying high tribute to the priestly career of Monsignor McMahon. Sixty brother priests honored the newly invested Domestic Prelate by their presence. It was an impressive ceremony—but not without its spectacular moment and a touch of humor in the end. In the interval prior to Benediction, the Very Rev. Vincent C. Egan, chaplain to Bishop Leipzig, caught the attention of the crowded church in dramatic fashion. Because of close quarters in the sanctuary, his surplice caught fire from a lighted candle at Our Lady's shrine.

"My God," cried one of the priests near us, "Vince is on fire!"

Instantly Bishop Leipzig went into action. By vigorously slapping the blaze with both hands, the bishop quickly extinguished the flames. It is fitting to mention that the bishop has been Honorary Fire Chief in Oregon as well as in Washington, D. C. There was momentary distraction, heightened by the amused smiles and well-controlled inclination to laugh on the part of the bishop and Father Egan.

Sister Clare Inez got so excited she stood up. Sister Maurina couldn't imagine what caused the tittering among the clergy in the middle aisle. I kept my eyes riveted on the pommeling meted out by the bishop to smother the flame.

Total loss is given as one surplice and some dignity, but the bishop carried off the affair as if smothering fires were in the execution of customary rubrics.

Chapter 13

At The End The Phone Rings

August 4 was much the same as any other bright, sunny summer day of 1956. Every Sister at Holy Family was endeavoring to do the greater part of her chores before the sweltering heat, after noon would slacken her efforts. Sister Maurina was at her favorite hobby, cultivating rosebushes, talking to them coaxingly, endearingly, to encourage them to bloom and flourish as much as they might. Through the open window came her vibrant, clear voice, "What's the matter with you? I hoped to have as nice a bush of roses as Father Delahunty had in 'Dainty Bess' last summer. Come on, perk up; you get the same attention the other roses do, but you look anemic or something like that. What's wrong? Do you miss the shade along Father's house in Condon?"

Sister regularly talked to her flowers as though they were children. To the flaming "Paul Scarlet," a climber along the garage, she had only words of praise and encouragement. No wonder her flowers did so well. She not only mulched and took care of them, but loved them as well. The "Charlotte Armstrong," radiantly beautiful in its crimson glory, and her "Peace Rose," delicately tinted with pink, cream and yellow shadings, received special praise. "Oh, you beauties, I am so proud of you. I'll reserve you for tomorrow. I like flowers for the altar during Mass."

Sister Lucilla was in the parlor, dusting and straightening the books on the table. Her heart is in music so she lets her fingers ripple along the piano keys, giving us a foretaste of what is in store for us when finally she is seated ready to rival the birds in their song.

Sister Clare Inez and I are both in the study going over the CCD Manual and studying the program for the next year. She has twitching fingers; as soon as we have spent an hour doing spadework for the coming scholastic year, she will join Sister Maurina on the lawn to enjoy gardening before the heat is too intense.

Everything is calm and serene. I find a new book on *Teaching Little Children to Pray,* that came in yesterday's mail. If it appeals, I will write a review of this handy little volume expressly for parents and primary school teachers. It has easy to read print, brightly colored illustrations, and a table of contents. My prayer-full thoughts are shattered by the piercingly shrill ring of the telephone, demanding instantaneous attention.

"Good morning, Holy Family Confraternity House," was my greeting over the phone.

"Hello there, Sister Presentina. Has your mail come this morning? . . . . Oh, that's too bad. We received the Community transfers. All the changes! The ones for your House are on the list. I am sure you won't like them. Want to hear them?"

"No. Thank you, Sister," I replied. "I'll wait until our mail comes."

It was Sister Liliosa, Superior of St. Francis Academy, calling. She was a very alert, dynamic, and active participant in all Community affairs, sometimes a little over-zealous, but none-the-less loyal to her colleagues. "Well, if you don't get word, I'll be glad to further the cause and spread the news. Aren't you worried?"

So many questions, all in one breath without waiting for an answer! Finally, I thanked Sister for her concern and hung up. No; I was not worried. I more or less expected a transfer, but did not know exactly what my destination would be. I looked at a possible transfer, more or less philosophically and had myself steeled for it. Businessmen, executives, and store managers all accept transfers as a matter of course. Why shouldn't I? My Community would place me where I could possibly do greater good or where my talents, such as they were, could be used to best advantage, where optimum possibilities could be developed.

I cannot deny that Sister's call made me wonder a bit. From that moment of 1956, my mind flashed back to 1937 when I had come West not knowing what the outcome would be. Little did I then dream that our newly-elected Superior General, Mother Veronica, would sanction Bishop McGrath's request that I be assigned to the Diocese of Baker for Confraternity work. Reverend Mother Veronica declared that this new field of service was entirely in accord with the pattern of life St. Francis had designed for his early followers. Mother Veronica expressed the further thought that our immediate Foundress, Mother Mary Francis Bachman, had initiated home-visiting and teaching as an apostolate for her pioneer Sisters in Philadelphia more than a hundred twenty years before. "You are doing what our Foundress saw as a great opportunity to spread the Kingdom of God. Keep on with the work."

With these thoughts in mind, I went about my work contentedly.

Thirty minutes had elapsed since Sister's call. I gave no further consideration to the matter. Then the telephone rang again. I answered. It was Sister Liliosa. She was on "pins and needles" as the saying goes. As soon as I lifted the receiver and gave the usual greeting, Sister came on fast and furious. "Did you get your changes? What do you think of them?"

"Our mailman has not been here," I explained. "He had no chance to get here yet. We usually get our mail about noon."

"That's all right," I heard Sister say. "Shall I read your changes to you? I have the list right here."

"Thank you, Sister. I would rather get the official notice first. I'll tell you what I will do. I will call you when our mail

225

comes. No, I won't forget. How could I?"

With that, all was quiet on the western front, excepting for the whirr of the mixer in the kitchen where Sister Lucilla was now whipping up a marble-cake for lunch. I took a stroll to the back porch where I surveyed our gardeners at work edging the lawn. Despite the fact that I had been twice told that I would not like the changes, I stoically refused the information that had been offered me by our seemingly agitated bearer of news. I had confidence enough in our Community to rely on their judgment.

As I was returning to my study, I heard the postman's steps coming up on the front porch to our mailbox. I waited a minute to give him time to walk to the corner, then went to the box. Oh, what a windfall! An official letter for Sister Maurina on the top; several communications from teachers outside Baker ordering some material for September; two newspapers, one *The Catholic Sentinel* from Portland, Oregon; a few other items such as catalogues and circulars; and finally two envelopes that looked very official and addressed to me.

I called Sister Maurina at once; Sister Clare Inez came in with her. Sister Maurina opened her mail and announced for all to hear, "I am going to Spokane, Washington."

When I heard that, I thought, "Well, that means I am not going to Spokane." Mother Agnes had told me earlier in June that only one of us was expendable.

Sister Maurina was excited; she wanted to know what my mail had brought. I assured her, "I don't know; but now is about as good a time as any to find out."

By this time, the general hubbub had brought Sister Lucilla into the study. I opened the first of the two official envelopes. It was the list of all the transfers in Sacred Heart Province for the scholastic year 1956-1957. It was this list that had given Sister Liliosa the news that almost a hundred Sisters were changed. I handed the list to Sister Maurina, who quickly gave it to Sister Clare Inez. Then I opened the next envelope. Here is what I read:

226

This is to inform you that you have been assigned to the Chancery Office in Spokane to supervise Catechetics. Please arrange to move to your new Mission as soon as possible.

"What is it, Sister? Are you changed?" All three of my companions were talking at once.

"Yes. I am changed. My assignment names Spokane."

"Then we are going to the same place," this from Sister Maurina.

"Who is coming in your place?" Sisters Clare Inez and Lucilla were interested.

"You have the list. Look carefully; the replacements must be there," I replied.

And then the telephone rang insistently. Instinctively I knew it was Sister Liliosa. "I am so sorry," I began, "not to have called you as soon as the mail came. We were so busy grasping the meaning of these transfers that I completely forgot to call you. Please forgive me."

"Well, that's all right; but what about the transfer? I will miss you, going more than two hundred miles away to Spokane. I won't be able to run over to your place anymore. I think it is unbelievable."

Trying to calm Sister a bit, I started, philosophically—I hoped—"Well, you know we have here no lasting city." I got no further. Bang! went the receiver at the other end! The phone was dead. Sister wanted no philosophical discussion of this very real situation. My reaction had been instantaneous; instead of pacifying Sister's ruffled feelings, I had riled her. An irresponsible, nervous laugh followed. To this day when I think of it, I smile; it seems so funny.

I called Bishop Leipzig on the phone; I wanted him to get the word from me and not at second-hand. He came to the House at once. After preliminary greetings, I asked, "Bishop, did you get any word from the Provincial?"

"No, I did not. Was I supposed to?" he asked.

I was searching for words. "Well, I thought you would

227

receive a notice. I am changed to Spokane."

"Well, there's still Sister Maurina. I am sure she will do well," replied the bishop.

"But," I began, "Sister Maurina has received a transfer, too; she is going to Spokane."

The bishop looked as though he had not heard. Then, "What is your Community trying to do, wreck the CCD?"

"No, Bishop; I hardly think so. Sister Clare Inez is staying here and there are two replacements coming—Sister Rosalinda, a native Oregonian and a teacher of many years, and Sister Christina, who has done CCD work before. I shall ease the transfer for them, by staying here and outlining the work that lies before them. Another thing, Bishop, I think your CCD will continue to prosper because the laity are well-grounded in their responsibilities."

"I hope so." The bishop continued, "After so many years here, your work will not collapse as long as someone takes over when you leave." Then he was on his way home.

And that was the end of our traversing the diocese from one end to the other. We stayed on three more weeks, writing, instructions for our successors; suggestions rather than instructions, for they would have to follow their own insights and judgments in the future. On the arrival of the "new" Sisters, we had many questions to answer as we tried to acquaint them with their new convent home and to introduce them to Confraternity ways and customs. This was the end of one era; a new one was to begin. The telephone had rung; but the mailman had brought the word.

However, the mailman came again! When the news broke that Sister Maurina and I were leaving the diocese for other fields, many letters of appreciation of our work came to us, particularly from priests. It was heartening to know that the priests had not looked upon us as operators, but had graciously accepted us as cooperators.

Monsignor Casey from Klamath Falls wrote to Sister Maurina and me a joint letter in August:

All of us seem to have taken for granted that you were

part of the diocese of Baker and I feel sure that Baker will not be the same without you.

In the twenty years that you have been working for us and with us in the diocese, great things have been accomplished for the glory of God and the spiritual welfare of our people, especially of our children.

"Isn't that thoughtful of Monsignor Casey?" I said to myself as I picked up another note from the Reverend John J. O'Hara, S.J., pastor of St. Mary's, Pendleton. It ran:

It is with great regret that I view your departure. During the years I have leaned heavily upon your zeal and generosity in forwarding our CCD program. You have made a definite contribution to the Catholic life of the children of the parish and their parents. . . .

Many things should be consoling to you as you leave for other fields whitened for the harvest. Praying God that He may again use you as a humble instrument . . .

I was pleased to learn of Father O'Hara's attitude, for I think that sometimes my insistence must have tried his patience.

The Vicar General of the diocese sent this message to Sister Maurina and me:

I feel you should not leave us without being told that the priests of the Baker Diocese are most appreciative of the wonderful work you have done for our children.

In my opinion your work, the work of teaching lay people to teach religion to the children, is the greatest and most important work in the diocese. You have brought to your task a single-minded devotion which accounts not only for the success of the Confraternity, under God, but the inspiration to us all.

There were many, many more expressions of appreciation, but these few examples show the caliber of the men we were dealing with. All of the letter-writers promised to offer a Holy Mass or two for us and extended invitations to visit them sometimes when we would be passing through.

Then all the bells of the widely scattered churches and

missions of the Baker diocese seemed to be ringing in my head. These letters brought home to me that I was leaving not a place, but people with whom almost twenty years of my life was involved. Tears filled my eyes for the first time since the phone rang and the news broke. My Religious stoicism towards transfers cracked a bit; I was a little dazed. The phone rang to interrupt the mood; I started to get up, but sat back and suggested that Sister Rosalinda answer it. I was "off duty." This was the eve of our "move"; early the next day Sister Maurina and I would be on the road. Spokane was the next stop. And away we went.

Oregon to Spokane

by Bishop Bernard J. Topel

August of 1956 was an unusually important month for our diocese. It was the month that Sisters Presentina and Maurina came from Oregon to Spokane to take over our CCD program. How much we needed them!

I first became acquainted with these two apostolic women early in October of 1955. On my way to Spokane to assume my responsibilities as Bishop, I attended in Boise a regional meeting of the Confraternity of Christian Doctrine. It was there that the experience and knowledge of these two Sisters became most apparent to me. How often others turned to them for answers and advice. How wise were their answers!

It never occurred to me then as even a remotest possibility that within a year these two Sisters would be working in our diocese. Yet in God's providence this is exactly what happened.

The two had done remarkable work in the CCD in the Diocese of Baker, Oregon. Pioneer work it was. They set up and developed their own unique and very effective CCD program. It featured teacher training. Their sacrifices to help CCD teachers were very great. The time had come, though, for others to continue the work that the Sisters had begun in Oregon. It marked them as real missionaries. It certainly would have been easier for them to stay on in Oregon. We needed help desperately—we needed them—and they agreed to come.

The difference their coming made was great. Perhaps I should say extraordinarily great. I remember telling our priests at that time that I did not think it necessary to impose this new program on them. I said I expected it would sell itself. It did. Anyone who had misgivings beforehand lost them completely when they saw the effectiveness of the program at work.

These two are truly remarkable and devoted religious. They have done a remarkable work. God will reward them most abundantly.

Devotedly yours In the service of Our Lady,

Bernard J. Topel
Bishop of Spokane